AFRICAN MARKET
WOMEN AND
ECONOMIC POWER

Recent Titles in
Contributions in Afro-American and African Studies

Financing Health Care in Sub-Saharan Africa
Ronald J. Vogel

Folk Wisdom and Mother Wit: John Lee – An African American Herbal Healer
Arvilla Payne-Jackson and John Lee; Illustrations by Linda Kempton Armstrong

Alice Walker and Zora Neale Hurston: The Common Bond
Lillie P. Howard, editor

A Journey into the Philosophy of Alain Locke
Johnny Washington

Time in the Black Experience
Joseph K. Adjayé

Folk Poetics: A Sociosemiotic Study of Yoruba Trickster Tales
Ropo Sekoni

Public Policy and the Black Hospital: From Slavery to Segregation to Integration
Mitchell F. Rice and Woodrow Jones, Jr.

Aunt Jemima, Uncle Ben, and Rastus: Blacks in Advertising, Yesterday,
Today, and Tomorrow
Marilyn Kern-Foxworth

A World of Difference: An Inter-Cultural Study of Toni Morrison's Novels
Wendy Harding and Jacky Martin

African Labor Relations and Workers' Rights: Assessing the Role of the
International Labor Organizations
Kwamina Panford

The Gong and the Flute: African Literary Development and Celebration
Kalu Ogbaa, editor

AFRICAN MARKET WOMEN AND ECONOMIC POWER

The Role of Women in African Economic Development

Edited by
Bessie House-Midamba
and Felix K. Ekechi

Contributions in Afro-American and African Studies, Number 174

Greenwood Press
Westport, Connecticut • London

Library of Congress Cataloging-in-Publication Data

African market women and economic power : the role of women in African
  economic development / edited by Bessie House-Midamba and Felix K.
  Ekechi.
    p. cm. (Contributions in Afro-American and African
  studies, ISSN 0069–9624; no. 174)
    Includes bibliographical references and index.
    ISBN 0–313–29214–0 (alk. paper)
    1. Women in development—Africa. 2. Women merchants—Africa.
  I. House-Midamba, Bessie. II. Ekechi, Felix K.
  III. Series.
  HQ1240.5.A35A397   1995
  381'.18'082–dc20   94–21082

British Library Cataloguing in Publication Data is available.

Library of Congress Catalog Card Number: 94–21082
ISBN: 0–313–29214–0
ISBN: 0069–9624

First published in 1995

Greenwood Press, 88 Post Road West, Westport, CT 06881
An imprint of Greenwood Publishing Group, Inc.

Printed in the United States of America

The paper used in this book complies with the
Permanent Paper Standard issued by the National
Information Standards Organization (Z39.48—1984).

10 9 8 7 6 5 4 3 2

Contents

Maps and Tables

Acknowledgments

We would like to express our debt of gratitude to several individuals and institutions who in one form or another helped in the preparation of this book. First, we would like to thank the Kent State University Research Council, which provided a travel grant to Dr. Felix Ekechi to collect the data for his essay in this volume, and the Kent State University Library, particularly the Interlibrary Loan Department, for providing books and documents. Moreover, we deeply appreciate the encouragement and support we received from Dr. Byron Lander, Chair of the Political Science Department, and Dr. Henry Leonard, Chair of the History Department. Our thanks, also, go to Dr. Milton Harvey, Dr. Howard Venegen, and Ms. Karen Andrews, all of the Geography Department, for assistance in redrawing Map 1.3 on page 16. Above all, we want to thank Nancy Myers, Ellen Denning, Bette Sawicki, Madelyn Thomas, and Carol Muhib for typing this manuscript. Last, we are grateful to our spouses without whose support and cooperation completion of this book would not have been possible. We also appreciate the cooperation of the contributors and the editor of *Ethnology* for giving us permission to reprint Dr. Catherine VerEecke's essay.

Introduction

Bessie House-Midamba and Felix K. Ekechi

The study of African women as an important focus of academic inquiry can be traced back to the decade of the 1960s, even though studies of African women go back to the colonial period. Since the 1970s, however, scholarly literature on women has grown with increasing rapidity, thanks to Africanist feminist scholars. Although the literature on the contributions of women in the economic development of sub-Saharan African states is abundant and still growing, few, if any, studies have attempted a regional and comparative analysis of African market women traders. Hitherto, attention had focused largely on the successful penetration of West African women in local markets, while very little attention has been given to women in East, Central, or Southern Africa. This book attempts to correct this apparent neglect by examining the economic role of women from a comparative perspective. Thus, the essays in this volume focus attention on the economic activities of women from Western, Eastern, Central, and Southern Africa in the precolonial, colonial, and postcolonial eras.

The ten chapters of this book deal with the theme of African market women and economic power. African market women's participation in trade is analyzed in terms of (1) the sexual division of labor in African societies; (2) the struggle and competition between men and women over certain market items and market centers; (3) the nature of resources available to them and the manner in which these resources are disbursed; (4) the cultural, social, and economic barriers that still exist and have, in one way or another, affected women's ability to participate fully in economic development; (5) the method by which African women exploit or manipulate economic, social, and political opportunities and thus promote their welfare and position; (6) the impact of European imperialism on the status and position of women; and (7) the effects of postcolonial structural adjustment programs, especially as they impinge on women's livelihood.

The issue of development is significant, more particularly now that most countries in Africa, especially in sub-Saharan Africa, are experiencing serious economic decline. Africa's developmental dilemmas have been characterized by low agricultural productivity, declining output in the industrial sector, poor export performance, spiraling debt, and deteriorating social conditions and resources. In short, as Barbara P. Thomas-Slayter notes:

Economic growth for Africa has averaged 3.4 percent a year for the last 30 years, barely staying ahead of population growth. Food production per capita was at best stagnant in the 1970s and declined in the 1980s. Agricultural exports have stagnated, and Africa's share in world trade has declined for many commodities. In fact, export volume has grown little in the last 20 years, and Africa's share in the world markets has fallen by almost half.[1]

A host of complex factors, both internal and external, are continuing to affect African economies. In recent years, the policies of the International Monetary Fund (IMF) and the World Bank (WB), through the implementation of structural adjustment programs (SAPs), have increasingly accelerated Africa's economic difficulties. The result has been the inexorable African indebtedness, increasing poverty, and the marginalization of Africa in the new world order. Several of the chapters appropriately link the activities of women to the consequences of the SAPs in their respective countries. In many countries, SAPs seem to have more seriously affected women. Hence, Horn, Osirim, and Musisi have particularly examined the impact of structural adjustment programs on women in Zimbabwe and Uganda and of women's adjustments to their changing economic conditions. House-Midamba and Robertson have also looked at the impact of the SAPs on women in Kenya. Bessie House-Midamba notes that its implementation has accelerated the rising costs of food, thus making it extremely difficult for women to feed their families. In addition, budget reductions in education and healthcare seem to have affected women more seriously.

In almost all these cases examined, it is remarkable that despite severe economic hardship, mounting social deprivation, and misery, women have found new avenues of economic survival and thus continue to play a vital role in the economic development of their societies and nations. In the process, women have also continued to assert a measure of economic independence or empowerment. Thus, it should be emphasized that the spirit of self-reliance has galvanized women to seek alternative sources of economic and social improvement. In this respect special recognition should be given to women's initiative and enterprise, which have led to the growth of small-scale enterprises throughout sub-Saharan Africa. Here Downing's essay makes an important contribution.

RETHINKING DEVELOPMENT

At this juncture, it may be necessary to state more clearly our concept of economic development, especially as it applies to African market women. Of course, "development" has been conceptualized in a number of different ways by scholars in different fields. Ester Boserup years ago defined economic development as "the progress towards an increasingly intricate pattern of labour specialization." By this she meant a situation in which "more and more people become specialized in particular tasks" and thus are able to contribute to the general welfare of the community. In her words, "The economic autarky of the family group is superseded by the exchange of goods and services."[2] More specifically, economic development involves the full and active participation of men and women in such fields as agriculture (farming), trade, or other productive economic enterprises that promote the socioeconomic progress of the community or nation. It is in this context that we have approached and examined the role of African women in economic development. This concept has little to do with modern notions of "development" in which development is perceived in terms of one-year to ten-year development plans, generally drawn by male-dominated governments and which relegate women to the background.[3] Rather, we acknowledge the active participation of men and women in all aspects of national endeavor, and especially in economic enterprises that ensure social progress.

Accordingly, this study departs from previous studies on women and development in the following ways. First, it places women at the center, rather than at the periphery, of economic analysis. This means that women are seen as "the vital social forces in economic development."[4] Market women in particular are acknowledged as invaluable to the African economy and overall development. Second, it places intrinsic value and worth on women's work and labor in the process of national development. In many African states, to be sure, women constitute more than half the population, and hence their vast reservoir of human potential must be harnessed; for "no national programmes will be meaningful and thorough if women are not fully involved."[5] Third, the study shows that the role of women in society should not be seen as a static phenomenon, for women's roles are characterized by fluidity and change. Indeed, as essays in this volume demonstrate, changes have occurred across time and space, and women have challenged, and continue to challenge, "the social construction of female and male gender characteristics."[6] It is indeed sobering that African states, perhaps responding to the goals of the United Nations Decade for Women (1975–1985), have now adopted progressive policies toward women's integration into the body politic, especially enhancing their economic improvement through the establishment of women's bureaux, financial and educational institutions, and cooperative societies. Yet, much more remains to be done to ensure the full participation of women in national development programs.

The unique feature of this volume is its multidisciplinary character. Thus we have attempted to analyze women's trading activities from an interdisciplinary approach representing the fields of history (Ekechi, Falola, Ogbomo, Musisi, Robertson), anthropology (VerEecke, Horn), political science (House-Midamba), geography and economics (Downing), and sociology (Osirim). Each contributor to this volume has individually carried out fieldwork on aspects of women's economic roles in the respective African countries. Thus, all the chapters are based on original research and (with the exception of VerEecke's and part of Ekechi's) none has previously been published. Also, the study reflects an interesting gender diversity. Works on African women are often written by female scholars; here, however, there are three men and seven women, drawn from Africa, Canada, and the United States. Although all the male contributors are Africans, only two of the female contributors are Africans—Nakanyike Musisi (Uganda) and Bessie House-Midamba (Kenya, by marriage). We attempted to include more African women in the study; but most of them, for various reasons, declined the invitation to participate.

Essentially, this volume articulates a truly Africanist feminist ideology—an ideology that grows "out of the objective reality of the masses of African women."[7] In this context, we have defined development from the perspective of the needs of the African people. To this end, we have advocated the liberalization of economic activities so as to include the full and active participation of all members of society, especially women. For as Robertson points out in this volume, "the economic health" of African societies may well depend on the full mobilization of the grassroots. In this regard, writes Robertson, "The fostering of women's trade offers an unexplored vehicle for development ignored in the Western experience, and could form a unique African contribution of alternative methods of development." We therefore argue in favor of "degendering" strategic economic and political activities in African societies. In doing so, we believe, the equality of men and women in matters of socioeconomic development would be solidly affirmed.

More specifically, Ester Boserup's pioneering book, *Woman's Role in Economic Development*, long ago "challenged the centuries old perception of the sexual division of labor between men as bread winners and women as homemakers."[8] Dismissing this demarcation of responsibilities as misleading, Boserup demonstrates women's important roles in agricultural or farming systems in Africa and warns us against following colonial development strategies that tended to devalue women's status and roles.[9] For example, colonialism discouraged women's involvement in certain aspects of economic activity, especially those involving cash crops. In the process, women's roles were restricted. The sociopolitical implications were obvious: colonialism "alienated" women from "the hierarchy of power."[10] Also, as Haleh Afshar writes, "Although the process of modernization with its emphasis on capital accumulation and the move away from artisan production is not of itself necessarily gender-specific, its effect has often been to deprive many poorer women of ready access to a reliable revenue based on subsistence production. This process has been reinforced by the male-oriented development projects and employment opportunities in the capitalist, waged sector which has reinforced the subordination of women."[11]

CULTURE, GENDERED SPACES,
AND THE SEXUAL DIVISION OF LABOR

One of the central themes of this book is the importance of the sexual division of labor. Essentially, traditional African society can be described as a society "with very marked and distinctive gender behavior. What males and females do in work, in the family, in general social life, and in aesthetics and rituals differ greatly. There is physical separation of the sexes, marked by separate living quarters for husbands and wives, distinct eating arrangements, generally different roles in farmwork, as well as separate and differing boys' and girls' initiations. These gender differences affect the manner in which children learn their own sex roles and the rules of gender behavior and interrelationships."[12] The concept can be further defined as the manner in which tasks were allocated within the family, meaning the distribution of work among husband, wife, children, and other members of the household.[13] The concept can be understood to be in operation not only at the household level, but also more broadly to encompass the social division of labor within the society as a whole. This includes labor relations between different social categories in the rural and urban communities.

The division of labor, especially in the economic arena, fosters some measure of empowerment. As indeed Tukumbi Lumumba-Kasongo has recently pointed out, "The division of labour within the African sociological, economic, and political structures did not necessarily mean in itself fostering inequality. Women are not atomistically isolated from the political processes and were not perceived as 'natural mistakes' as in the Republic of Plato. In fact, [in] most parts of Africa, men and women's relationship was based on the notion of complementarity."[14]

As stated earlier, there is now a large body of literature about the dominance of West African women in trade. Through trade, as studies show, West African women have achieved a considerable measure of economic independence. Therefore, in a discussion of the linkages between gender, dominance, and economic power, the region of West Africa is an appropriate place to start our analysis. Hence, the first four chapters provide case studies from this region.

In Chapter 1, Onaiwu Ogbomo analyzes the role of Esan women traders in the precolonial era in Nigeria. In doing so, he traces the historical origins of Esan society and the evolution of markets. He demonstrates that the Esan polity was a part of the famous Benin kingdom and therefore adopted aspects of Benin's cultural lifestyle, such as the taking of titles and other features that symbolize social status. While explaining the political system that undergirds the cultural and political organization of precolonial Esan society, Ogbomo argues that Esan women's tenacity enabled them to preserve for themselves "various productive industries which secured them autonomous economic avenues." These economic activities included participation in palm oil processing, soap making, food processing, as well as active involvement in various craft industries. In fact, their participation in these and other productive sectors of the economy enabled them to effectively compete with men in trading activities.

In Chapter 2, Toyin Falola analyzes the role of the Yoruba market women who, through their participation in trade, are able to exercise a significant power and control over market space and market ritual. He argues that "their predominance in market transactions, as sellers and buyers, enables the acquisition of control over an important sector of the economy. It is this control—of a space that is so central to production and exchange—that provides considerable spin-off values and influence."

Of course, African women, like most of their counterparts elsewhere, live in a largely male-dominated society. They nevertheless tend to use their economic power as an instrument of social and political emancipation. Thus, in many African societies women have used their wealth to obtain titles or even chieftaincy. These titles not only confer social status but also "bring prestige to the title taker."[15] In Nigeria, for example, Ekechi, Falola, and Ogbomo have demonstrated how women assumed leadership roles both in the precolonial and colonial eras as a result of their economic achievements. Because of their involvement in trade, also, many women acquired considerable property (especially real estate) like their male counterparts.

Yet, however important women's contributions have been in the area of economic development, their control over certain strategic institutions and resources has not gone unchallenged. In fact, their control over market spaces, as in any other spaces (i.e., political, social, and cultural), has generally been contested by men. This fact is clearly demonstrated in Ekechi's essay, which focuses on the male–female struggle over access to the market (a gendered space), as well as the types of market items being traded.

Using archival and published secondary sources, Ekechi skillfully examines the dynamics of economic change in colonial Nigeria, focusing attention on the male–female struggle for dominance in the palm oil and cassava trades. In discussing Igbo palm oil and cassava trade, Ekechi stresses the importance of trading among the womenfolk in Igbo society, noting that traditionally, "marketing has been a central feature in the life of every Igbo woman. A husband's favour is bestowed or withheld largely according to the degree of his wife's success in the market."[16] Indeed, the mark of success for an Igbo woman is having many children "and making money that she can call her own (not her husband's) through trade."[17]

Following on this same theme, Catherine VerEecke focuses on Muslim Fulbe women of Yola in Northern Nigeria. She compares and contrasts Muslim Fulbe women with Muslim Hausa women, noting that whereas Hausa women are generally noted for their active involvement in trade over the centuries, Muslim Fulbe (Fulani) women of Yola have been averse to trading for cultural and religious reasons. Yet, because of changes in economic circumstances, they now do some trading. Thus, while most of West African women's trading activities have been longstanding, the Muslim Fulbe women of Yola have only recently engaged in trade because of economic changes. As VerEecke notes, "Trading has 'always' been the responsibility of other groups, to the extent that Fulbe leaders often invited traders, such as the Hausa of Kanuri, to develop this necessary activity in their communities. . . . Spending unnecessary time in the market is shameful (*chemtu'dum*)." Nevertheless, Muslim Fulbe women participate in various forms of the "hidden" or household trade.

The next three chapters, by Bessie House-Midamba, Claire Robertson, and Nakanyike Musisi, respectively focus critical attention on women's trading activities in East Africa. (Robertson, of course, makes a comparative analysis of Ghanian and Kenyan women's trade.) Although the important economic roles of women traders in East, Central, and Southern Africa have been understudied, or have attracted less attention in the scholarly literature, our study reveals that women in these three regions have been involved in entrepreneurial activities as much as their "better known" counterparts in West Africa. Therefore, these essays challenge the erroneous assumption that women in East, Central, and Southern Africa have not made significant contributions in trade and economic development.

Bessie House-Midamba discusses the trading activities and contributions of Kikuyu women traders in the Mathare Valley. Trading provides avenues through which they have been able to empower themselves economically. This chapter also highlights the cultural and structural constraints that affect Kenyan women's participation in economic and commercial activities. House-Midamba also assesses the factors that have enhanced women's involvement in trade.

Claire Robertson provides a historical analysis of the similarities and differences in the experiences of Ga women traders in Accra, Ghana, and Kikuyu and Kamba women traders in Nairobi, Kenya. Basing her analysis on archival and extensive interviews with market women traders in both countries, she argues that women's participation in trade is inexorably intertwined with their respective histories and cultures. Thus, women's participation in trade is directly related to the dire economic circumstances of African economies, as well as the population growth in both countries. Equally important, women's entry into trade is influenced by such variables as landlessness and changing residential patterns among the Kikuyu and Kamba, as well as ethnicity and education—issues that are more fully developed in House-Midamba's, Musisi's, Horn's, and Osirim's chapters.

Nakanyike Musisi assesses the increasing participation of Baganda women in night market trade activities in Uganda, known locally as *toninyira mukange*. She argues that their recent large-scale entry into this area has been affected by the economic crises that have plagued Uganda since the 1970s. These include economic mismanagement under the leadership of Idi Amin, perennial civil wars, as well as the imposition of structural adjustment programs (SAPs). Baganda women's increasing involvement in night market trade illustrates the significance of social networks, class relationships, as well as a number of important linkages between the formal and the informal sectors of the economy.

The remaining three chapters, those by Nancy Horn, Mary Osirim, and Jeanne Downing, provide interesting insights on women's entrepreneurial activities in the Central and Southern African states. These studies demonstrate that the implementation of SAPs in these countries has severely affected the economic viability and status of women. As Downing notes, "As the income-generating and employment opportunities of men have been increasingly reduced as a result of structural adjustment programs and declines in commodity prices on the world market, the displacement of women from traditionally female-controlled activities has equally intensified."

Nancy Horn and Mary Osirim focus attention on urban women's trading activities in Zimbabwe. Horn's analysis focuses on Shona women's participation in the sale of fresh produce in Harare, while Osirim discusses the role of women traders in Harare and Bulawayo. Throughout the decade of the 1980s, the Zimbabwean economy faced many challenges, including the war in Matabeland, world recession, drought, and destabilization brought by South Africa's frequent raids on member states of the Southern African Development Coordination Conference (SADCC).

Furthermore, Horn and Osirim argue that economic necessity has been a major factor in explaining Zimbabwean women's increasing involvement in trade. Furthermore, in the case of Shona women, cultural ascription in terms of women fulfilling their role of providing food for their families, has also been an important factor in their entry into the fresh produce trade. As Horn notes, through the development of fresh produce enterprises, women have been able to adapt and transform their skills in order to meet the economic needs and challenges of an urban environment.

Jeanne Downing provides documentation on women's entrepreneurial businesses in the four countries of Lesotho, Swaziland, South Africa, and Zimbabwe. She skillfully analyzes the growth patterns of female entrepreneurship and their strategies for generating income. She also gives examples of women who have been able to make the transition from low-growth and low-return enterprises to higher-profit-oriented businesses.

It is particularly noteworthy that women in South Africa and Lesotho in particular have been able to achieve meaningful successes in trade in spite of the oppressive and restrictive system of apartheid. According to Downing's study, there are many more African female entrepreneurs in retail trade than men in South Africa. The study reveals that in all four countries women are heavily involved in small-scale enterprises. The resultant effects of women's marketing and entrepreneurial activities are twofold: the breakdown of stereotypes of African women on the one hand, and their continuing challenge to the status quo on the other hand. Indeed, as Musisi put it poignantly in her chapter, "Social relations can be modified and reinforced within the indigenous social-cultural, political, and economic arena."

NOTES

1. Barbara P. Thomas-Slayter, "Class, Ethnicity, and the Kenyan State: Community Mobilization in the Context of Global Politics," *International Journal of Politics, Culture and Society*, Vol. 4, No. 3, 1991, p. 303.

2. Ester Boserup, *Woman's Role in Economic Development* (London: George Allen & Unwin, 1970), p. 15.

3. See Solomon Izieben Agbon, "Class and Economic Development in Nigeria, 1900–1980," Ph.D. dissertation, University of Texas, Austin, 1985.

4. Tulkumbi Lumumba-Kasongo, "Dynamic Factors," in *West Africa*, 5–11 July 1993, p. 1140.

5. President Ibrahim Babangida, quoted in *West Africa*, 1–7 November 1993, p. 1970.

6. Cf. Patricia Stamp, *Technology, Gender, and Power in Africa* (Ottawa: International Development Center, 1989). See also Ivy Florence Matsepe, "African Women's Labor in the 'Political Economy of South Africa, 1880–1970,'" Ph.D. dissertation, Rutgers University, New Brunswick, 1984.

7. Marjorie Mbilinyi, "Research Priorities in Women's Studies in Eastern Africa," *Women's Studies International Forum*, Vol. 7, No. 4, 1984, p. 292.

8. Irene Tinker, ed., *Persistent Inequalities: Women and World Development* (New York: Oxford University Press, 1990), p. 187.

9. Boserup, *Woman's Role in Economic Development*.

10. Lumumba-Kasongo, "Dynamic Factors," p. 1141.

11. Haleh Afshar, *Women, Development and Survival in the Third World* (London: Longman, 1991), p. 3.

12. Simon Ottenberg, *Boyhood Rituals in an African Society, An Interpretation* (Seattle: University of Washington Press, 1989), p. xvi.

13. Boserup, *Woman's Role in Economic Development*, p. 15; Per Kongstad and Mette Monsted, *Family Labour and Trade in Western Kenya* (Uppsala: Scandinavian Institute for African Studies, 1980), p. 18.

14. Lumumba-Kasongo, "Dynamic Factors," pp. 1140–1141.

15. Ottenberg, *Boyhood Rituals*, p. xvii; Sandra Barnes, *Patrons and Power. Creating a Political Community in Metropolitan Lagos* (Bloomington: Indiana University Press, 1986), Chap. 5.

16. G. T. Basden, *Among the Igbos of Nigeria* (London: Frank Cass and Company, 1966), p. 194.

17. Ottenberg, *Boyhood Rituals*, p. xxii.

Chapter 1

Esan Women Traders and Precolonial Economic Power

Onaiwu W. Ogbomo

The African woman as entrepreneur is not a twentieth century phenomenon, but an aspect of reality deeply rooted in the history of African social, economic, and political structures. In Western Africa, in particular, women as merchants and traders have become legendary.[1]

A number of studies, most of which focus on women in prominent empires, kingdoms, and majority ethnic groups, have examined the exploits of West African female traders.[2] On the other hand, the economic activities of women in segmentary and noncentralized societies have been overlooked. Consequently, an erroneous impression is created that the latter group of women has consisted of passive participants in their societies. It cannot be overemphasized that an understanding of the activities of women in these smaller political entities will lead to a better appreciation of the lives of African women. This chapter sets out to reconstruct the commercial initiatives of one such neglected group—the Esan women of Nigeria (see Map 1.1).

The interviews on which this chapter is based were conducted in August and September 1987 as part of the defunct Esan History Research Project at the Bendel State (now Edo State) University, Ekpoma-Nigeria. The project was abandoned as a result of lack of funding. I also benefited from the field notes of Mr. A. I. Okoduwa of the Department of History, Bendel State University, Ekpoma. Last, I wish to acknowledge the support of the Frederick Douglass Institute for African and African-American Studies for a postdoctoral fellowship from September 1993 to May 1994 which enabled me to write up my research findings.

Map 1.1
Nigeria Showing States and Their Capitals

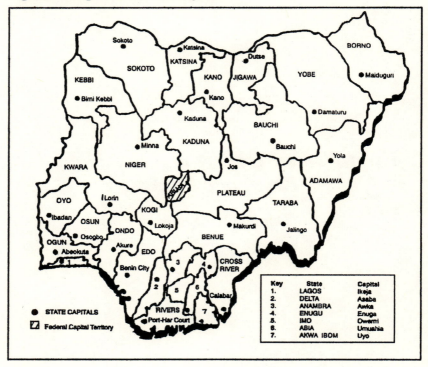

ESAN PEOPLE AND THE ENVIRONMENT

The Esan people at present inhabit four local government areas (Esan West, Esan East, Esan Northeast, and Esan Southeast) of Edo State, Nigeria (Map 1.2). The majority of Esan people claim Benin origins. The name Esan is a Benin word meaning "jump" or "flee." It explains the manner in which they fled from harsh rulers of the Benin kingdom. Oral traditions from many of the Esan chiefdoms claimed their founders migrated into the region during the reign of Oba Ewuare (c. 1455–1482). This was undoubtedly a turbulent period in the history of the great kingdom. Following the death of the oba's sons, he enacted "a strict law forbidding anyone in the land of either sex to wash and dress up, or to have carnal intercourse for three years."[3] This law occasioned mass exodus from the kingdom. As Jacob Egharevba, the Benin historian pointed out, "This law . . . caused great confusion for a large number of citizens migrated to various places."[4] Consequent upon advice, the oba revoked the law and requested all Benin migrants to return. Nevertheless those who settled in Esanland refused to return. To ensure the iden-

Map 1.2
Edo State Showing the Local Government Areas

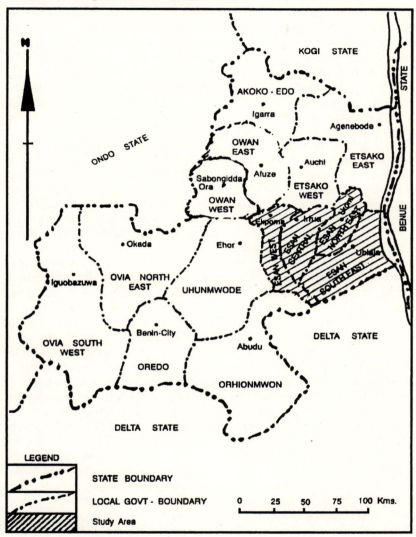

tification of Benin migrants in neighboring territories, Oba Ewuare ordered them to tattoo their bodies. According to C. G. Okojie:

Oba Ewuare, after being repeatedly beaten in attempts to get the recalcitrant subjects to return to Benin, tried body tattooing to make identification of deserters easy; that did not help, as, very soon, everybody in Ishan [Esan] began tattooing . . . in an . . . attempt to be like the superior migrants.[5]

As a result of the failure of this strategy, the oba decided to approach or resolve the impasse diplomatically. As a first step, he extended to the leaders (*Ekakulo*) a general amnesty to pave the way for them to return to the kingdom. This also failed. Oba Ewuare in 1463 "invited all the leaders to Benin and formally installed them Enigie (Dukes) . . . owing allegiance only to the Oba himself."[6] The investiture ceremony became a major watershed in the political development of Esan communities.

While oral tradition claims this marked the foundation of the chiefdoms, the correct historical interpretation of this period was the centralization of political authority by Benin migrants over existing aboriginal sociopolitical arrangements.[7] Presumably this transition also marked the end of the egalitarian period in the history of the Esan people. The period of egalitarianism is synonymous with the sociopolitical arrangement that anthropologists tagged the communal kinship system. A similar reorganization has been identified in the same period (c. 1455–1482) in the history of Iyede people of Nigeria.[8] While the structural changes affected authority and power relations between the settlers and the aboriginal population, it also tilted the existing gender balance in favor of male titled chiefs.

As a consequence of the reorganization efforts, Esan communities were transformed into chiefdom political structures under *enigie* (chiefs) who were descendants of the *Ekakulo* (war leaders).[9] While the Onojie headed each Esan chiefdom, the political organization comprised three major elements: the age-grade system, the title system, and a hereditary chieftainship. All Esan chiefdoms comprised between one and twenty villages.[10] Individual villages were administered by a council of elders called the *edion*. The council was headed by an *odionwere* or village head whose qualification was based on the fact that he was the oldest man.[11] The *ekhaemon* (chiefs) acted as the representatives of the *onojie* in the villages. The titles of the ekhaemon included iyase, edogun, ezomo, oliha, oshodi, and unwangue, which were patterned after those in the Benin Kingdom.

Most Esan communities are located on a plateau northeast of Benin. According to Bradbury, the "plateau rises from the Orhiomo River in the south-west to an east-west ridge along the northern borders of [the region] on which are situated the chiefdoms of Irrua and Ekpoma. Egoro, Ukhun, Idua, and Ewu lie on the northern slopes of this ridge, which is drained by small streams flowing north then east to the Niger."[12] The lowland communities are located in regions with abundant water, forests, hills, and valleys.[13] Some of the lowland communities include Ohuesan, Emu, Ewatto, Ewohimi Ebelle, Ewossa, and Amahor. There are two vegetational zones. On the vegetation, Bradbury notes that

most of the area is high tropical forest with an abundance of good timber. There are areas of orchard bush in the north-eastern part of Ukhun, in Ujagbe, Northern Uzia [Uzea], Egoronokhua, and the adjoining south-western part of Ekpoma, and patches of orchard bush and elephant grass on the surface of the plateau, especially in the more densely populated areas where the forest cover has been removed. The eastern, south-eastern, and south-western sectors, where the population density is low, are heavily forested.[14]

ESAN WOMEN AND FARMING

As a background to the discussion of the commercial activities of Esan women during the precolonial period, it is important first of all to examine their agricultural and manufacturing roles. As was true of most precolonial economies in Africa, the mainstay of the Esan economy was essentially agriculture. Hence it has been asserted that "pre-colonial Esan society rested on agriculture which provided a suitable foundation on which other economic pursuits were based."[15] Farming as an occupation was the affair of both men and women. As a result, there was a sexual division of labor in the Esan farming system. Esan farmers grew yams, maize, cocoyam, tomatoes, beans, cassava, pepper, cotton, groundnuts, melons, bananas, and plantains.[16] Although men, women, and children supplied the labor for the cultivation of these crops, yam was regarded as a male crop because of its status as "king of crops."[17] Invariably all other crops were regarded as those of women who paid special attention to their cultivation. For instance, it has been pointed out that in "Ishan 'A' . . . most women have separate cocoyam and groundnut farms . . . such crops as beans, melon, groundnuts . . . cotton, pepper, etc." were women's.[18] Despite the sexual division of labor in farming activities, the functions performed by men and women were complementary. Thus men carried out such tasks as bush clearing, tree felling, and land preparation. From the period of the planting of yams to the harvesting, men, women, and children participated in all stages of the different activities. In addition to supplying labor for yam farming, women, with the support of children's labor, also cultivated the so-called subsidiary or female crops.

Because of the level of Esan women's involvement in agricultural production, it is important to examine their status vis-à-vis the organization of production processes and the control and utilization of agricultural products. In assessing the relationship between women's participation in production and their position in society, some scholars "have hypothesized that in societies where men and women are engaged in the production of the same kinds of socially necessary goods, and where widespread private property (and therefore class structure) has not developed, women's participation in production gives them access to and control over the products of their labour, as well as considerable freedom and independence."[19] Judging from the development of Esan political history, it is easy to identify two major periods, the prestratification and poststratification eras. As noted earlier, in the traditions of origin of the people, the period of egalitarianism and absence of extreme social stratification can be dated to before c. 1455–1482. On the other hand, the poststratification phase occurred from about 1463 when Oba Ewuare invested the Esan leaders with the onojie titles. From then on, political centralization culminated in the entrenchment of male dominated power and authority structures. While conventional scholarship has interpreted this as part of the prevailing political upheavals in the Benin kingdom, the present writer has argued elsewhere that they were in many respects related to gender struggles in the kingdom at the time.[20] Moreover, the period coincided with the beginning of and subsequent boom in the cotton and cloth trade, which was designated a female occupation in the region. It seems that the centralization of political authority was intended to deny women gains from this boom. This development tends to confirm the hypothesis that as society becomes stratified, the status of women deteriorates. However, it must be noted that the tendency toward male dominance in Esanland never resulted in a clean sweep of power and authority. It undoubtedly caused a tilt in the balance of power between genders.

One of the noticeable areas the imbalance affected had to do with the control and utilization of land resources, which were said to be communally owned.[21] Following the introduction of the chiefdom-style administration, land was designated the property of the onojie. Although Bradbury and Okojie claimed the onojie held land in trust for the people, where disputes arose as to its use, he was the final arbiter.[22] Precolonial Esan land-allocation policy did not recognize the rights of women to direct access to land. Because the power of control resided with lineage elders and the onojie, the women remained subject to the whims and caprices of the men. They had to rely on the good will of their fathers, husbands, brothers, and sons for access to land use. Hence women had to employ all the wits and tact they could muster to ensure continuous access to land resources. In precolonial Esan chiefdoms, women were never known to own farmlands. Rather, their male kins allocated them plots to cultivate female crops. Such crops as pepper, plantain, maize, tomatoes, and bananas were intercropped with yams. Since yam was the major crop, the farming calendar revolved around its cultivation. Men recruited the labor of their wives, children, relatives, and slaves toward its successful production.[23] The quantity of seed yams was also crucial in the size of a farmer's field.

In addition, the amount of a farmer's farmland was defined by the strength and size of the labor force available to him. According to A. I. Okoduwa, "The amount of land acquired by individual [farmers] for farming depended on the amount of labour put in during the initial work of clearing and burning the bush; hence, the wealth of a man was determined by the number of wives and children he had to provide him with the necessary helping hands."[24] The importance of women in the scheme of things demanded that men look up to them to be part of their labor force and also bear them children who would not only be labor hands but also extend the life of their patrilineages. Thus in many respects women were crucial to the survival of the lineages. In order to satisfy these yearnings, Esan men practiced polygyny. It has been pointed out that in the agriculture and polygyny marriage system, "women only have limited rights of support from their husbands, but they may have some economic independence from the sale of their own crops."[25] The evidence from Esan society supports this view. While women may have benefited from the fact that certain crops were designated as theirs, the profits from the sales of agricultural products were very marginal. The explanation for this can be found in the reproductive roles of women in the precolonial Esan economy.

These reproductive roles took the form of biological reproduction, social reproduction, and reproduction of the labor force. Whereas biological reproduction essentially has to do with childbearing, social reproduction is the process of reproducing the conditions that sustain a social system.[26] The major issue in sustaining the social system becomes the definition of "what structures have to be reproduced in order that social reproduction as a whole can take place."[27] The reproduction of the labor force included both its maintenance and the "allocation of agents to positions within the labour process."[28] For precolonial Esan women, the second aspect of reproduction of the labor force involved training the children in agricultural techniques—in both producing and processing food items. Of note is the fact that while women expended their time and energy in the transfer of agricultural knowledge, they spent whatever agricultural and economic profits accrued to them from independent sources on the maintenance of the labor force. Clearly Esan women were compelled as mothers to utilize their personal gains for the good of their families.[29] Contrary to women's concerns for the well-being of their families, adult males employed their major resources—yams and cattle—for such personal gains as titles and manhood ceremonies.[30] Under such conditions where the women were dispossessed of their resources by catering to family members, the question arises as to what options were left for them. Without doubt the women made up for the shortfall from such other sources as craft production and trading activities. Before an examination of these vocations can be undertaken, it is important to examine another social practice in precolonial Esan society that prompted other economic choices open to women.

ESAN WOMEN AND INHERITANCE

The laws of Esan society excluded a woman from inheriting anything substantial from either her patrilineage or from that of her husband. This exclusion is well expressed in two proverbs: "Okhuo ila aghada bhu uku (A woman never inherits the sword!)" and "Ei bio omokhuo heole iriogbe" (literally, "You do not have a daughter and name her the family keeper!").[31] The patrilineal and patrilocal nature of Esan society made it impossible for wives and daughters to inherit either their husbands' or their fathers' property. The implication of the second proverb was that the Esan people felt any property handed over to a daughter would ultimately end up in her husband's patrilineage. As a result, families were not prepared to transfer to their daughters inheritances that would enrich in-laws. On the other hand, wives were considered strangers among their husbands' kin, which again does not qualify them for any form of inheritance. Another curious notion is the belief that women were themselves inheritable. As Okojie noted, in Esan customary laws of inheritance "the woman had no place, . . . she was one of the inheritable properties!"[32] Thus, to ensure that women were prevented from inheriting any property, a number of cultural norms were established. As a case in point, a woman was not allowed to perform the burial ceremonies of her father. It was a custom that whoever performed the burial ceremonies inherited a man's property.[33] Knowing full well that some women might have been wealthy enough to perform funeral rites, it was deliberately stated that women were prohibited from such rites. Tradition also claims that because women were not permitted to handle an *ukhure* (a family staff), it was inconceivable for women to want to perform burial ceremonies for their dead fathers.[34] Hence they could not inherit the family shrine where the ukhure was placed. It was therefore logical for a woman not to dream of owning family property. These constraints no doubt prompted women to search for individual ways of amassing wealth that they could hand over to their daughters in the form of either bridewealth or inheritance.

Despite the strong patrilineal descent system of the Esan people, there was matrifocality within lineages and households. The matrifocal families were very much the same as those Uchendu identified among the Igbo. According to him, these families could be described as follows:

Sometimes called a matricentric family, it is a mother-centered segment of the polygynous family. Two or more matrifocal units "linked" to or sharing a husband (who may be male or female) result in a polygynous family. . . . A matrifocal household consists of a mother, her children, and other dependents. Among the Igbo it is essentially a cooking unit and eating unit.[35]

The residential pattern created a situation whereby each wife in a polygynous household had a separate living space. The living arrangements made it possible for each woman to be the focal point of her children. Also, because of the competitive nature of polygynous households, women were very much concerned about how their children fared against children of other co-wives. This in effect meant that women had to look for independent sources to improve their own lives and those of their children.

Since women relied on their sons for access to such critical resources as land at the death of their husbands, they had to save for the rainy day by working to improve and consolidate their sons' position within the polygynous family. As noted earlier, because the polygynous family was very competitive, women had to strike special bonds with their children. These bonds were created by extending economic benefits to the children which ordinarily might not be forthcoming from their fathers. Again to be able to dispense these favors to her children, a woman sought independent economic avenues. More important, because female children were not in a position to inherit from their patrilineage, the only people they pinned their hopes on were mothers.[36] Since it was a cultural practice for mothers and daughters to demonstrate reciprocity in their relations, the mothers felt they had to cater to their daughters when age was on their side.[37] And in their old age, it became their daughters' turn to care for them. It is clear that a number of factors spurred Esan women to look to independent sources of income. If anything, they were determined to guarantee for their children a secured future.

SEXUAL DIVISION OF LABOR IN MANUFACTURING

As with other economic endeavors in precolonial Esan society, a sexual division of labor operated in the manufacturing industries, which included wood carving, metal smithing, basket weaving, cloth weaving and dyeing, pottery making, soap making, palm oil production, and food processing. While men were involved in wood carving, metal smithing, and basket weaving, women were in the cloth-weaving and dyeing, pottery-making, soap-making, palm-oil, and food-process-ing industries.[38] The division of labor in craft production in Esan society has been rationalized by the claim that it was conditioned by local taboos. As one scholar noted in the case of Yoruba and Igbo societies:

Women and men often desire to keep their artistic [craft and manufacturing] domains sepa-rate and it is through taboos and other means of social avoidances that the lines of division are kept intact. One frequently hears of taboos which prevent women from doing men's wood-carving and iron-work, but it is also true that taboos prevent men from entering arts dominated by women. Weaving in the Yoruba town of Oyo and the Igbo village of Akwete is strictly a woman's domain, and it is believed that men who attempt weaving will become impotent.[39]

Conversations with female informants in Esan communities indicate that many of them were delighted that separate economic domains existed and still exist. They believe that taboos have ensured that they were not deprived of independent sources of income. Consequently, they have relied less on their husbands.

In spite of the separate spheres of male and female craft and manufacturing activities, these efforts have nevertheless been complementary. As expected in both precolonial and postcolonial periods, they have been accorded due respect. The male craft activity of wood carving provided various objects for both spiritual and secular needs. As an example, wood carvers produced such items as the family staff (*ukhure*) and other shrine objects with which Esan people performed numer-ous religious rites.[40] Of note was the masks (*okpodu*) for masquerade societies. Since masquerade societies were limited to male participation, women were pre-vented by taboos from carving them. The Esan smithing industry supplied farm implements and weapons of war. Like wood carving, the industry also catered to religious needs. Following the tradition in Benin, whereby the oba controlled the guilds, in Esanland the *enigie* (plural *of onojie*) granted the iron workers royal charters to produce their wares.[41] However, they were not organized into guilds as was the case in Benin. Because blacksmiths were granted charters by the *enigie*, they were expected to pay them tributes.

One of the outstanding female craft industries in precolonial Esan society was cloth weaving and dyeing. It has been difficult to date the beginning of the cloth industry in Esanland because informants claim it began "long ago." Nevertheless, both male and female informants are very firm on the fact that the industry has always been controlled by women. Although cloth weaving was carried out in virtually all Esan chiefdoms, the women of Uromi and Ohordua were the most famous weavers. While growing cotton crops has been the work of almost every Esan woman, the more specialized work of ginning and spinning were done by elderly women. It has also been pointed out that even though cloth weaving and dyeing has been a female job, not all women learned the trade.[42] There was also specialization of functions between women who wove and those who dyed the cloth. The most valued product of the weavers was the *ukpon-ododo* (multicolored cloth) brand. Also important were the red ones, which were sought after by Benin traders. It became a major article of trade with the Europeans—Portuguese, French, English, and Dutch—from about 1500 to 1700. The red cloth became very important because it was part of the royal emblem in Benin and formed the basis of many rituals. But more important was the economic consideration. As Ray A. Kea has shown, in the Gold Coast trade in the seventeenth century, Bini (Benin) cloth was exchanged for gold by the Europeans.[43] Thus the involvement of Esan women in the very important cloth-weaving industry set them on the path to independent economic enterprise. How this affected their lives is explored more fully when their trading activities are examined.

Other principal craft objects Esan women produced were ceramic products. Writing generally about pottery in Africa, Lisa Aronson claimed that the technique of making ceramic products "is the most pervasive and perhaps the most important of art forms which African women perform."[44] She went on that "in addition to serving important religious and political purposes, it is economically vital as is indicated by the degree to which women impose rigid boundaries and controls to protect their profession and the processes with which it is associated."[45] The ceramic products manufactured by Esan women included pipes for smokers, ritual objects, and various types of pots. Among the different types of pots, the outstanding ones were the cooking, ritual, and ceremonial pots.[46] In addition to these uses Esan pots were also used in storing water, oil, and other cooking ingredients. The major centers of pottery making were located in Idegun-Ugboha, Ibore-Irrua, and Asukpodudu-Uzea. Despite the recognition of these Esan chiefdoms as centers of pottery, other Esan communities such as Iruekpen, Egoro-Amede, and Ekpoma secured their ceramic pieces from the neighboring Owan people. Because of the significant uses Esan ceramic products were put to, the women who produced them were highly regarded within their communities. This was the logical outcome of the demand for their products. The Esan women potter's experience tallies with Peggy R. Sanday's postulation that "in societies where control and production are linked and a competitive market exists, female power is likely to develop if females are actively engaged in producing valued market goods."[47] Without doubt Esan women were able to achieve this level of importance because they exercised direct control over their vocation and ensured that men did not interfere.

Other important trades of women included palm oil processing, soap making, and food processing. Informants pointed out that palm oil in the early stages of the development of Esan communities was produced only for household consumption. However, with the development of the legitimate commerce following the abolition of the transatlantic slave trade, palm produce (palm oil and kernels) became major export commodities. Whereas women controlled palm oil processing in the pre-European era, the advent of the export trade witnessed the involvement of men in the trade in palm produce. Despite this development, women were not completely displaced.

As an extension of palm produce processing, soap making became a predominantly female occupation. Most of the ingredients for soap making were derived from the waste materials from the processing of palm oil. Again, as with other female trades, Esan women successfully prevented men from encroaching upon the soap-making industry. Through the tenacity of Esan women, they were able to preserve for themselves various productive industries that secured them autonomous economic avenues. From this solid foundation established in productive ventures, they were able to propel themselves into trading activities.

ESAN WOMEN AND TRADE

In Nina Mba's analysis of women's role in precolonial Benin economy, she claimed:

There was much less economic autonomy among Bini women than among Yoruba women. They were not involved in the key area of the economy—trade with the Europeans—and not actively involved in long-distance trade. This meant that men had greater opportunities than women for amassing wealth.[48]

Even though her fieldwork revealed that Benin women were involved in long distance trade in beads from Ilorin, she chose to dismiss it as "limited degree" on very scanty evidence. Her major explanation was based on the claim by informants that the women "more often employ[ed] young male slaves or freeborn males to make the journey for them."[49] The fact that the women did not carry out the buying and selling of the goods themselves is not sufficient to lead to the conclusion that they were not in control. Is this not indicative of the women's power rather than their helplessness? For no justifiable reason, Mba chose to ignore the evidence. She also argued that because women were not involved in the long-distance trade with the Europeans they were economically dependent. This again is an untenable argument. Granted that men dominated the coastal trade with Europeans, there is no evidence to show that Benin women were completely excluded.

Furthermore, research has shown that even in the case of Yoruba women, "some women did engage in inter-urban trade, by far the majority traded in their local town markets."[50] It is therefore clear that economic autonomy did not go only hand in hand with long-distance trade. From all indications, Mba based her deductions on limited, male-biased information. For instance, out of six of the sources she relied on for her conclusions, four were males and two females. Last, the fact that "men had greater opportunities than women for amassing wealth" does not lead the latter to be dependent on the former. More detailed research must be done before such generalizations can be made.

A generalization similar to that reached by Mba has also been put forward for Esan women by Okojie. According to him, the Esan people were generally "poor traders," the Uromi being the notable exception. Okojie's explanation for this is that "until the advent of the white men, people hardly ventured beyond the confines of their settlement."[51] Again this is a conclusion based on very scanty information. It is difficult to understand how Uromi women developed trading skills that other Esan women could not copy. More important, while Okojie claims there was no external trade in precolonial Esanland, he seems to believe that Esan society was in a state of anarchy before the advent of the Europeans. There is no doubt that this is a twisted version of the discredited Eurocentric depiction of African societies, which claimed Africans were soaked in barbarism before the arrival of the "carriers of civilization"—the Europeans. This is clearly ahistorical.

Tracing the origins of exchange procedures in precolonial Esanland, Okoduwa identified two forms—formal and informal exchanges.[52] He argued that informal exchanges began as tribute paying, gift giving, help or assistance from a junior member of a family or lineage to an elder or lineage head. This transfer of resources further extended to the enijie, the chiefdom heads who expected annual tributes from their subjects. On the other hand, formal exchanges can be classified into two categories—local and long-distance trade. A. G. Hopkins defines local trade as "transactions which took place within a radius of up to about ten miles of the production. This was the range which could be covered in one day by foot or by donkey, while still allowing time to exchange products and return home."[53] Long-distance trade, on the other hand, "can be regarded as an attempt by African entrepreneurs to overcome the limitations of local commerce."[54] One such limitation was the failure of local trade to cater to the demands of the consumers. Thus traders had to look for larger markets to satisfy their needs. Transactions in both formal modes of exchange were carried out in markets, which were locations where buying and selling took place.

It has been suggested that in West Africa women dominated local trading activities. As Hopkins argues:

They were mainly female because local trade was a convenient adjunct to household and, in some societies, farming activities; they were part-time because trade was regarded as a supplement, though often an important one, to primary, domestic occupations; they were small scale because they lacked the capital to be anything else, they were mobile (except in the towns) because the most efficient way of connecting buyers and sellers was by bringing them together in periodic, rotating markets; and they were numerous because local trade was a generally accessible way of adding to farm incomes, since it required few managerial or technical skills and little capital.[55]

The evidence from the precolonial Esan economy confirms Hopkins's assertion. According to Esan traditions, local trade began with women displaying items such as soap, coconuts, pepper, tomatoes, and groundnuts in front of their houses for sale to those who needed them. A woman could be working on the farm while she displayed her wares in front of the family home. This practice was referred to as silent trade.[56] This meant that the seller shared her articles into units that were exchanged for *ogbolo* (twenty cowries). The customer came by, took his or her requirements, and left the equivalent amount, only for the seller to collect her money at dusk. The silent trade was essentially based on the honesty of both parties. Since the seller was expected to place the approximate quantity of goods on the frontier, the consumer was also required not to cheat. Gradually the silent trade gave rise to small markets in village squares. These were called *ekiolele*—literally "outside markets." As a result of economic forces, a more dependable market system had to evolve.

As demand increased the need arose to establish larger chiefdom or village markets to cope with the local volume of trade. The creation of chiefdom markets followed the centralization of sociopolitical organization in most chiefdoms. Sometime in the sixteenth century, Ekpoma, Irrua, Ugboha, and Uromi founded larger markets to cater to the growth in population and trade. For instance, the foundation of the Uromi chiefdom market has been linked with the onojie Agba, whose reign is dated at c. 1488–1504. This generation followed the era in which many Benin migrants moved into the Esan region. There is every indication that the migrants might have moved away in search of greener pastures in Esan land.[57]

The establishment of village markets became a reality when two or more villages struck agreements to that effect. In Okojie's analysis:

Two villages, usually bound by OKOVEN (a covenant), deciding to have a common market, would come together round about the Okoven, to clear a piece of ground; . . . they took the oath of friendship and faithfulness, and the market was established, fixing a day for it and also fixing prices.[58]

The establishment of markets through the cooperation of villages ensured there was no duplication of efforts at encouraging local trade. Periodicity and market rings were other avenues through which duplications were checked. The most common periodicity of precolonial Esan markets was the four-day week. By these arrangements, unnecessary competition between different village and chiefdom markets were avoided. Precolonial Esan market rings were organized as shown in Table 1.1.

As local markets expanded, women became placed in vantage positions to enhance their economic independence. For instance, the development of new markets responded to increased output in primary "production sites which attracted those traders who bought on wholesale to resell" in larger markets.[59] Consequently Amaru, a fishing village, Asukpodudu, Uzea (famous for pottery making), and Uromi (a major cloth weaving town) developed into principal trading centers. The major commodities of trade—cloth, soap, and pots—were basically female products, an observation that supports the contention that increased trade had direct effects on the economic well-being of the women. The major factor that worked in favor of Esan women's economic success was the fact that the products they produced were generally required for societal use. In many cases, the goods were essential commodities. It should be pointed out, however, that even though agricultural products were also exchanged in the local markets, women were not able to reap much profit from them, largely because they were expended on feeding members of the households and extended family. Having established a foot-

Table 1.1
Principal Market Days in Esan Chiefdoms

Week Day	Markets
First Day (Ede no odion)	Ekpoma, Ibore, Okhuesan Ugboha, and Ekpon
Second Day (Ede no zeva)	Irrua, Opoji (nearness did cause trouble), Ebelle, Ubiaja, and Ohordua
Third Day (Ede no zea)	Uromi, Iruekpen, and Ewohimi
Fourth Day (Ede no zenen: Uhen Edeken or Ede Izele)	Ewu, Illushi (Ozigolo), Igor, and Ewatto

Source: Based on Okojie, *Ishan Native Laws,* p. 139; and Okoduwa, "Economic Organization," p. 104.

hold in local markets, Esan women were advantageously positioned to venture into long-distance trade. However, Okojie wants us to believe that interethnic and chiefdom wars prevented women from being involved in long-distance trade. In his words,

In those days of terrible inter-tribal wars, . . . markets as they exist today were unknown. There were the EKIOLELE—small markets in the village square. . . . It would be suicidal for a woman to leave her husband's village at Uromi, for instance, to attend a market at Irrua and Ekpoma. If she attempted it, she might, if lucky, be caught and made the wife of the captor, otherwise she would be sold to slave dealers.[60]

There are a number of contradictions in Okojie's statements both in the quotation given here and in others given earlier. For instance, Okojie claimed that the essence of covenants established between villages in the precolonial period was to ensure friendship. How is it possible for insecurity to reign in a friendly atmosphere? If insecurity was the order of the day, what was the importance of the covenants? A diametrically opposite argument has been made for the dominant position of women in rural trade in Yoruba societies.[61] However, such propositions have been shown to contain serious flaws.[62] It has to be recognized that "the existence of markets depended in the first place on the existence of a political structure which could guarantee the security of the traders and the maintenance of peace in the markets themselves."[63]

The Esan experience reveals that most of the chiefdom markets were established after 1500, following the installation of the enijie by Oba Ewuare and the formal centralization of political authority. Okoduwa has also shown that because chiefdom markets were located close to the palaces of the enijie, these officials appointed market guards who took charge of security matters.[64] Even when the chiefdoms lacked the means to protect the markets from attacks, it is inconceivable that the oba would have allowed pillaging to take place in his vassal territories, which were economically useful to the kingdom. From available data, Okojie's characterization of precolonial Esan chiefdoms as perpetual regions of anarchy cannot be sustained. Thus the claim that women were excluded from long-distance trade does not hold water. A more credible argument would be that for a long time men dominated the long-distance trade. This is understandable in that it could have been the result of the gender division of spheres of influence in precolonial Esan society. In any case, some female informants recalled instances when their mothers and aunts traded various commodities to distant markets.[65]

The incorporation of Esan chiefdoms into Benin's imperial trading formation began from about 1463 when Oba Ewuare appointed the enigie as his representatives in the region. This prepared the grounds for the assimilation of Esan chiefdoms and other neighboring groups into two centuries of economic exploitation of the region by the obas. Coincidentally, between 1500 and 1700 there was a flourishing coastal trade between the Benin kingdom and the Europeans—the Portuguese, French, English, and the Dutch. The major articles of trade were woven cloth, beads, pepper, and slaves. This trade linked the hinterland markets such as those in Esanland with the coast. As R. A. Sargent reported, "The cloth industry, in fact, emerged as the economic mainstay of Benin's export production, and thereby contributed to the expansion of cotton production, weaving and dyeing skills. These apparent multiplier effects in the cloth trade provided additional incentive for the increase in the cloth industry."[66] Although it is not possible to measure the level of benefits Esan women derived from increased trade in the cloth industry between 1500 and 1700, there is every indication that they benefited. It is significant that they had firm control of the industry within the Esan economy.

A major indication that women in peripheral economies such as that of the Esan people benefited directly from increased trade in cotton cloth can be seen in the manner in which Uromi resisted Benin's attempt to monopolize the trade. By the reign of Onojie Agba, Uromi had become an important center of cloth production in Esanland. As Okoduwa stated, this "attracted Benin's efforts to control or monopolize such a flourishing free enterprise. This attempt by Oba Ozolua [c. 1482–1509] however, produced strong local opposition. All yearly tributes from Uromi to Benin were stopped and deriding scorn was directed at those Enijie who persisted in paying homage."[67] Since women were in control of the cloth industry, it is logical to think that they might have been responsible for the initiative to curtail Benin control by stopping tributes to the kingdom.

Another primary article in the trade between the Esan chiefdom and the Benin kingdom was red pepper. As with cotton cloth, women were the dominant producers in the precolonial Esan economy. The climate undoubtedly was conducive to the production of red pepper. The trade began in the fifteenth century when a Portuguese trade envoy, d'Aveiro, took samples of the commodity to a Portuguese factory at Antwerp.[68] Records show that between 1498 and 1505 the quantity of Benin red pepper received there amounted to about 75 quintals annually.[69] Ryder,

Map 1.3
Esan Precolonial Trade Routes

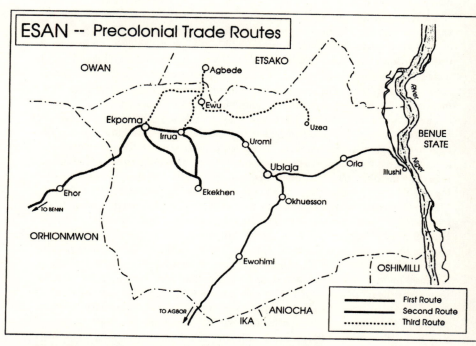

Source: Okoduwa, "Economic Organisation of Pre-Colonial Esanland."

however, argues that the quantity must have been more. Clearly the level of trade in Benin pepper had some effect on the economic status of Esan women because of their incorporation into Benin's imperial trading formations.

In addition to the trade with Benin, Esan chiefdoms also established trading links with neighboring groups. According to Okoduwa, three major precolonial trading routes linked Esan communities with other trading centers (see Map 1.3). The first ran from Uromi through Irrua, Ekpoma, and Ehor to Benin. This was the route through which Esan traders imported beads (*akpono*), cowries, tobacco, and gin. In exchange, Esan traders exported cloth, pepper, goats, sheep, and slaves.[70] The second trade route began from Uromi through Ubiaja to Oria and Illushi (Ozigolo). A subdivision of the route branched out to Okhuesan and Ewohimi and then to Agbor.[71] Esan traders imported from the Igala people such items as decorated calabashes, iron, wooden spears, and smoked fish. In return, Esan women sold them cloth. The third route proceeded northward from Irrua through Ewu to Alegbette, and from Ewu to Uzea. Salt and coral beads came into Esan communities from this route.[72] Of the three trade routes, the route that linked Esan chiefdoms with Benin became the major one. This is certainly understandable in that the route linked Benin with the Europeans.

Informants claim that in the organization of the trading activities Esan women relied on different sources to raise capital. Some claimed traders in precolonial times started long-distance trade with the capital they raised from local trade. However, a more reliable source of capital was informal credit institutions called *osusu*. The Esan *osusu* was similar to the *esusu* of Yoruba land.[73] The major component was that each member of the credit institution had specific economic goals which it wanted to achieve. In coming together, the members of the savings club raised capital for one another to start a given project. Another source of capital was individuals who pawned either themselves or members of their families to secure loans from more affluent people. A nineteenth-century female Uromi merchant, Iroro, is said to have granted loans to individuals to commence commercial activities.[74]

The medium of exchange changed with time and the sophistication of the economy. At the early stage, exchange was carried out through bartering of goods. At a point, Esan cloth was adopted as a medium. It is very likely that since the Esan economy was tied to that of the Benin kingdom, trading activities in the former responded to developments in the latter. This can be seen in the switch from cloth to cowrie currency. It has also been reported that tobacco leaves were used.[75] The adoption of cowries as currency is associated with the reign of Oba Esigie of Benin. Its introduction into Benin economy by the oba "provided the opportunity for the establishment of wider palace controls over commercial exchange, and eventually contributed to the expansion of stringent elite supervision of all standards of Exchange."[76] With the introduction of a sophisticated currency system such as cowries, it became easily possible for traders to reckon their wealth. Esan women, for example, began to invest their profits in valuables such as clothes (both local and imported), beads, and gold. This marked the beginning of women's attempt to amass wealth that their daughters ultimately inherited. Thus the involvement of Esan women in local and long-distance trade led to the emergence of a wealthy group who became economically independent of men. Another category of women, who emerged out of independent economic exploits of female traders in precolonial Esan, were those who married other women. The practice of "woman marriage" was prompted by childlessness, the wealth of the female husbands, and the need to have an heir who eventually inherited the woman's wealth. According to Okojie:

A childless but very rich woman not wanting her property to pass to her husband and desiring fitting burial ceremonies, "married" a girl by paying the full bride price and bringing her to live with her. She [the girl] was allowed to be "kept" by any serviceable man of the guardian's [female husband's] choice. All the offsprings [*sic*] of this association were the lawful children of the rich woman.[77]

While the practice demonstrates the independence of a group of women in precolonial Esan society, it also reveals how flexible the concept of gender was in the past. Clearly, this gender flexibility became effective only when the women were able to exercise control over economic resources. Hence they were able to take their destinies into their own hands.

CONCLUSION

In summary, this chapter has examined the avenues through which precolonial Esan women wielded self-reliant economic power. While they were very visible in agricultural production, agriculture did not guarantee them independent sources of income because of their commitment to social reproduction and reproduction of the labor force. Thus they expended surpluses in feeding members of their family. Nevertheless, their vital role in other productive sectors, such as craft production, provided them the basis on which they effectively competed with men in trading activities. Furthermore, their strong economic base was enhanced by the existing sexual division of labor, reinforced by societal taboos that prevented men from encroaching on such industries as soap making, cloth weaving, and pottery making. Since Esan women were able to stave off any possible interference by their male counterparts, they were able to engage in commercial ventures that guaranteed them independent sources of income. Last, the inheritance laws of the Esan people, which denied female children any opportunity to share from the property of their patrilineages, may also have spurred many mothers to seek autonomous means of livelihood. If anything, it ensured that they bequeathed some inheritance to their daughters. On the whole, a number of factors worked together in ensuring female economic power and independence in precolonial Esan society.

NOTES

1. Ruth Simms, "The African Woman as Entrepreneur: Problems and Perspectives on Their Roles," in *The Black Woman Cross-Culturally*, edited by Filomine Chioma Steady (Rochester, Vt.: Schenkman Books, Inc., 1985), p. 141.

2. Claire Robertson, "Economic Woman in Africa: Profit-Making Techniques of Accra Market Women," *Journal of Modern African Studies*, Vol. 12, No. 4, Dec. 1974, pp. 657–664; Claire Robertson, "Ga Women and Socioeconomic Change in Accra, Ghana," in *Women in Africa: Studies in Social and Economic Change*, edited by Nancy J. Hafkin and Edna G. Bay (Stanford: Stanford University Press, 1976), pp. 111–133; Niara Sudarkasa, *Where Women Work: A Study of Yoruba Women in the Market-Place and in the Home* (Ann Arbor: University of Michigan Press, 1973); Felicia Ekejiuba, "Omu Okwei: Merchant Queen of Ossomari," *Journal of the Historical Society of Nigeria*, Vol. 3, No. 4, 1967, pp. 61–84; Barbara Lewis, "The Limitations of Group Action among Entrepreneurs: The Market Women of Abidjan, Ivory Coast," in *Women in Africa*, pp. 135–156.

3. Jacob Egharevba, *A Short History of Benin* (Ibadan: Ibadan University Press, 1968), p. 15.

4. Ibid.

5. C. G. Okojie, *Ishan Native Laws and Customs* (Yaba: John Okwesa & Co., 1960), p. 181.

6. Ibid.

7. It is remarkable that Okojie noted the existence of "primitive settlements" before Ewuare's era. (See Ibid., p. 181). This is indicative of an aboriginal population before the Benin migrants settled in the area.

8. See O. W. Ogbomo and Q. O. Ogbomo, "Women and Society in Pre-Colonial Iyede," *Anthropos*, Vol. 88, 1993, pp. 434–435.

9. Okojie, *Ishan Native Laws*, p. 21.

10. R. E. Bradbury, *The Benin Kingdom and the Edo-Speaking Peoples of South-Western Nigeria* (London: International African Institute, 1957), p. 67.

11. Ibid., p. 73.

12. Ibid., p. 61.

13. Okojie, *Ishan Native Laws*, p. 25.

14. Bradbury, *The Benin Kingdom*, p. 62.

15. A. I. Okoduwa, "Economic Organization in Pre-Colonial Esan," M.A. dissertation, University of Benin, Benin City, 1988, p. 33.

16. Okojie, *Ishan Native Laws*, p. 26.

17. See Okoduwa, "Economic Organization," p. 36. This information was also confirmed by male and female informants during my field research.

18. Okojie, *Ishan Native Laws*, p. 26.

19. Leith Mullings, "Women and Economic Change in Africa," in *Women in Africa*, p. 243; see also Eleanor Leacock, "Introduction," in Frederick Engels, *The Origin of the Family, Private Property and the State* (New York: International, 1972); Ester Boserup, *Woman's Role in Economic Development* (London: George Allen & Unwin, 1970); Kathleen Gough, "The Origin of the Family," *Journal of Marriage and the Family*, Vol. 33, No. 4, Nov. 1971, pp. 760–770.

20. See Onaiwu W. Ogbomo, "Men and Women: Gender Relations and the History of Owan Communities, Nigeria c. 1320–1900," Ph.D. dissertation, Dalhousie University, Halifax, Nova Scotia, 1933, Chaps. 5, 6.

21. Interview with Pa. Ivbhagbosoria Akhidenor (c. 85), Eguare Opoji, Aug. 6, 1987; and Pa. Odion Omobhude (c. 80), Ehanlen-Ewu, Sept. 2, 1987.

22. Bradbury, *The Benin Kingdom*, p. 76; Okojie, *Ishan Native Laws*, p. 98. The point was further reinforced when Okojie asserted that, "If there was a dispute over a piece of land in the village, the Edion (elders) looked into and effected settlements. If it was a dispute involving two villages, the Onojie decided the matter" (p. 98).

23. Interview with Chief Ojiekhebho Idiake (c. 90), Ikekogbe-Iruekpen, Jan. 6, 1987; Mr. Itua Iduhon (76), Uhiakhen quarters, Okalo, Jan. 19, 1987; and D. Aikienede (80), Ihumidumu-Ekpoma, Jan. 25, 1987.

24. Okoduwa, "Economic Organization," p. 42.

25. Henrietta L. Moore, *Feminism and Anthropology* (Minneapolis: University of Minnesota Press, 1988), p. 45. The same point was made by Boserup, *Woman's Role in Economic Development*, p. 50.

26. Lourdes Beneria, "Reproduction, Production and the Sexual Division of Labour," *Cambridge Journal of Economics*, Vol. 3, 1979, p. 205.

27. F. Edholm, O. Harris, and Kate Young, "Conceptualising Women," *Critique of Anthropology*, Vol. 3, Nos. 9 and 10, 1977, p. 105.

28. Beneria, "Reproduction, Production," p. 205.

29. This was confirmed by female informants interviewed. For instance Madam Agbonmalelenwai Ajayi of Idumebo, Irrua, stated that precolonial Esan women were more

concerned with feeding their families than with personal profits they could make from their crops. She also said contemporary Esan women still have such considerations in their daily agricultural work.

30. Okojie, *Ishan Native Laws*, pp. 127–128.

31. Ibid., pp. 92–93.

32. Ibid., p. 93.

33. Interview with Mr. Okosun Ogbebor (73), Efandion-Uromi, Jan. 23, 1987; and Mr. Ebekhile Idede (60), Okalo, Feb. 27, 1987.

34. Interview with Pa. Obhiose Azaka (c. 80), Ihumidumu-Ekpoma, Feb. 12, 1987; and Pa. Irebhale Jacob (c. 90), Ujoenlen-Ekpoma, Feb. 12, 1987.

35. Victor C. Uchendu, *The Igbo of Southeast Nigeria* (New York: Holt, Rinehart and Winston, 1965), p. 55.

36. Similar practices have been observed among the Ga of Accra, Ghana. See Claire C. Robertson, *Sharing the Same Bowl: A Socioeconomic History of Women and Class in Accra, Ghana* (Bloomington: Indiana University Press, 1984), p. 55.

37. Interview with Madam A. Aigbochie (68), Ujueolen-Ekpoma, Aug. 23, 1987.

38. Interview with Madam Omoduwa Odion (c. 80), Eguare-Uromi, March 20, 1987; and Madam Isimenmen Aberalo (60), Uwalor-Uromi, Feb. 28, 1987.

39. Lisa Aronson, "Women in the Arts," in *African Women South of the Sahara*, edited by Margaret Jean Hay and Sharon Stichter (London: Longman, 1984), p. 121.

40. See Eugene O. Erunahikhor, "Pre-Colonial Economic Production," B.A. Research Essay, Department of History, Bendel State University, Ekpoma-Nigeria, 1987, p. 56.

41. Okoduwa, "Economic Organization," p. 65.

42. Ibid., p. 74.

43. Ray A. Kea, *Settlements, Trade and Politics in the Seventeenth-Century Gold Coast* (Baltimore: Johns Hopkins University Press, 1982), p. 25.

44. Aronson, "Women in the Arts," p. 127.

45. Ibid.

46. Okoduwa, "Economic Organization," p. 87.

47. Peggy R. Sanday, "Female Status in the Public Domain," p. 200.

48. Nina E. Mba, *Nigerian Women Mobilized: Women's Political Activity in Southern Nigeria, 1900–1965* (Berkeley: University of California, Institute of International Studies, 1982), p. 19.

49. Ibid., pp. 18–19.

50. Sudarkasa, *Where Women Work*, p. 26.

51. Okojie, *Ishan Native Laws*, p. 26.

52. Okoduwa, "Economic Organization," p. 98.

53. A. G. Hopkins, *An Economic History of West Africa* (London: Longman, 1973), p. 53.

54. Ibid., p. 58.

55. Hopkins, *Economic History*, p. 56.

56. Interview with Madam Akharia Eriakha (c. 85), Uwalo-Usogho, Uromi, March 20, 1987; and Madam Amasowoman (c. 83), Oyomon, Uromi, March 21, 1987. See also Okojie, *Ishan Native Laws*, p. 137.

57. This thesis has also been put forward for the intrusion of Benin migrants into Owan communities. See Onaiwu O. Ogbomo, "Men and Women."

58. Okojie, *Ishan Native Laws*, p. 137.

59. Okoduwa, "Economic Organization," p. 100.

60. Okojie, *Ishan Native Laws*, p. 137.

61. Sudarkasa, *Where Women Work*, pp. 25–26.

62. Ibid., pp. 26–37.

63. Jan Vansina, "Trade and Markets among the Kuba," in *Markets in Africa*, edited by Paul Bohannan and George Dalton (Evanston, Ill.: Northwestern University Press, 1962), p. 193.

64. Okoduwa, "Economic Organization," p. 102.

65. Interview with Madam Agbonmamelenwai Ajayi (c. 74), Idumebo, Irrua, Aug. 24, 1987; Madam Oseria Evboeruan (c. 90), Emuado-Ekpoma, Aug. 11, 1987; and Madam A. Aigboichie (68), Ujuolen-Ekpoma, Aug. 23, 1987.

66. Robert A. Sargent, "Politics and Economics in the Benue Basin, c. 1300–1700," Ph.D. dissertation, Dalhousie University, Halifax, Nova Scotia, 1984, p. 147.

67. Okoduwa, "Economic Organization," p. 77.

68. See A. F. C. Ryder, *Benin and the Europeans, 1485–1897* (New York: Humanities Press, 1969), p. 31.

69. Ibid., p. 38.

70. Ibid., p. 108.

71. Ibid., p. 109.

72. Ibid., p. 110.

73. William Bascom, "The Esusu: A Credit Institution of the Yoruba," *Journal of the Royal Anthropological Institute*, Vol. 82, 1952, pp. 63–69.

74. Okoduwa, "Economic Organization," p. 117.

75. Ibid., p. 112.

76. Sargent, "Politics and Economics," p. 140.

77. Okojie, *Ishan Native Laws*, p. 89.

Chapter 2

Gender, Business, and Space Control: Yoruba Market Women and Power

Toyin Falola

As defined by the agenda of this volume, this chapter sets out to show a linkage between an economic activity (trade) and power, as it relates to a segment of the population (women) and one subset (traders). Such a linkage is possible, as it is indeed of any two other aspects of the structure and institution of society. In this specific case, the assumption is that wealth translates into power. This is true, but there are limitations that must be borne in mind from the beginning. Wealth is only one criterion of power or indeed of upward mobility. There are ascriptive factors as well, like the membership in ruling families, age, and sex, to mention but a few. In addition, in a male-dominated society, gender is built into the construction of power. No matter how wealthy a woman is, she cannot become an *oba* (king) or *balogun* (war commander) in most towns or wield the highest title in many lineages. Power and reward are in general distributed by a male hierarchy, concerned with articulating its own interest.

Nevertheless, as this chapter makes clear, women constitute part of the *political landscape* in a number of ways. Their predominance in market transactions, as sellers and buyers, enables the acquisition of control over an important sector of the economy. This control—of a space that is so central to production and exchange—provides considerable spinoff values and influence. One spinoff value is the ritual control of space in a society operating within a framework of a nonmechanical world view that seeks spiritual balance with the universe. The marketplace is part of the *religious environment* that is integrated into the *religious pantheon*. Since women in Yorubaland control the market space, they also control the market rituals. Cases have been reported of powerful women heads of market who double as priestesses. One nineteenth-century example makes the linkage between such control and power so clear that it deserves to be quoted:

The Eni-Oja[1] is at the head of all the devil worshippers[2] in town. She also has charge of the King's market, and enjoys the perquisites accruing therefrom. She wears a gown like a man, on her arms the King leans on the day he goes to worship at the market, i.e., to propitiate the deity that presides over the markets. She has under her (1) the Olosi who has joint responsibility with her for the market, and (2) the Aroja or market keeper, an officer whose duty it is to keep order, and arrange the management of the market, and who actually resides there.[3]

As we point out below, the rituals cannot be ignored; they must be discussed as part of the makeup of the *political configurations*. Productivity and prosperity underline the concern for rituals by the power elite. Power is threatened without prosperity and productivity, and women become part of the means of maintaining both and, of course, of the spiritual balance. Thus, goddesses of wealth, productivity, and fertility must be seen as part of the process of explaining this intricate relationship between gender and power. Control of ritual power is crucial to the control of space and to the way interpersonal and intergroup relations are intricately constructed to distribute power and resources in a society.

Still on the control of the marketplace, the bulk of the financial transactions takes place here, bringing together people, goods, and money in a single setting. The very nature of the interaction in this space is useful in such ways as information exchange, social interactions, social control, influence building, and networking. Women are able to participate in all the privileges conferred by this space. It is because of the *relevance* of the market to the articulation of gender image and influence that I have chosen to underscore *space control* as part of the title of this chapter. In the more formalized power structure, women are marginalized and tend to operate within a clientele framework—serving as clients and agents to a male power elite—to tap opportunities. Gender and clientelism are also beyond the scope of this chapter, but it is important to point out that women flourish more within the framework of space control than anywhere else.

One dimension the specific concern of this project does not address is that of power acquisition through other means. For instance, there were several female leaders of substance in precolonial formations, including Queen Kambassa of Bonny and Queen Amina of Zaria. In both contemporary colonial and postcolonial settings, resistance to British rule and a new political process toward democracy have thrust a number of women leaders into the limelight. Studies of women have been more concerned with these high-profile political women—the queens of African history, for want of a more appropriate description[4]—than with market women, in order to demonstrate more glorified aspects of the political worth of women and their contributions—a justifiable reaction to male-dominated historical accounts. No one should dismiss this emergency rescue operation to construct the history of women of political substance, a part of creating a balance in historiography and of correcting a generation-old lapse in methodology. Nevertheless, an *archeology* of the queens limits the range and possibility of social and political history.[5] As the case of market women demonstrates, the less structured, informal sector produces its own "queens," its own mythology, and its own conception of order and values: it may be less dramatic, but it is more revealing of the dynamics of power interplay and social institutions.

The strength of this chapter lies in the elaboration of the linkage identified above. The data are limited to the domestic, informal arena of trade and politics from the precolonial period through the colonial to the present. One limitation is that the case studies to illuminate general points are rather limited, a function of the state of gender historiography. Studies are few and far between, and their rationale is uncoordinated.[6] As I have pointed out elsewhere, the weakness in gender studies may result, among other factors, from the paucity of information in both oral and written sources on the contribution of women to the emergence and development of Yoruba kingdoms, the patrilineal nature of the Yoruba family, which emphasizes the supremacy of men over women, and the low position occupied by women in the policy and decision-making machinery.[7]

WOMEN AND TRADE

Like members of most other societies, the Yoruba believe that everyone must work, irrespective of gender, as a means to avoid starvation and poverty, and to earn respect, fame, and prowess. While a number of activities associated with women are designed to help their husbands and raise their children, the society does not frown on women creating the opportunity to make money for themselves. Women spend money on household maintenance, social functions, and chieftaincy titles. In the process of achieving a variety of ambitions and fulfilling mutually related roles, women appear to have devoted more time to work than men, in a variety of activities ranging from the domestic to the high-profile ones of public administration and the priesthood of important cults.[8]

In precolonial formations, there was a sexual division of labor: men were farmers and craftsmen and women engaged in food processing and trading.[9] In general, women's entry to many occupations was unrestricted, although they avoided the military and certain crafts. They were not excluded from the new occupations created during the colonial rule and beyond, even if they were marginalized by the very fact that a colonial society was male dominated.[10] In the precolonial domestic economy, farming was the leading occupation, although Yoruba women were less involved in farming, compared to, say, the Ijo and Igbo of eastern Nigeria, the Akan of Ghana, or the Tio of the Middle Congo.[11] Yoruba women contributed to harvesting, processing for final consumption and storage, livestock keeping, and the selling of farm products.[12] Women of means were able to plough their profits into large-scale farming, as in the case of the nineteenth-century celebrity, Efunsetan Aniwura of Ibadan, who had more than a thousand slaves on her farms.[13] Women were active in the manufacture of a variety of goods like oil, dye, ceramics, and textiles.

By far the most important precolonial activity of women was trade, a professional occupation. The emphasis was on selling what they or their husbands produced from their farms, what they manufactured on their own, and the goods they bought from others for the purpose of reselling them. One of the earliest students of Yoruba markets, W. Hodder, was fascinated with the prominent role of women and dated this domination to the nineteenth century, "to the conditions of internal insecurity in which it was unsafe for men to move away from their farms, while women enjoyed relative immunity from attacks."[14] That there was turbulence in the nineteenth century and women received better protection than men, there can be no doubt.[15] However, there is no strong evidence to associate the wars of the nineteenth century with women's dominance in trade. Earlier records reveal this domination as well.[16]

Two studies by Gloria Marshall (now Niara Sudarkasa) have established a close correlation among the roles of women as wives, mothers, and traders. There was the expectation that a man would assist his wife by providing some capital to start a small trade. As the relationship between the husband and wife developed and the woman had borne a certain number of children, she increased her trading business, unhindered by occasional or regular separation from the husband, who could then take another wife. The woman could assist her husband with money; but more important, she had to take care of her children in the context of competition with the children of rival wives.

With the introduction of formal Western education, the need to sponsor children was to further justify trading, especially in cases when the husband refused to pay for female children or had to limit the number of sons he could train.[17] Women also paid for the upkeep of their children and supplemented domestic expenses on food. The common pattern appears to be that a younger wife stayed closer to home to bear children and assist her husband with limited farm work. When the children grew up, she had more time for herself, and the husband could fulfill the aspiration of taking another wife. Thus, Yoruba marriages matured in such a way that women were able to acquire their independence and men were able to divert their sexual exploits elsewhere.

The process of capital accumulation in the precolonial setting is best described by N. A. Fadipe, the first to write a sociology of his own people. A husband and network of relations furnished the necessary capital for a woman to start a trade:

A percentage of the payment made as bride price by her husband was passed on to her before her marriage. A few days before marriage her own relatives made her, in addition to clothing and other articles of personal wear, presents of cash. . . . A few days after her marriage . . . she has an opportunity of receiving presents of money not only from the various households in her husband's compound, but also from some members of the neighborhood, and from principal members of her husband's kindred group. . . . Out of it she buys an animal (goat or sheep) or two and some fowls for rearing. If a wife was not brought in any trade, these animals and fowls would remain her principal investment. If she was skilled in some trade, part of it would be used for starting it.[18]

Here is perhaps the best description of the "sentiments of kinship and social solidarity" in creating mobility for a woman who had to start from scratch, sentiments devoid of "mercenary motives" or expectations of interest. A new wife benefited from more "sentiments" in the form of gifts and other support until the birth of her first child. Thanks also to Fadipe, the continuation of the practice of accumulation is reported for the colonial period as well:

With regard to a woman who is not married in the customary sense of the word—i.e., who lives with a man as his wife without the consent of her parents—a more generous amount for trading purposes is usually granted. Women of this type are usually of the town-dwelling class, and are generally sophisticated Muslims or Christians. They usually have not learnt any craft. But when in their husband's house, they usually ask for and receive a sum of money with which to start trading in one line of goods or another—generally cheap articles of European manufacture. These women must get all they want for the purpose from their husbands, since they cannot rely upon the sources which are open to women married in the socially approved way.[19]

Starting in such small ways, the enterprising woman expanded by plowing capital back in, raising more capital, obtaining credit, and manipulating market opportunities.

Still on the precolonial society, women traders could be found everywhere hawking cooked food. Many women held their trading activities in their homes where they sold a variety of items like foodstuffs, cosmetics, and tobacco. Such traders were patronized by those who could not attend the market. The practice of staying home for the purpose of trading was common among older women and new brides who might not be permitted to begin full-time trading until they had spent a few years at home. There were women commissioned agents, obtaining supplies from craftsmen to sell.

Women traders were predominant in the village and town markets, the daily and periodic ones. Their activities were many, from preparations to actual selling and buying. Other trading activities took place outside the marketplace, with women hawking their wares, scouting around for goods from producers and farmers, intercepting other traders in order to buy cheap, and so on.[20] Women took part in the regional and long-distance trade, carrying their businesses to areas far away from home. Like men, they withstood the physical hardship of long journeys and the risk traveling involved, especially in periods of political instability. Those married to highly placed men like the *oba* and chiefs were also able to participate, either as independent operators or through proxies.[21]

Colonial and postcolonial rule has not diminished the role of women in trade.

Throughout this century, the complex web of marketing that links villages with cities and one region with the rest of the country is dominated by women. Trade expanded considerably, thanks to the growth of cocoa, a major cash crop, improvements in transport systems, urbanization and, since the 1960s, substantial revenue from petroleum. Surveys on the division of labor conducted in the 1960s and 1970s show that higher percentages of women worked as traders—for instance in the case of Oje, a neighborhood in Ibadan where 84 percent of the women were traders, and in Lagos, where women made up 70 percent of traders.[22] Certainly, older institutions of the market and trade continued until the recent period, as the study by Hodder clearly demonstrates.[23]

WOMEN AND POWER: POLITICAL SYSTEMS AND MYTHOLOGIES

One fact must be recognized: the Yoruba political systems create titles specific to women and recognize the need to incorporate successful women into the system. Opportunities are not many, compared to those offered men, and the distribution of principal functions and roles are no doubt male dominated. Within the avenues created for women, however, and the opportunities open to them can be found all the successful cases of women who exploit and benefit from them. In the precolonial polities, women wielded political influence that varied in degree from one community to the other. Although the validity is yet to be ascertained, a few women are reputed to have reached the apex of authority as *oba*. Ile-Ife tradition mentioned, for instance, the reign of the tyrannical *Ooni* Luwo,[24] and there were similar cases in Akure[25] and Ilesa.[26] There was no town without a woman chief of some kind, although the power attached to such offices varied. For instance, in Ondo the *lobun* was a powerful woman chief, excluded from farming and secluded to her palace like the male *oba*. She took part in the selection of a new king, settled quarrels among the male chiefs, and officiated in the opening of new markets. In addition, she was also regarded as the priestess of *Aje*, the god of money.[27] In Ilesa, another kingdom, the head of the women chiefs was the *arise* supported by the *Risa Arise, Odofin Arise*, and *Yeye-Soloro*. Each ward had a female head, as well.[28] Other towns and villages had their *Iyalode* as heads of women chiefs.[29] A few women chiefs constituted part of the membership of secret societies responsible for executive and judicial functions in a number of communities.[30]

As an integral part of the palace system, the oba's wives (*aya oba* or *olori*) occupied a strategic position to hear and spread news and to influence major policies of state, especially in matters relating to their own lineages or communities. Many quarters in a town tried to be represented in the palace not only through the palace servants but also through marriage ties. There were marriage ties, too, with the neighboring states in order to use women to cement existing friendships or create new ones. Women were also employed to monitor and influence foreign-policy decisions.[31] The *olori*, together with other palace officials, were assigned duties of much social and political significance.[32] Women of rank, royal wives, and princesses often formed organizations to protect their own interests, as in the case of Akure.[33]

WOMEN AND POWER: THE RITUAL
AND MARKET DOMAINS

Fertility, productivity, and wealth are some of the key elements associated with female power. Goddesses of wealth and productivity are many, dominated by female worshippers. Several goddesses were associated with market protection. The goddess of the river, *Yemonja*, derives her relevance from the power to give children and general prosperity. Some traditions call *Yemonja* the mother of all gods and the "mother earth," the fountain of life and productivity. For combining life with water, Yemonja personifies greatness, which perhaps explains the widespread nature of her worship.[34]

Many localized studies have revealed the centrality of the female goddess in the Yoruba pantheon.[35] One recent example is on Ondo where Jacob Olupona shows how the *Obitun* and the *Odun Aje* demonstrate the significance of women in the economy and politics.[36] The *Odun Aje* in particular is more focused on wealth, as a celebration and worship of the goddess *Aje*, usually by the majority of adult females. According to Olupona, the *Aje* rituals bring out the dimensions of human reproduction and economy, symbolizing success in trade and prosperity. He provides the English version of an important lyric:

> Aje excreted on my head;
> Whoever Aje touches is made human.
> Aje slept on my head;
> Whoever Aje touches acts like a child.
> Aje elevates me like a king;
> I shall forever rejoice.
> Aje is happy, so am I.
> Aje is happy, so am I.[37]

This lyric and others sing the gains of trade, gains attributable to this goddess.

By participating in various trading activities, women had the opportunity to become wealthy and could therefore enjoy the high sociopolitical status associated with people of wealth, such as collecting titles, building a following, and acquiring symbols of status like clothes and horses. The connection between the market and power is, however, much broader than the one-to-one relation of wealth and power.

To start with, there is the influential one of the control and management of the marketplace. The marketplace is an important aspect of local and national politics not only for its influence but also for its communication and social functions. It is the place where the bulk of community wealth circulates. To the political class, the market is a place to collect revenues (such as taxes, tolls, fees, dues, levies, gifts), benefit from corruption (by way of stall allocation), and exercise power (by making laws to establish control or using physical coercion or violence). In all these facets, the target is the market women. In the modern era, political parties have extended the building of machine solidarity and opposition mechanisms to the marketplace, urging women to collaborate or resist. In periods of military rule, the marketplace is a venue of propaganda to announce and spread reforms; and the target is again the market women. Building a political constituency or a sphere of influence has always been one criterion to attain prominence, seek office, or wield and retain power. The incorporation of market women into such a sphere has been recognized since the 1930s by the early political parties like the Nigerian Youth Movement, and virtually all subsequent political parties have adopted a similar strategy. In the process, power seekers pursue the means to penetrate market women. In so many instances, competition for control of the marketplace by prominent women traders becomes part of the complications of local politics itself: one recent case study of the Mushin district in Lagos has explained very convincingly how the market, with its "large bloc of support," occupies a prominent part of power struggle and political factionalism.[38]

Invisible to buyers and other visitors to the marketplace are the powerful associations and guilds that try to dominate the space in order to maximize economic gains, create order, and wade through the muddy terrain of politics. Traders dealing in a similar commodity organize into a guild. A guild has an executive that admits new members and discusses issues relating to pricing and market administration. In recent times, organizations of women traders control and discipline their members and oversee the recruitment to the marketplace. In major urban markets, the right to participate has to be negotiated cleverly, and it is difficult to bypass women's organizations. Expulsion from the market, enforcement of discipline, checks on the activities of illegal traders, improvement of market facilities, all are part of the activities and duties of market women associations. Because the unions are powerful, they are able to police the market, and they set up microadministrations respected and recognized by the state.

Presiding over the association is the *iyalode* or *iyaloja*, a woman of means and influence. An *iyalode* wields a lot of power derived from her individual capacity and charm, her personal resources, and the role of the association that she represents. She is the link between the market, market women, and the political authorities, both formal and informal. She implements the wish of the association with regard to stall allocation and the admission of members, she knows all the traders with stalls, and she keeps an eye on a floating population of street traders and hawkers. She supervises the internal administration of the market, settles disputes, and interacts with external suppliers to ensure fairness.

The market political paraphernalia is more elaborate than the office of the *iyalode*. The *iyalode* herself has a long list of lieutenants, in some cases elected by the women's association and in some others appointed by the town's traditional political authority. In Ibadan for instance, there are such subordinate titles as *otun, osi, balogun, asipa, ekarun, abese, maye, are alasa*, and *ikolaba*. There are honorary titles, too, to reward successful and prominent women. As if to create a forest of titles, each guild runs a parallel order, headed by an *iya egbe* with subcommittees presided over by chairwomen known as the *alaga*. For those who could mobilize adequate capital to expand the scale of their operations, considerable scope exists to benefit socially and politically from their business acumen.

If the established political order dominated by men assumes that it can freely manipulate the marketplace and women traders through women's association and leadership, it is wrong. These women also manipulate prominent men and political order, seeking the extension of their influence. The subject of female manipulation requires more treatment than is possible here, but its mechanisms can be highlighted briefly. Prominent male members are incorporated into market organizations through offices and honorary titles. Men are appointed as honorary consuls and to functional positions such as secretary or treasurer. These appointments are no indication that women could not perform these tasks or manage their affairs, but they are clever ways of forging alliances with men. Incorporated male members and others are expected to deliver crucial linkages with power, authority, resources, and groups external to the market in ways defined or suggested by the women.

COPING WITH STATE POWER

What looms large in the discussion has been the role of the state. The state has always been interested in drawing women into its revenue network by collecting market levies, dues, and tolls from them. In trying to attain legitimacy and to govern, the state also makes use of the marketplace for propaganda and for building a constituency. In other words, the state understands the relevance of women. There was an argument in the 1950s that women did not understand the state and that market women are, in general, politically passive and are not "alive to demand their rights."[39]

Akin Mabogunje, a geographer of international renown, responded to this position by saying that political response is a function of the interpretation of one's rights. He cited the Aba women's riot of the 1920s which arose when women were asked to pay tax. As long as women's trade is not interfered with, Mabogunje contends, they are politically quiet. However, whenever there is an economic injustice, they tend to join in male-led protest against the state.[40] He is ambivalent in his conclusion: while on the one hand there is the assumption of passivity, on the other hand, there is an acknowledgment of the market women's political role as objects of manipulation. Whenever politics have been studied as a *social phenomenon*, beyond the highbrow boardroom negotiations and cutthroat competitions, women have been seen to play an active role. This is made clear in the study by Cheryl Johnson, to mention one important case study.[41] Mabogunje, too, underscores this point when he refers to the protest in the 1950s by women against the badly run Free Education Scheme of the Eastern region and a Yoruba oba who was using his power to control commerce to his advantage.[42] In spite of his example of women's protest, Mabogunje still sees gender-based weakness: he concludes that women are more interested in deriving profits from their trade than participating in politics.[43]

We cannot undermine women's understanding of politics as Mabogunje does, an error born of a limited conception of politics and trade. The marketplace itself is a *political space* dominated by women. We can move the discussion in yet another direction to show the limitation of Mabogunje's understanding and broaden the conception of women and politics. This direction is to see how women, by means that can be described only as political, confront the state.

Politics is about interest. To search for market women's role in the male-dominated arena is to abandon the substance in pursuit of a shadow. We must understand their interest: the pursuit of trade and the benefits arising therefrom. It is this interest that determines their political role, which explains why they fight the state over the allocation of market stalls, price control, regulation of street trading, and the location of new markets, to mention some of the important issues. These conflicts are many, as reading any of Nigerian newspapers and magazines will reveal. Conflict is an expression of politics: it is public, challenging, and result oriented.

There is also resistance; a common, almost daily, occurrence is to ignore the state and disregard laws that are considered stupid or injurious to their interests. For example, most price-control measures have failed simply because the market women refused to cooperate.[44] So also is commodity rationing in moments of scarcity.[45] Rather than succumb to pressure, market women are known to close down their shops, thus bringing economic activities to a halt. Resistance is politics, a most intense manifestation of a hostile social and political intercourse between the market women and the agents of the state. To repeat an important point: in seeking data to validate assumptions about market women and politics, let us look in the right place, which is the space they dominate and manipulate better then men.

PRECOLONIAL CASE STUDIES

So far, I have exposed the contours of the linkage. Now I turn to a few cases to illustrate the theme, drawing from four experiences of women who use the marketplace to obtain power. There are two cases of *iyalode* of the nineteenth century who attained their positions because of their trading connections and wealth. In the turbulent history of the nineteenth century, women took part in the decision to go to war, financed military expeditions, saw to the efficient organizations of markets, and competed with their male counterparts.

The first case is that of Tinubu, the famous Egba woman who achieved fame because of her trade. She left her town of Owu and settled in Badagry where she traded in salt and tobacco and acted as a middleman to Brazilian traders. The trade brought her an immense wealth; and Akitoye, the exiled king of Lagos, met her in Badagry in 1846 as one of the most influential citizens of the town. In 1851, Tinubu followed Akitoye to Lagos where she decided to settle. The change did not affect her fortune, and she was able to increase the number of her slaves.[46] She became very influential in Lagos politics and participated actively in the attacks both on the Lagos government and on the foreign merchants whom she saw as monopolists denying the indigenes of their economic rights. By 1856, this lady, now known to her opponents as "the terror of Lagos,"[47] could no longer be tolerated. She was forcibly expelled from Lagos by Consul Campbell who breathed a sigh of relief after her departure. The move was not without local protest against the British by hundreds of Tinubu's supporters. She resettled in Abeokuta where in a short while she reestablished herself as an astute politician and a patriot who supplied the town with weapons during warfare. Her contribution to trade and Egba politics fetched her the highest title of *iyalode* in 1864.

The second case is that of Efunsetan Aniwura of Ibadan who, through trade and large-scale farming, was able to rise to the leading position of *iyalode*. Her wealth was such that she could afford to build a private army of personal guards. She was active in local trade and built an extensive network of regional trade, which included the profitable articles of salt, guns, and gunpowder.[48] Her success generated considerable resentment among the male chiefs. Such a resentment took a turn for the worse in the 1870s when the political head of the city-state, *Are Latosa*, instigated her brutal murder on May 1, 1874. The official reasons for this murder were all tied with her political influence and wealth: a male leader of the town accused her of political insubordination and arrogance.[49] Her death almost led to civil war, and the authorities had to use a face-saving device of executing the slaves who carried out the assignment.[50]

There were perhaps many more examples of rich and powerful women contemporaries of Tinubu and Efunsetan, although records of their careers did not survive. For instance, Aniwura's predecessor as *iyalode* is described as a rich woman who "lost her wealth."[51] Another lady, Adu of Ijanna, a town under Ijaye, is also mentioned in the tradition as "a rich lady" of influence.[52]

CONTEMPORARY CASE STUDIES

A few biographies and case studies are emerging, indicating a positive shift to the recent period. As was to be expected, the biographies have focused more on those active in political life.[53] To keep our concern, we take two examples of traders. One prominent example in the colonial period is Alimotu Pelewura of Lagos,[54] whose concern was to protest colonial policies that threatened the interest of Lagos market women. Her leadership of a market association 8,000 strong lasted four decades and derived from a recognition by other traders of the need to unite for a common cause. An illiterate fish trader, Pelewura emerged as a stronger leader in 1923, in alliance with the newly formed Nigerian National Democratic party led by Herbert Macaulay, the "father of Nigerian nationalism." Pelewura became a member of the Ilu Committee, the traditional executive of the town. There was a row in the mid-1930s over the attempt by the government to relocate Eleko market, a decision that met with popular protest led by her. She also successfully opposed the move to ask women to pay tax in the 1930s and 1940s, and she vigorously protested the price-control measures introduced during the Second World War.

She participated in party campaigns; on one occasion at Abeokuta, she reminded the audience that there was nothing men could undertake without the support of women. She mobilized market women to accord a decent burial to Herbert Macaulay in March 1946, hosted receptions for party dignitaries, and was picked to be part of a team in 1947 to travel to London to protest the Richards Constitution although illness prevented her from traveling. She became the *erelu* of Lagos in 1947, a traditional chieftaincy that conferred upon her the right to represent women's interests. When she died in 1951, a crowd estimated at 25,000 people attended her burial.

My final example is a living legend, Humoani Alade, the current *iyalode* of Ibadan.[55] Born in the late nineteenth century, Humoani did not have the privilege of Western education but received apprenticeship as a trader in textiles. With little capital, she gradually built up her trade until she became wealthy and influential. She is the president of the Oyo State Market Traders' Association (*iyaloja*) and the *iyalode* of Ibadan. In a noncombative manner, she has contributed to a number of women's causes, ranging from market palaver to conflicts with the government. The general perception of her is that of a leader who wants peace, mediating between the government and market women. In the 1980s, she assisted the state government in seeking and building a new market and preventing a clash over street trading. She has also participated in party politics since the 1940s, identifying with the Obafemi Awolowo–led party of the Action Group (AG) and the Unity Party of Nigeria (UPN). She provided support for the AG and the UPN, mobilizing people to support the party and its programs. She never sought any party elective office, nor was she ever appointed to any political position in the government; but she is a moderating influence on the party and a mediator in intraparty rivalry. In addition, she is a member of the *Egbe Ilosiwaju Yoruba* (Yoruba Progressive Union), seeking the progress of the Yoruba people. She is a philanthropist. As the *iyalode*, she receives dignitaries to the town on behalf of women, and attends the meeting of the Olubadan-in-council, where issues relating to the town are discussed. She is the link between the women and the traditional chieftaincy. Many of her contemporaries, including political rivals, are full of praise for her. In the words of Lam Adesina, a prominent educator:

She has been a true leader of women and a lover of the less fortunate . . . Iyalode is a very successful trader. She is also a first-class manager of human beings. Since the old Western Region, Iyalode Alade has been leading the Market Women and Traders Association. The association likes her and respects her. She commands them and they obey her. She is able to do this because her leadership is acceptable and respected.[56]

And to take a second testimony, this time from Archibong Nkana, a former commissioner of police in Oyo state:

She is a dynamic traditional chief in Ibadan, Oyo State. She is diligent, patriotic and very honest. This respectable woman is ever willing to assist the police for the common good of the people. She has used her position as President of Oyo State Market Traders Association to foster peaceful co-existence and mutual understanding between the police and the market traders in the state. I also want to emphasize that this special mother was a serving catalyst to my glorious tenure as commissioner of police in Oyo State. I wish her well in life.[57]

CONCLUSION

Yoruba women have plenty of scope and opportunity to trade, and they dominate the marketplace. Since the colonial period, complex factors of migration, urbanization, and Western influence have brought a number of changes to women's lives and roles, but without diminishing their domination of the marketplace. The linkage between the marketplace and power takes several forms. First, there is the power and influence that accrue to those who grow wealthy. Second, the control of the marketplace confers ritual and symbolic power. Third, domination of the marketplace and of business provides opportunities to relate and negotiate with the political authorities, traditional and modern.

The case studies have revealed women who were able to actualize power in traditional and modern settings. Some dominated national politics, and others influenced local politics. A number of other interpretations can be drawn from these case studies. The women were able to mobilize capital to enlarge trading opportunities. They were enterprising, calculating, and shrewd. They faced considerable risk: Tinubu was expelled from Lagos, and Efunsetan was assassinated, to mention two examples. In general, they faced considerable resentment and antagonism from the male power elite. The women were independent, rejecting the stifling conditionalities of marriage, or at least overcoming the barriers that marriage and child rearing posed. They demonstrated courage in breaking from traditions that constrained their activities; and in the case of Tinubu, of fighting powerful political authority and vested interest. Once they acquired economic power, they were astute and wise enough to add political power unto it. Economic power also changed the conduct of social relations: a rich woman would certainly reject undue subordination. In general, as many studies have pointed out, Yoruba women enjoyed economic independence and limited constraints on their movement, thus enabling not a few to exercise freedom and associate with a constituency of their own choice and creation.

In spending their wealth, they behaved in ways similar to those of the male chiefs by acquiring followers, showing generosity to a large number of people, and obtaining titles for themselves and their supporters. They received *oriki*, great eulogies that captured their lives in grandiose ways and beautiful language. Part of the *oriki* of Efunsetan will suffice for our purpose, but it needs to be emphasized that *oriki* is not a peculiar trademark of this lady:[58]

Efunsetan, Iyalode
One who has horses and rides them not.
The child who walks in a graceful fashion.
Adekemi Ogunrin!
The great hefty woman who adorns her legs with beads
Whose possessions surpass those of the Aare

Owner of several puny slaves in the farm.
Owner of many giant slaves in the market.
One who has bullets and gunpowder,
Who has the gunpowder as well as guns,
And spends money like a conjurer,
The Iyalode who instills fear into her equals.
The rich never give their money to the poor;
The Iyalode never gives her wrappers to the lazy.[59]

Localized within its Yoruba setting and idioms, this is a brilliant rendition, made more powerful by the drumming and dancing that would accompany it. It encapsulates a message, with all the metaphors of greatness. The abundant slaves, the horses, the "graceful fashion," the guns, and gunpowder are all evidence of wealth and success. Power is adequately reflected in the references to slaves, the poor, access to weapons of violence, and warfare. There is rivalry, too: "The Iyalode who instills fear into her equals." And there is the bold comparison with the male political head of this city-state, with the *iyalode*'s possessions surpassing that of the *Aare*. Grace resonates beautifully: the horses in the compound, the "great hefty" woman, "the child who walks in a graceful fashion." And here is a woman so rich in money that she spent like someone who was conjuring (i.e., minting) her own currency.

From this *oriki* and other evidence, we see how aspirations centered on the "good things of life": money, long life, power, children, and good health. In this focus on aspirations, there is no difference from how men too defined what they wanted.

The case studies should not obscure the problems women faced. Access to large amounts of capital was always a problem, and men tended to have more opportunities. Not every woman grew wealthy or powerful from trade; indeed, for the majority, trade did not translate to wealth or power. Trade was competitive, losses were recorded, and some high-profit-yielding commodities like cocoa and cattle were in the hands of male dealers. Women experienced other constraints, such as domestic responsibility, which curtailed activities in the early years of marriage; many lost a lot of time to social and religious events and to illness.[60] Since the colonial period, obstacles to mobility and ingrained prejudices linger. Contemporary concerns of women are focused on the penetration of the more formal, public sector by better access to school, jobs, and promotion;[61] and current studies tend to ignore the informal sector, including the dynamic marketplace that has played such a significant role for so long.

NOTES

1. This is the same as the *iyaloja* (head of market).

2. This is a reference to the god *Esu*, misunderstood by Christian writers of the nineteenth century who adopted his name for the biblical devil. Now variously interpreted, *Esu* can also be described as the god of order.

3. Samuel Johnson, *The History of the Yorubas* (Lagos: Church Missionary Society, 1921), p. 66.

4. See, for instance, David Sweetman, *Women Leaders in African History* (London: Heinemann, 1984); Nina Emma Mba, *Nigerian Women Mobilized: Women's Political Activity in Southern Nigeria, 1900–1965* (Berkeley: Institute of International Studies, University of California, 1982); Cheryl Johnson, "Grassroots Organizing Women in Anti-colonial Activity in Southwestern Nigeria," *African Studies Review*, Vol. 25, Nos. 2 & 3, 1982, pp. 137–157; F. Coker, *A Lady: A Biography of Lady Oyinkan Abayomi* (Ibadan: Evans Brothers, 1987); Bolanle Awe, ed., *Nigerian Women in Historical Perspective* (Lagos and Ibadan: Sankore and Bookcraft, 1992).

5. For the celebration and limitation of gender historiography in Africa (with little stress on the Yoruba, however) among others, see Margaret Strobel, "African Women," *Signs: Journal of Women in Culture and Society*, Vol. 8, No. 1, 1982, pp. 109–131; Margaret Jean Hay, "Queens, Prostitutes, and Peasants: Historical Perspectives on African Women," *Canadian Journal of African Studies*, Vol. 22, No. 3, 1988, pp. 431–447; Audrey Wipper, "Reflections on the Past Sixteen Years, 1972–1988, and Future Challenges," *Canadian Journal of African Studies*, Vol. 22, No. 3, 1988, pp. 409–421; Kathleen Staudt, "Women Farmers in Africa: Research and Institutional Action, 1972–1987," *Canadian Journal of African Studies*, Vol. 22, No. 3, 1988, pp. 567–582.

6. Among others, see E. Ward, "The Yoruba Husband-Wife Code," in *Catholic University of America Anthropological*, No. 6, 1938; Aidan Southall, ed., *Social Change in Modern Africa* (London: International African Institute and Oxford University Press, 1961); J. Harris, "The Position of Women in a Nigerian Society," *Transactions of the New York Academy of Sciences*, Vol. 2, No. 5, 1940; Phyllis Mary Kaberry, *Women of the Grassfields* (London: Her Majesty's Stationery Office, 1952); S. Leith Ross, *African Women* (London: Faber and Faber Ltd., 1939).

7. Toyin Falola, "The Place of Women in the Yoruba Pre-colonial Domestic Economy," *Seminar Proceedings*. Ile-Ife: University of Ife Press, 1978.

8. See, for instance, Johnson, *History of the Yorubas*, pp. 64–65; and E. B. Idowu, *Olodumare, God in Yoruba Belief* (London: Longman, 1962), Chap 8.

9. Several works have described the sexual division of labor among the Yoruba. See, for instance, N. U. Beier, "The Position of Yoruba Women," *Presence Africaine*, 1/2, 1955, pp. 39–46; A. Izzett, "Family Life among the Yorubas in Lagos, Nigeria," in *Social Change in Modern Africa*; and Niara Sudarkasa, *Where Women Work: A Study of Yoruba Women in the Marketplace and in the Home* (Ann Arbor: University of Michigan Press, 1973), Chap. 2.

10. See, for instance, "The Rise of the New Elite amongst the Women of Nigeria," *International Social Science Bulletin* (UNESCO), Vol. 8, No. 3, 1956, pp. 481–488.

11. A more intense role is described for women elsewhere, as in the case of the Ijo. See N. Borric Leis, "Economic Independence and Ijaw Woman: A Comparative Study of Two Communities in the Niger Delta," Ph.D. dissertation, Northwestern University, Evanston, Ill., 1964, p. 55.

12. For a gender-based discussion of farming, see N. A. Fadipe, *The Sociology of the Yoruba*, edited by F. O. Okediji and O. O. Okediji (Ibadan: Ibadan University Press, 1970), Chap. 5.

13. Johnson, *History of the Yorubas*, p. 393.

14. B. W. Hodder, "The Yoruba Market," in *Markets in Africa*, edited by Paul Bohannan and George Dalton (Evanston, Ill.: Northwestern University Press, 1962), p. 110.

15. See, for instance, Toyin Falola and Dare Oguntomisin, *The Military in 19th Century Yoruba Political Systems* (Ile-Ife: University of Ife Press, 1984).

16. See, for instance, G. Marshall, "Women, Trade and the Yoruba Family," Ph.D. dissertation, New York: Columbia University, 1964, pp. 73–78.

17. Sudarkasa, *Where Women Work*. See also B. Belasco, *The Entrepreneur as Cultural Hero* (New York: Praeger, 1980).

18. Fadipe, *Sociology of the Yoruba*, p. 156.

19. Ibid.

20. See, for instance, the remark by Dr. Irving, who traveled in Ibadan, Egba, and the Ijebu territories between December 1854 and January 1855, in *C. M. S. Intelligencer*, 1859, p. 259.

21. A number of nineteenth-century sources specifically mentioned encounters with these women. See, for instance, John Lander and Richard Lander, *Journal of an Expedition to Explore the Course and Termination of the Niger*, Vol. 1 (New York: J. and J. Harper, 1833), p. 122; *C. M. S. Intelligencer*, January 1856, p. 20.

22. B. Lloyd, "Indigenous Ibadan," in *The City of Ibadan*, edited by Peter Cutt Lloyd, Akin L. Mabogunje, and B. Awe (Cambridge: Cambridge University Press, 1967), p. 71; Peter Marris, *Family and Social Change in an African City* (London: Routledge and Kegan Paul, 1961), p. 68; Sandra T. Barnes, *Patrons and Power: Creating a Political Community in Metropolitan Lagos* (Manchester: Manchester University Press, for the International African Institute, 1986), p. 160.

23. B. W. Hodder and U. I. Ukwu, *Markets in West Africa* (Ibadan: Ibadan University Press, 1969), Part 1, "Markets in Yorubaland." See also William Bascom, *The Yoruba of Southwestern Nigeria* (Prospect Heights: Waveland, 1984 [reprint]), Chap. 3.

24. M. A. Fabunmi, *Ife Shrines* (Ile-Ife: University of Ife Press, 1969), pp. 23–24.

25. The thirteenth *deji* of Akure is said to be a woman who did not wear a crown. Nigerian National Archives, Ibadan (N.A.I.), "Intelligence Report on Akure" compiled by N. A. C. Weir, 1935, p. 10.

26. Toyin Falola, "A Descriptive Analysis of Ilesa Palace Organization," *The African Historian*, Vol. 8, 1976, pp. 78–79.

27. N. A. I., "Intelligence Report on Ondo," by A. F. Bridges, 1934/5, p. 10. There were other women chiefs to assist the *lobun*: these included the *lisa lobun* who settles quarrels among the women, the *ogese lobun*, and *sara lobun*, both of whom were "remembrances" to the *lobun*. These offices were duplicated in the Ondo nonmetropolitan area, where the *oloja* (*baale* or village head), together with his chiefs, appointed a *lobun*. In villages such as Ajua and Aiyesan, women chiefs were called *iyalode*, not *lobun*.

28. Falola, "Descriptive Analysis," p. 69.

29. N. A. I., "Intelligence Report on Abeokuta," by John Blair, 1937, p. 48; N. A. I., "Intelligence Report on Ijebu Ife," by E. A. Hawkersworth, 1935, p. 9. For an overview on this institution, see Bolanle Awe, "The Iyalode in the Traditional Political System," in *Sexual Stratification*, edited by Alice Schlegel (New York: Columbia University Press, 1977).

30. For instance, in Ago, an Ijebu village, "female members, known as *Erelu*, were allowed in the society (i.e. Osugbo society). The *Erelu* were consulted in all matters that concerned the female community, though they did not sit with the other members in judicial matters." See "Intelligence Report on Ago," by A. F. Abell, 1934, p. iii. Women membership of secret societies was, however, uncommon.

31. One interesting and mythical example of this is that of Moremi of Ile-Ife. The Igbo people are said to have repeatedly attacked Ile-Ife with success until the beautiful Moremi married the king of Igbo from whom she was able to learn the secrets of Igbo's military success. She returned to Ile-Ife and exposed the secrets. This enabled Ile-Ife to resist and defeat the Igbo.

32. For instance, Samuel Johnson (*History of the Yorubas*) mentions eight women of

"the highest rank" whose roles could not be dispensed within the Oyo palace (*Iya Kekere, Iya Oba, Iya Naso, Iya Monari, Iyalagbon, Orun Kumefun,* and *Are Orite*). On *Iyakekere,* Johnson writes: "She has the charge of the king's treasures. The royal insignia are in her keeping, and all the paraphernalia used on state occasions, she has the power of withholding them, and thus preventing the holding of any state reception to mark her displeasure with the king's head at the coronation" (p. 63). Other women holding important offices were mentioned besides those eight, and their roles within and outside the palace reveals the political influences they could wield on state matters (pp. 64–66).

33. In Akure, there was an Apate club, with a membership restricted to fifty people at a time. They were "not expected to carry loads on their heads." Other clubs included the *Ukoji,* comprising daughters of titled men, and *Esari,* daughters and granddaughters of all late obas (Weir, "Intelligence Report on Akure," p. 21).

34. On this goddess, among others, see Jonathan Olumide Lucas, *The Religion of the Yorubas* (Lagos: C.M.S. Bookshop, 1948), pp. 218–219; J. Gleason, *Orisha: The Gods of Yorubaland* (New York: Atheneum, 1971), p. 137.

35. See yet another example in Henry John Drewal, *Gelede: Art and Female Power among the Yoruba* (Bloomington: Indiana University Press, 1983).

36. Jacob Obafemi Kehinde Olupona, *Kingship, Religion, and Rituals in a Nigerian Community: A Phenomenological Study of Ondo Yoruba Festivals* (Stockholm: Almqvist & Wiksell International, 1991), Chap. 6.

37. Ibid., p. 156.

38. Barnes, *Patrons and Power*, Chap. 7.

39. Akin Mabogunje, "The Market-Woman," *Ibadan,* No. 11, Feb. 1961, p. 16.

40. Ibid.

41. Cheryl Johnson-Odim, "Nigerian Women and British Colonialism: The Yoruba Example with Selected Biographies," Ph.D. dissertation, Northwestern University, Evanston, Ill., 1978.

42. Mabogunje, "The Market-Woman," p. 17.

43. Ibid.

44. See, for instance, Wale Oyemakinde, "The Pullen Marketing Scheme: Trial in Food Price Control, 1941–47," *Journal of the Historical Society of Nigeria,* Vol. 4, 1973, pp. 413–423.

45. See, for instance, Toyin Falola, "Salt is Gold: The Management of Salt Scarcity in Nigeria during World War II," *Canadian Journal of African Studies,* Vol. 26, No. 3, 1992, pp. 412–436.

46. Public Record Office (P.R.O.), London, Foreign Office (F.O.) 84/950, Campbell to Clarendon, 11 Aug. 1854.

47. P.R.O., F.O. 84/920, Fraser to Malmesbury, 20 Feb. 1853.

48. For one interesting account of this lady, see Bolanle Awe, "Iyalode Efunsetan Aniwura (Owner of Gold)," in Awe, *Nigerian Women,* pp. 55–72.

49. Johnson, *History of the Yorubas*, p. 391.

50. For the political background to the crisis, see Toyin Falola, *The Political Economy of a Pre-colonial African State, Ibadan, ca. 1830–1893* (Ile-Ife: University of Ife Press, 1984).

51. Johnson, *History of the Yorubas*, p. 392.

52. Ibid., p. 331.

53. See, for instance, Tola Adeniyi, *The Jewel: A Biography of Chief (Mrs.) H. I. D. Awolowo* (Ibadan: Gemni Press Ltd., 1993); Johnson-Odim, "Nigerian Women and British Colonialism."

54. The account of Pelewura is based on the evidence of C. Johnson, "Madam Pelewura and the Lagos Market Women," *Tarikh*, Vol. 7, No. 1, 1981, pp. 1–10.

55. This reconstruction is based on a pamphlet by T. A. Layonu, "Iyalode Hunmoani Alade (The Embodiment of Truth)" (Ibadan: Famlod Books, 1990).

56. Ibid., p. 32.

57. Ibid., p. 35.

58. On this genre, see K. Barber, *I Could Speak until Tomorrow: Oriki, Women, and the Past in a Yoruba Town* (Edinburgh: Edinburgh University Press, 1991).

59. Translation by Awe, *Nigerian Women*, p. 57.

60. Fadipe, *Sociology of the Yoruba*, p. 166.

61. See, for instance, Bosede Sola-Onifade, *The Nigerian Woman* (Lagos: Julia Virgo Enterprises, n.d. [1980s?]); O. A. Adeyemo, ed., *Women in Development* (Ibadan: National Center for Economic Management and Administration, 1991), Chap. 3.

Chapter 3

Gender and Economic Power: The Case of Igbo Market Women of Eastern Nigeria

Felix K. Ekechi

"African traditional society had certain steadfast beliefs, especially when it came to gender differentiation. The woman was seen as subordinate to the male, and the male provider was not to be easily contradicted in either the public or the private sphere. . . . The female was brought up to believe she had a limited part to play in the day to day affairs outside her domestic domain."[1] This enduring stereotype of male–female relations needs modification so as to reflect the African reality. "For too long the western observer, accustomed to gaze through a veil darkly, has accepted formless shadows as tangible objects of reality."[2] In other words, the supposedly static "African world" presented in popular literature seems quite misleading. First of all, this static model never existed; instead, change characterized both past and present African society. In any case, women's activities were by no means limited to the domestic domain. On the contrary, as studies now show, men and women have played and continue to play vital roles both in the domestic economy and elsewhere. In fact, where there have been gender limitations, women have continually challenged the status quo.

In the agricultural and commercial spheres, for example, women were not only active participants; they actually dominated these sectors of the local economy prior to the advent of the Europeans in the nineteenth century. With special reference to agriculture, Jeanne Henn writes, "Women usually carried out all the major farming tasks—breaking up the soil, planting, weeding, harvesting, and carrying the harvest home."[3] Not surprisingly, Africa has been described as "the region of female farming par excellence."[4] In short, women not only dominated the farming system but also fed the household. "It is the women who own us," acknowledged an Igbo elder, meaning that it is the women who cooked and "gave men food."[5]

Yet, women's activities in the domestic economy should be better understood in terms of the sexual division of labor. For in Africa, men and women traditionally performed different roles, generally defined along sex or gender lines. Hence in the agricultural sphere, certain activities were (and still are) defined as men's or women's work. Thus, while women's work on the farm included the planting and weeding of crops, as well as "carrying the harvest home," men were responsible for clearing the brush and preparing the farm for planting. In the case of yams, men were solely responsible for stalking them. On the whole, "The men help with the heavier parts of the farm work. . . . But there are months when they have little if nothing to do in the farms whereas all year round, though particularly in the wet season, the women are occupied in weeding, planting, [and] tending crops."[6]

Furthermore, there was a clear distinction between men's crops and women's crops. Hence, just as in the social sphere, where men and women were segregated according to sex, so it was in the economic arena: roles were allocated on the basis of gender. Take the case of the palm oil industry: "Only men climbed palm trees, whether to cut nuts or to tap for wine. The idea of women climbing was unthinkable."[7] Some feminist writers, however, have argued that there is a direct correlation between the sexual division of labor and men's assumption of political and economic power over women. Thus, Susan Martin writes,

This sexual division of labor was accompanied with a complex division of authority and responsibility between the sexes and the generations, which ensured that while women did the bulk of farm work the male head of each *Ezi* (a patrilineal group . . .) received the bulk of any cash proceeds from the farming.[8]

Just as women virtually dominated the farming system, they also predominated in the local trading or distributive system. For example, the sale of farm products and other locally produced goods was generally undertaken by women. Indeed, as Green said of Igbo women, "Trade is second only to agriculture as a means of livelihood."[9] As elsewhere in Africa, trading was of great importance to Igbo women. A European visitor underscored the significance of trade among Igbo women,

Marketing is the central feature in the life of every Ibo woman, and to be successful in trade is the signal for generous congratulation. By this a woman's value is calculated: it affects her position and comfort; a man considers it in the choice of a wife, and a husband's favor is bestowed or withheld largely according to the degree of his wife's success in the market.[10]

As a matter of fact, Igbo women traded in a variety of items including vegetables, cassava, palm oil and palm kernel, pots, and baskets. Some women even traded in elephant tusks with the Europeans and in the process made large amounts of money. Such accumulation of wealth, as Professor Henderson has shown, enabled successful women to take coveted titles, as was the case of Madam Nwagboka, who was crowned as queen of Onitsha in 1884 by the Obi of Onitsha, Anazonwu I.[11]

In this chapter, I examine and analyze the dynamics of economic change in Nigeria in the era of European imperialism, especially as it affected women. I also examine patterns of male responses to economic opportunities. Emphasis is given to the nature of male challenges to Igbo women's commercial enterprises in the palm oil and cassava trades. Conversely, the chapter highlights the impact of colonialism on the economic status and position of women. Special attention is given to the cultural, historical, and economic factors that enabled men to effectively challenge women's predominance in the palm oil and cassava industries. Attention is also drawn to the nature of women's responses to and protests against the intrusion of men into their erstwhile economic domain.

WOMEN AND THE PALM OIL TRADE

The commercialization of palm oil in the Igbo region began in the 1830s, when British merchants gained access into the area, following the so-called discovery of the Niger by the Lander brothers. British encounter with the peoples of the coastal hinterland resulted, as Professor Dike has convincingly demonstrated, in a "phenomenal rise" in palm oil exports.[12] From about the 1870s, palm produce trade (i.e., palm oil and palm kernel) had become the major source of wealth. For Igbo market women, the decades from the 1870s were ones of relative economic prosperity, arising from the exploitation of the palm produce trade and cassava. In more specific terms, this expansion of palm produce trade and the adoption of cassava "gave women increased autonomy within the household economy."[13]

Of course, women have generally seized commercial and economic opportunities for their social, economic, and political improvement or empowerment. For example, during the era of the slave trade, Igbo market women provided cooked food for traders and slaves. In the process, they not only profited economically but also gained a measure of economic independence as well.[14] And during the period of legitimate trade, which began with the abolition of the slave trade, as well as in the era of European colonial rule (from c. 1900), Igbo market women also played critical roles in the development of trade. They served, for instance, both as producers of palm oil and palm kernel and as commercial entrepreneurs. With special reference to Ngwa women, a subgroup of the Igbo people, Martin states that "the most important economic change in the period 1884–1914 was that [women] began to earn cash in their own right from the export industry."[15] As a matter of fact, women dominated the palm produce transactions in the local markets well into the 1920s. As is discussed later, two important developments directly enhanced market women's role in the palm produce trade, namely the expansion of trade from the coast to the hinterland and the proliferation of imported goods from the coast to the hinterland markets. Indeed, as imported commodities like salt, snuff, stockfish, fish, tobacco, soap, and iron pots proliferated, women became the major distributors in the village markets.[16]

Unfortunately, the expansion of trade during the colonial era resulted, in large measure, in the whittling down of the importance of women in the colonial economy. During this period, men by and large seized the opportunities provided by improved river, road, and railway transportation "to break the women's stranglehold upon the palm produce bulking trade."[17] Reporting of the lure of hinterland trade, a British colonial official described the aggressive male (Kalabari) penetration of the interior from the coastal states thus:

The plentifulness of oil palms in the N.E. part of the [Owerri] Division brings traders from the sea-board towns via Imo River, and they [have] set up trading on the banks: Buguma, Okrika, Bakana, Bonny, and Opobo (and Akwette) are represented at Okpala, and Bonny and Opobo at Udo; at Ife [Mbaise] too there are several of them. They buy kernels and palm oil and pay in cash and tobacco. The journey to Bonny and back takes them about three weeks with one of their big canoes (about 8 puncheons). Some of them are also at Ihiagwa [near Owerri].[18]

Kalabari presence at Oguta and other places slowly but definitely altered the character of palm oil trade in the area.[19] Hitherto, the local traders, especially women, dominated the trade, serving as the main channels through which palm produce reached the European firms at Aba, Oguta, and Umuahia stations. In essence they were the chief middlemen. Some of these Igbo businesswomen in time rose to positions of prominence. The life of Omu Okwei (1872–1943), the merchant queen of Ossamari, provides an interesting illustration of the economic role of women in indigenous African enterprise.[20]

The male challenge to women's position in the palm oil trade, as might be expected, engendered a clash of economic interests between men and women. On the one hand, according to Martin, men responded to the higher prices of palm oil between 1900 and 1913 by insisting on "higher oil production," with the view of ensuring "that the level of income under male control was maximized." As for women, on the other hand, even though they sought to profit from the rise in the price of palm oil, just as the men, they nevertheless were deeply concerned with the corresponding fall in the price of palm kernel.[21] Since women had exclusive claims to the proceeds of palm kernel production, it was natural that they would react angrily to the fall in kernel prices. Their dilemma, therefore, was how to solve the problem of the decline in kernel prices while at the same time profit from the rise in the price of palm oil. For increased production of oil, it seemed, implied increased profits from palm oil and palm kernel as well.

As recent studies have now demonstrated, commerce and colonialism both significantly affected the structures of village life and transformed the traditional relationship between men and women.[22] In other words, colonialism fostered the democratization of wealth and power, and thus accentuated the "stratification of African societies."[23] Furthermore, adventurous young men perceived accurately that trade, currency dealing and wage "labour were the main sources of rapid, if unpredictable, earnings within the colonial economy."[24] For all practical purposes, as is discussed later, the "new political order" proved to be disadvantageous to women, especially in the commercial arena.

ECONOMIC IMPACT OF COLONIAL INNOVATIONS ON MARKET WOMEN

"Every innovation alters many existing features" of local life.[25] This observation is particularly relevant to our discussion here about the impact of European colonial innovations on Africa, and on Nigerian women in particular. As previously indicated, transportation improvements enabled men "to break the women's stranglehold upon the palm produce bulking trade." This male challenge was specially made possible by the construction of the Eastern Railway (1913–1926) and the introduction of bicycles and motor lorries from about the 1920s. These new means of transport enabled male merchants to transport increased volumes of goods from the local markets to the coastal stations or to the new European trading centers in such places as Aba, Oguta, Onitsha, and Umuahia. As a matter of fact, up until about 1920 women figured prominently in the palm oil trade in these trading stations. From this time on, however, the trade, especially its long-distance sector, was monopolized by men. The chief factors that enabled them to do so were their ability to control the new European currency (silver coins and currency notes) and initiative to engage in bulk trade via the use of railways, bicycles, and lorries. Equally important was the use of canoes for hauling volumes of palm produce, as was the case with Kalabari merchants.

Ordinarily, women carried relatively small quantities of palm oil and kernel to the new palm oil centers. With the advent of the new modes of transport, women were invariably shortchanged: "It is notable [for instance] that no women were reported as riding bicycles in the early [1920s and] 1930s."[26] Why was this so? The reasons are many but include both economic and social factors. On the economic sphere, "women's social roles and in particular their responsibility for spending on household needs had held them back from buying bicycles and joining the ranks of the enterprising and ambitious [male] retail traders."[27] Furthermore, whereas the male traders, notably the Kalabari merchants, freely accepted the European currencies, which had become the official tender or medium of exchange, market women resisted the new currencies and thus seemed unable to accumulate sufficient funds necessary to purchase bicycles.[28]

Of course, women experienced other economic disadvantages. For example, Igbo market women, who traded at Oguta, one of the major palm oil centers, were edged out of their middleman role by the Kalabari merchants. As I have argued elsewhere, "Prior to the Kalabari settlement, many local women traders traded directly with the European factories, but after 1920 or so, the situation seems to have changed substantially. Instead of trading as independent entrepreneurs, indigenous traders were now employed as agents or sub-agents of the Kalabari merchants." Contemporary reports clearly indicated that women had thus lost their ability to trade directly with the European firms and that whatever trading was done with the European factories was simply 'chance trade' regulated by events and circumstances."[29] In short, men had replaced women as the direct suppliers of palm produce to the European factories, notably the United African Company. African middlemen purchased palm oil and palm kernel directly from the local markets; and after cleaning and blending the produce, they then resold the produce to the firms at higher prices.

Moreover, sociocultural factors significantly affected women's commercial roles. For example, until recent times, cultural prejudice prohibited women from owning bicycles or even traveling on the railways. It was generally believed that access to the new modes of transportation would corrupt women's morals.[30] Therefore, unable to secure bicycles, women remained handicapped in the competition with men, especially in the more lucrative long-distance trade. While male cyclists were able to transport their oil in tins and drums to distant markets where prices were relatively higher, women were unable to do so for lack of bicycles and thus remained as petty traders in the local markets. Nor were they able to afford the motor lorries, which also gave men a decisive economic advantage over women in the palm oil trade.[31] Thus, cultural and social constraints, as well as colonial innovations, acted as barriers to women's economic progress. Susan Martin has described the impact of colonial innovations on women in these words: "While colonial transportation innovations provided junior men with fresh opportunities to travel and enter into trade, women remained tied to their homes and families, both in their daily lives and in their loyalties."[32]

Oddly enough, mechanization of the palm oil industry equally affected the role of women, for it enabled men to effectively challenge women's predominance in the production of palm oil. Hitherto, women had been mainly responsible for the gathering and processing of palm oil and palm kernel. But the introduction of oil presses changed the situation and further "altered the balance of economic power" between men and women. Palm oil mills were introduced into Eastern Nigeria as early as 1915,[33] but it was not until the 1930s that palm oil presses were widely adopted in the Igbo regions, the Pioneer oil mills being the most common. The Duchscher presses for extracting kernel were also in use. In point of fact, oil mills (presses) offered "fresh sources of profit to a few of the entrepreneurially minded people," notably men.[34] For one thing, mechanization of the oil industry enabled men to produce larger quantities of oil, in contrast to the traditional hand-processing methods, often described as "crude and wasteful." Ideally, increased production meant increased profits (even though this was not always the case), and therefore ensured men's greater economic power.[35] In addition, while the oil mills "provided job opportunities for local men as wage laborers and technicians," women could only improve their economic condition largely through palm oil production and cassava cultivation.[36]

Ironically, while the colonial administration enthusiastically encouraged increased palm oil production through the use of oil presses and the cultivation of new palm plantations, prices of palm produce continued to fall precipitously.[37] Consequently, farmers, particularly women, faced with declining incomes, protested strongly against government economic policy, which tended to impoverish them. Hence Igbo market women demanded, among other things, "that the government should guarantee higher prices for palm produce." In effect, women believed that the government and the European firms were "hand-in-glove over the question of price control" of local products.[38] One colonial official acknowledged in 1919 that "the recent decline in the price of palm oil has been a very serious blow to the people, and it is now a matter which occupies their minds to the exclusion of all else."[39] Worse still, while palm oil prices plummeted, the prices of imported goods rose substantially, thus making the economic situation even more serious. Responding to the local agitation against higher prices for imported goods, the district officer (DO) for Owerri Division smugly admonished women that "the days of cheap goods are over during the lifetime of the present generation."[40]

Colonial officials nevertheless seemed quite concerned with the continued fall in the prices of palm oil and palm kernel. Increasingly fearful of the consequences of women's protests which gained momentum by 1938, the DO for Owerri Division hoped a way could be found to stabilize produce prices "at a reasonable level." Unless some practical action was taken to assuage the anger of market women, he informed his seniors, "we are in for a difficult time" indeed.[41] Interestingly, it was the Igbo women's protests against falling prices of palm oil and palm kernel, as well as rumors of colonial taxation of women, that triggered the women's uprising of 1929, popularly known as the Women's War.[42] It was this Women's War or Revolt that toppled the British Indirect Rule System in Eastern Nigeria; hence the colonial administration's anxiety about the 1938 women's movement. On the whole, the long-term decline of palm produce prices not only affected the economic position of women but ultimately led to the collapse of the palm oil industry by the 1950s. In this regard, the roots of persistent rural poverty today, especially among women, can be traced, at least in part, to the "falling cash incomes" from the palm oil trade. Using her Ngwa study as a case in point, Martin lays the blame for local poverty squarely on colonial exploitation, adding that "poverty arising from poor terms of trade has been a major impediment to capital-using innovation."[43]

THE CASSAVA PALAVER

Just as men's entry into the palm oil trade resulted in the relegation of women to the status of petty traders, so also did men's intrusion into the cassava trade threaten market women's economic preeminence in that industry. It is not exactly clear when men first "invaded" this sphere of women's business; but by the 1930s, women's protests against men's intrusion "in the sphere of women's crops, especially cassava," had become widespread. This cassava palaver, which raged from the 1930s up to the 1950s, is the theme of this section of this chapter. As it turned out, men slowly but steadily replaced women as the major force in the commercialized cassava industry.

First, a brief history of the adoption of cassava as a staple food is essential to understand the premier role women played in the cassava industry. Cassava, sometimes known as manioc, was introduced into West Africa, presumably by the Portuguese, during the era of the slave trade. Originally, it was used to feed slaves. According to Ohadike, who has studied the diffusion of cassava into the Igbo region, cassava was adopted by the Igbo after 1914. Prior to that time yams were the main food crop—the chief staple food. Before 1914, therefore, "no one ate cassava" in the Igbo hinterland. Why, then, was cassava adopted? "The shift from yams to cassava has been the direct result of British imperial presence . . . as marked by the punitive expeditions . . . , the First World War, and above all, the influenza pandemic of 1918–19."[44] More specifically, the death toll and the dire food shortage, which accompanied these disasters, are said to have induced pragmatic Igbo people to adopt cassava as an alternative source of food. This explanation fits well, of course, into Igbo utilitarian philosophy. Being a very cautious and pragmatic people, the Igbo, like most other Africans, tend to accept innovations, essentially if they are seen to be "obviously useful." Otherwise, new ideas are treated with characteristic indifference.[45] In short, the Igbo are receptive to change, but not change for the sake of change.

The crucial question is this: Will the acceptance of this innovation "make the individual or the town get up"? If the answer is in the affirmative, there is a great possibility of immediate acceptance; but to be retained, the innovation "must work." The material and symbolic evidence of "getting up" must be demonstrated.[46]

Whatever the reasons for its adoption, cassava remained a "poor man's food" for quite a long time, implying that yams continued to predominate as the chief staple food. In some areas of Igboland, to be sure, "some of the old people were still afraid of [cassava] and refused to eat the new fangled foodstuff" as recently as 1947.[47] In fact, wealthy men (ogaranya) did not eat cassava until the hardship of the Biafra War (1967–1970) forced almost everybody to embrace cassava and *gari* as the new staple foods.

For all practical purposes, cassava was (and still is) a woman's crop, reflecting the traditional division of labor on gender lines. Indeed, from its inception, cassava was regarded as a woman's crop, while yam was a man's crop. In short, women were the chief cassava growers. And while yam was "king," meaning that it was the main staple foodstuff, cassava remained essentially a secondary food item. But cassava became increasingly important, largely because it was available all year around, whereas yams were a seasonal crop. Thus cassava significantly "helped to alleviate periodic hunger and famine, especially in the months when yams were not ready for harvesting."[48] For women, the adoption of cassava as a cash crop also meant economic empowerment.

Women's acceptance of cassava has meant not only the alleviation of the traditional famine period preceding the yam harvest but also a profound alteration in the economic and social relations between husbands and wives. In precontact [i.e., precolonial] days if a woman's husband did not give her food, she was in a sorry plight; now it is possible for her to subsist without her husband.[49]

Seen from this perspective, cassava symbolized women's economic independence; it provided the potential for capital accumulation. Thus, by selling cassava in its root form, in its processed form (*jiapu, akpu*), or even as *gari* (cassava flour), a woman could boast of some private income. This sense of economic autonomy was articulated by an Afikpo woman in 1952: "If a woman has any money she buys land and plants cassava. The year after she does this she can have a crop for cassava meal, which she can sell and have her own money. Then she can say, 'What is man? I have my own money!'"[50]

Cassava was not only used for *fou-fou* (cassava meal) but also for snacks in the form of tapioca (*eberebe, jigbo, mpataka*) or as *akara japu* (like bean balls). Besides selling cassava roots in the rural markets, women also sold cooked cassava meals (*japu* or *gari*) in the market and at makeshift roadside restaurants. Thus cassava provided women the opportunity for making money and for feeding the family. The income generated from the cassava business not only enabled women to exercise a measure of economic independence; it also enabled them to finance the education of their children. Many women, too, used their resources to pay for their husband's taxes. Equally important, women often used the fortunes derived from trade to take titles.[51] Therefore, whatever threatened women's sources of income would naturally be viewed with serious concern. And, since the cassava trade was a vital source of income, as well as a means of social mobility, interference in this sphere of women's activity was almost "tantamount to social and economic subjugation."[52]

MALE ENCROACHMENT IN THE CASSAVA TRADE

As already indicated, women monopolized the cassava industry—from the cultivation, harvesting, and marketing of the cassava product. But, as in the case of palm oil, men invaded this sphere of women's economic domain in the 1930s. Data from the colonial archives reveal that in 1938, women complained loudly against men's encroachment in the cassava business. In August 1938, for example, the DO for Owerri Division reported of a women's protest movement precipitated by alleged "unfair male competition in the sphere of women's crops, especially cassava."[53] In addition, women are said to have complained bitterly about the fall in the prices of locally produced goods, especially palm oil and palm kernel. For Nigerian farmers, to be sure, 1938 was particularly a difficult year because of the continued decline of the prices of palm oil and palm kernel.[54] And there was also the apprehension that the government was about to tax women, which naturally upset women. It should be remembered that it was the rumor that the government was about to tax women that actually triggered the Women's Revolt of 1929. Hence, fear of the recurrence of the 1929 episode significantly shaped the colonial officials' attitude toward the women's protest movement.

To the colonial officials, it initially seemed that the fall in produce prices and the proposed tax rates "were more in [the women's] minds" than perhaps the cassava issue, the exact character of which remained nebulous. Thus it was thought that when women "say one thing they [probably] mean twenty."[55] However, officials were in no mood to dismiss the matter out of hand; and hence the determination to "nip" the protest movement "in the bud." In other words, the women's protest was to be not only taken seriously but contained. Otherwise, as the officials admitted, the protest movement could become so explosive as to turn into another revolt similar to that of 1929.[56]

Therefore, in September 1938, the colonial administration at Owerri asked the Oratta Clan Council to carefully look into the nature of the women's cassava complaint. The council reportedly took up the matter with great enthusiasm, and "made an extensive tour" of the division and beyond, collecting evidence from women and others. After the investigation, the council reportedly submitted an official report to the DO, written, as the DO remarked, in a "true 'Commission of Inquiry' style." The report, according to the DO, contained, among other things, the council's "findings and recommendations." Regrettably, my searches in the Nigerian Archives at Enugu have failed to locate the actual report, now probably lost.[57] However, commentaries on the women's protest movement and the Oratta Clan Council's report are scattered in several of the DO's annual reports. What follows is therefore a reconstruction based largely on these reports, supplemented by local interviews.

According to the reports, the council members deeply appreciated the seriousness of the women's complaints, particularly their grievance about the decline in the price of palm produce. A careful reading of the annual reports suggests that the council seems to have tackled its task with the conviction that women were to be approached with careful diplomacy. Hence, it made an attempt to assure women that the government was their friend and would in no way undermine their economic well-being; that rumors that the government was about to tax women were false; that the government would do its best to ensure a better price for palm produce; and finally that the government was prepared to listen to their grievances, both individually and collectively.[58] Yet there was no direct mention in the official reports of the cassava palaver.

Indeed, it appears from available evidence that what the women actually got were assurances of government's good will towards them. In this regard, the measures taken by the council seem to have been mere palliatives rather than solutions to the critical issues affecting women. Without a doubt, assurances of government's good will toward women and the encouragement given to them to "talk" to government officials seem intended to dissuade women from resorting to violence.[59]

Nevertheless, the colonial administration heaved a sigh of relief inasmuch as the women's protest did not disrupt the tax collection for the year, thanks to the "outstanding" services of the Oratta Clan Council. "Looking back on the events of the past four months," the DO wrote with obvious appreciation, "it seems more than likely that had this [women's] movement not been nipped in the bud, the story of the 1938–39 tax collection in this Division might have been a different one."[60] Still applauding the "spectacular achievement" of the council and his administration, the DO remarked,

The collection of the bulk of the tax during the month of November [1938] is possibly the most noteworthy achievement of the year. This would not call for special comment in any ordinary year, but the combination of the September crisis, low produce prices and a whole series of fantastic rumors had so unsettled the people that it was obvious from the outset that we were in for a difficult collection. This being so it was decided to insist as far as possible, on a quick collection. Strong opposition was encountered during the early part of November.[61]

And yet, the DO was not complacent. He was well aware that, unless some positive action was taken to stem the persistent fall in the prices of palm oil and palm kernel, women might probably revolt again. Said the DO, "If only some means could be devised of stabilizing produce prices at a reasonable level, it would make the task of the Administrative Officer a much happier one."[62] But despite assurances of government's good intentions, market women and others enjoyed no economic relief and hence blamed the colonial administration and the European firms for their economic predicament.[63]

In any event, the colonial officials appreciated the seeming appeasement policy of the Oratta Clan Council toward women insofar as it gave women the illusion that the government was on their side. Hence the DO assured his seniors that the Council's recommendation for direct "talks" with women had been fully adopted. Said the DO:

The privilege of easy access to a European Officer for the individual has been maintained and although a large proportion of these interviews are frivolous it is highly important that this privilege be not denied for many years to come. Particularly is it important that the women who in many ways are the backbone of the community, should know that they will find a sympathetic ear for any reasonable complaints.[64]

Even though we know very little about the government's handling of the women's complaints about men's "unfair competition in the sphere of women's crops, especially cassava," the district officer nevertheless congratulated his administration for a job well done. "Despite low produce prices and the unsettling effect of events in Europe," he wrote in 1939, "the people of the Division remain on the whole contented. They have seen a good return for their tax in the way of Native Administration works in the past years and in the year under review, and politically the Administration had done all in its power to meet their wishes, particularly in the matter of Court Membership."[65]

Because of the "good work" of the Oratta Clan Council in containing the woman's movement, it is no surprise that the DO enthusiastically supported the reelection of the council members, arguing that they were "the best material in the Clan." He was realistic enough to know that the Igbo resent political monopoly, either by an individual or by a group. Hence, the DO seemed willing to allow the purging of some of the members so as to give "a fair number of the people . . . the experience of Council membership at this stage of the development of the Clan."[66]

For all practical purposes, as the foregoing discussion suggests, it would certainly appear that the colonial administration seemed more concerned with maintaining law and order and raising revenue, than with seriously redressing women's grievances. And despite the seemingly benign attitude of the colonial administration toward women's complaint of "unfair competition" in the cassava business, women's concerns over cassava issues continued to run high indeed.

It must be remembered that from about the 1930s cassava had increasingly become an important foodstuff, as well as a profitable cash crop in Eastern Nigeria. In the Ngwa region, for instance, cassava was reportedly "the main food crop" by the 1950s. Similarly in the Ibibio area, cassava was the chief starchy food.[67] Consequently, any perceived threat to this women's vital source of livelihood and income invariably provoked hostile reaction. Also, the phenomenal growth of population in the region meant that any interference in the cassava cultivation would attract angry protests.[68]

Thus, when in 1944 it was rumored that the colonial government would take over cassava farms, tempers naturally flared up. According to Martin, women organized a series of demonstrations against the government. In the Ikot-Ekpene Division, for example, the uprising is said to have involved about 5,000 women.[69] Unfortunately, details of this 1944 uprising are not readily available, but it appears that the diversion of *gari* to Northern Nigeria added to the crisis. According to Martin, "*gari* was now one of the items exchanged for northern cattle. [However,] official fears that *gari* production would crowd out palm production, together with more immediate awareness of localized food shortages in Aba and Umuahia, led to a temporary ban on railings to the north."[70]

Earlier, it was pointed out that the official sources are regrettably silent on the exact nature of the 1938 women's complaint against men's "unfair competition" in the cassava trade. Fieldwork undertaken in Nigeria in the late 1980s, however, provides some clues to the male–female question. First and foremost, it seems that the commercialization of cassava probably induced men to enter into the cassava trade. Indeed, as Martin has aptly observed, "Adventurous young men perceived accurately that trade [was one of] the main sources of rapid, if unpredictable, earnings within the colonial economy."[71] Therefore, men's entry into both the palm oil and cassava trade can be rationalized in terms of men's desire for economic self-improvement.[72] Furthermore, colonial exactions, particularly the imposition of taxation, tended to induce young men not only to engage in trade, but also to resort to wage labor, albeit reluctantly. Utilizing the modern transportation facilities, therefore, men ultimately succeeded in gaining control of the cassava industry, especially the lucrative long-distance trade. As I have pointed out elsewhere, this phenomenon prevailed in the 1940s and 1950s.

From the 1940s, to be sure, marketing of the cassava crop in "far-away markets" lay practically in the hands of men, particularly those with the modern means of transport. In the

1950s, for example, when this writer served as a headmaster in places like Mbieri and Ogwa, centers of cassava trade in the old Owerri Division, it was a common scene to witness men on Sunday mornings evacuating carloads of fermented cassava brought from the Rivers State. The cassava was sold to local women who, in turn, retailed it in the local markets. Thus, while men engaged in wholesale trading, women seemed to be playing the role of ubiquitous petty traders.[73]

What is equally significant is this: Men were able to relocate or migrate to other regions where they established cassava plantations. For example, men from Owerri and Aba Divisions colonized parts of present Rivers State from about the 1940s. Colonies of Igbo farmers thus sprouted in such places as Elele, Omanelu, and Diobu, where cassava, rubber, and palm oil plantations dotted the landscape. Since this colonization entailed "being away from home,"[74] it invariably meant that only men were mainly involved in this entrepreneurial innovation. As a matter of fact, social and cultural conventions prevented women from venturing into this pattern of economic enterprise. For example, it was not considered "culturally proper" for women to be away from home for long periods of time.[75] Even women who habitually returned home late from market were often reprimanded; and they were also objects of gossip, because lateness was perceived as reflecting moral laxity. Besides, "domestic responsibilities and social expectations" demanded that women stay at home.[76] Without a doubt, women's commercial initiatives tended to be inhibited by cultural factors.

CONCLUSION

The palm oil and cassava issues, which we have examined closely here, clearly illustrate the gender problem in African economic development. Furthermore, this study demonstrates that men were more likely to seize economic opportunities afforded by the new political order than were women. Equally important, this study highlights the implications of the introduction of Western capitalism into a preindustrial society like that of Nigeria. The transformation of the economy was profound and its impact on women was equally far reaching. Dr. Nina Mba has summarized the impact of colonialism on women rather nicely when she writes, *inter alia,*

The position of women in Southern Nigerian society was both diminished and enhanced under colonialism. In government and administration, there was almost total loss of their traditional areas of responsibility and participation because they were excluded from all levels of administration. In the economic realm, while colonialism provided increased opportunities for some women in trade, it also led to a takeover by men of many areas formerly reserved for women and to a gross underutilization of women in their traditional roles in agriculture.[77]

But, as we pointed out at the beginning of this chapter, change has been the constant leitmotif in the African economic and political landscape. Thus, while colonialism brought subjugation, it also fostered political awakening. Thus today, women are assuming important new roles and positions as politicians, civil servants, and business magnates. The struggle for change, especially among the womenfolk, seems eternal. It was against this background that President Ibrahim Babangida of Nigeria said of women at the Fourth Regional Conference on Women in 1989:

There are compelling reasons why African women must be integrated in the development process. First is their numerical strength [55 percent]. They are industrious and enterprising. . . . They are good managers. . . . No national programmes will be meaningful and thorough if women are not fully involved.[78]

Women's struggle for full integration into the development process, especially in the economic realm, is still an uphill battle. However, given the intensity of the women's movement, their determination and sense of purpose, it is perhaps only a matter of time before gender discrimination, as we know it, becomes a thing of the past. In Nigeria and elsewhere in Africa, both the urban, educated and rural, illiterate women have joined hands to promote the economic welfare of women and to campaign for the passage of legislation "for the advancement of women and the protection of women." These objectives were poignantly articulated at the 1992 seminar organized by the Better Life Programme for Rural Women in Nigeria and the Federation of Women Lawyers (Imo State Chapter). Among other things, the seminar directed attention to the promotion of women's rights, including the expansion of women's economic, educational, and political opportunities. Given that women "suffer disabilities" particularly reflected in their "inability to have access to funds for reasons of gender," it was therefore strongly felt that "income generating activities by women should be encouraged." In addition, women were urged to participate in politics so as to insure their political and social emancipation. Said the chairperson, "Women have no justification in playing shy when the issue of politics arises. The law empowers them to participate actively in politics and the governance of this nation."[79]

NOTES

1. *West Africa*, "Breaking the Mould," 18–24 January 1993, p. 54.

2. David Waines, "Through a Veil Darkly: The Study of Women in Muslim Societies. A Review Article," *Comparative Studies in Society and History. An International Quarterly*, Vol. 24, No. 4, October 1982, p. 643.

3. Jeanne K. Henn, "Women in the Rural Economy: Past, Present, and Future," in *African Women South of the Sahara*, edited by Margaret Jean Hay and Sharon Stichter (London: Longman, 1984), p. 2.

4. See Ester Boserup, *Woman's Role in Economic Development* (London: George Allen & Unwin, 1970), p. 16.

5. Margaret Makeson Green, *Ibo Village Affairs* (New York: Frederick A. Praeger, 1947),

p. 174. Cf. Simon Ottenberg, *Boyhood Rituals in an African Society: An Interpretation* (Seattle: University of Washington Press, 1989), p. xvii.

6. Green, Ibo *Village*, p. 171. For a useful discussion of "boundary development" in African socialization process, see Ottenberg, *Boyhood Rituals*, Chap. 4.

7. Green, Ibo *Village*, p. 175; Ottenberg, *Boyhood Rituals*, p. xvi.

8. Susan Martin, "Gender and Innovation: Farming, Cooking and Palm Processing in Ngwa Region, South-Eastern Nigeria, 1900–1930," *Journal of African History*, Vol. 25, 1984, p. 417.

9. Green, *Ibo Village*, p. 12.

10. G. T. Basden, *Among the Ibos of Nigeria* (London: Frank Cass & Co., 1966 [first edition 1921]), p. 194.

11. Richard N. Henderson, *The King in Every Man: Evolutionary Trends in Onitsha Igbo Society and Culture* (New Haven: Yale University Press, 1972), p. 464.

12. Kenneth Onwuka Dike, *Trade and Politics in the Niger Delta, 1830–1885* (Oxford: Clarendon Press, 1956), p. 96.

13. Susan M. Martin, *Palm Oil and Protest, An Economic History of the Ngwa Region, South-Eastern Nigeria, 1800–1980* (Cambridge: Cambridge University Press, 1988), p. 140.

14. Boniface I. Obichere, "Slavery and the Slave Trade in Niger Delta Cross River Basin," *Actes du Colloque International sûr la traite des Noirs Nantes 1985*, Paris: Center de Récherche sûr l'histoire du Monde Atlantique Societé Française d'histoire d'Outre-Mer, Vol. 2, pp. 48–49.

15. Martin, *Palm Oil and Protest*, p. 47; Green, Ibo *Village*, p. 47; John N. Oriji, "A Study of the Slave and Palm Produce Trade amongst the Ngwa-Igbo of Southeastern Nigeria," *Cahiers d'Études Africaines*, Vol. 91, 1983, pp. 322–326. "Indeed," Oriji writes, "the major role which women played in the economic life of the Ngwa during the period of palm produce trade is one of the most outstanding developments in Ngwa history" (p. 324). Also, "These women who dominated the palm produce trade were said to be so influential that when the British penetrated into Ngwaland in the latter part of the nineteenth century, they thought of appointing them warrant chiefs" (p. 326).

16. Martin, *Palm Oil and Protest*, p. 50. Cf. Anthony G. Hopkins, *An Economic History of West Africa* (New York: Longman, 1973), Chap. 5.

17. Martin, *Palm Oil and Protest*, p. 49.

18. Nigerian National Archives, Enugu (NNAE): OWDIST 346/17.RIVPROF 8/5/353. "Half Year Report on Owerri Division 1917."

19. See Felix K. Ekechi, "Aspects of Palm Oil Trade at Oguta (Eastern Nigeria), 1900–1950," *African Economic History*, Vol. 10, 1981, pp. 41–58.

20. See Felicia Ekejuba, "Omu Okwei, the Merchant Queen of Ossomari: A Biographical Sketch," *Journal of the Historical Society of Nigeria*, Vol. 2/4, June 1967.

21. Martin, *Palm Oil and Protest*, p. 54.

22. Ibid., *passim*; A. Adu Boahen, *African Perspectives on Colonialism* (Baltimore: Johns Hopkins University Press, 1987), Chap. 4.

23. Martin, *Palm Oil and Protest*, p. 55; Boahen, *African Perspectives*, p. 17.

24. Martin, *Palm Oil and Protest*, p. 104.

25. Jan Vansina, "Lessons of Forty Years of African History," a review essay of *The African Experience: Major Themes in African History from Earliest Times to the Present*, by Roland Oliver, in *The International Journal of African Historical Studies (IJAHS)*, Vol.

25, No. 2, 1992, p. 397. See also David Dorward, "The Impact of Colonialism on a Nigerian Hill-Farming Society: A Case Study of Innovation among the Eggon," *IJHAS*, Vol. 20, No. 2, 1987, p. 214 and *passim*.

26. Martin, *Palm Oil and Protest*, p. 106.

27. Ibid.

28. Ekechi, "Aspects of the Palm Oil Trade," pp. 48–49.

29. Ibid., p. 42.

30. Felix K. Ekechi, *Tradition and Transformation in Eastern Nigeria: A Sociopolitical History of Owerri and Its Hinterland, 1902–1947* (Kent: Kent State University Press, 1989), p. 46. Cf. Innocent Uzoechi. "The Social and Political Impact of the Eastern Nigerian Railway on Udi Division, 1913–1945," Ph.D. dissertation, Kent State University, 1985, p. 174.

31. Ekechi, "Aspects of the Palm Oil Trade," pp. 58–59.

32. Martin, *Palm Oil and Protest*, p. 90.

33. Ibid., p. 62.

34. Ibid., p. 66.

35. Ekechi, "Aspects of the Palm Oil Trade," pp. 57–58; Martin, *Palm Oil and Protest*, p. 129.

36. Martin, *Palm Oil and Protest*, p. 128.

37. Ekechi, "Aspects of the Palm Oil Trade," pp. 55–57; Gerald K. Helleiner, *Peasant Agriculture, Government, and Economic Growth in Nigeria* (Homewood, Ill.: Richard D. Irwin, 1966), p. 19.

38. NNAE: OWDIST 10/1/3. Annual Report on the Owerri Division, 1938.

39. NNAE: "Intelligence Report on the Ngwa Clan, Aba Division," 1933, by J. C. Allen, para. 18.

40. NNAE: OWDIST 9/5/6. Half Yearly Report on Owerri Division, January 1–June 30, 1919, by E. Falk.

41. NNAE: OWDIST 10/1/3, Annual Report on Owerri Division, 1938.

42. On the Women's War of 1929, see: Harry Gailey, *The Road to Aba* (New York: New York University Press, 1970); Adiele Eberechukwu Afigbo, *The Warrant Chiefs, Indirect Rule in Southeastern Nigeria, 1891–1929* (New York: Humanities Press, 1972); Nina Emma Mba, *Nigerian Women Mobilized: Women's Political Activity in Southern Nigeria, 1900–1965* (Berkeley: University of California Press, 1982); Martin, *Palm Oil and Protest*, Chap. 9; Ekechi, *Tradition and Transformation*, pp. 164–168. Caroline Ifeka-Moller, "Female Military and Colonial Revolt: The Women's War of 1929, Eastern Nigeria," in *Perceiving Women*, edited by Shirley Ardener (New York: John Wiley & Sons, 1975), pp. 127–157.

43. Martin, *Palm Oil and Protest*.

44. D. C. Ohadike, "The Influenza Pandemic of 1918–19 and the Spread of Cassava Cultivation on the Lower Niger: A Study in Historical Linkages," *Journal of African History (JAH)*, Vol. 22, 1981, p. 380.

45. Felix K. Ekechi, "Colonialism and Christianity in West Africa: The Igbo Case, 1900–1915," *JAH*, Vol. 12, 1971, p. 104.

46. Victor C. Uchendu, *The Igbo of Southeast Nigeria* (New York: Holt, Rinehart and Winston, 1965), p. 19.

47. Green, *Ibo Village*, p. 172.

48. Felix K. Ekechi, "The Cassava Palaver: The Gender Problem in African Economic Development," *Proceedings* (12th Annual Third World Conference), Vol. 1, 1986, p. 134.

49. Phoebe V. Ottenberg, "The Changing Economic Position of Women among the Afrikpo

Ibo," in *Continuity and Change in African Cultures*, edited by William R. Bascom and M. J. Herskovits (Chicago: University of Chicago Press, 1959), p. 215.

50. Ibid.

51. Cf. Ekejuba, "Omu Okwei."

52. Ekechi, "The Cassava Palaver," p. 135.

53. Ibid.

54. Margery Perham, ed., *Mining, Commerce and Finance in Nigeria* (London: Faber & Faber, 1948), Chap. 3.

55. NNAE: OWDIST 10/1/3, D.O. to Resident, July 17, 1939, in Annual Report on Owerri Division, 1938.

56. Ibid.

57. Information from the Chief Archivist, Enugu, 1975. According to the Archivist, some papers being transferred from the National Archives, Ibadan, to Enugu, after the Civil War, were destroyed by fire.

58. NNAE: OWDIST 10/1/4, Annual Report 1939—Owerri Division.

59. This observation is based on impressions rather than empirical evidence.

60. NNAE: OWDIST, Annual Report on Owerri Division, 1938.

61. Ibid.

62. Ibid.

63. Ibid.

64. NNAE: OWDIST 10/1/4, Annual Report 1939—Owerri Division.

65. Ibid.

66. Ibid.

67. Martin, *Palm Oil and Protest*, p. 124.

68. Ibid.

69. Ibid., p. 123.

70. Ibid.

71. Ibid., p. 104.

72. Owerri field notes—interviews at Owerri, 1979, 1983, and 1986.

73. Ekechi, "The Cassava Palaver," p. 137.

74. Owerri field notes—colonists interviewed at Owerri and elsewhere in 1983 stated that "being away from home" often resulted in hardships on their families or even the breakup of marriages.

75. Owerri field notes—informants suggested that the public image of a woman who stayed away from home for long periods of time in pursuit of trade was that of a prostitute.

76. Ekechi, *Tradition and Transformation*, p. 185.

77. Mba, *Nigerian Women Mobilized*, p. 67.

78. Quoted in *West Africa*, "Struggle for Change," 1–7 November 1993, 1970.

79. Susan Onyeche, "Rights of Women," Address Delivered at the Seminar at Nwaorieubi Mbaitoli L. G. A. (Imo State, Nigeria), August 17, 1992, pp. 4–5.

Chapter 4

Muslim Women Traders of Northern Nigeria: Perspectives from the City of Yola

Catherine VerEecke

Since Polly Hill's pioneering work on the economics of households in a northern Nigerian town,[1] devoted largely to the analysis of what she termed the "hidden trade" among Hausa women, there has been a proliferation of related studies.[2]

These and many other works show that a vast majority of married Hausa women from such cities as Kano, Katsina, and Zaria and their rural environs often earn a sizable income from petty or large-scale trade while participating in the Islamic institution of *purdah*, in which they must remain secluded in the house. As a result of this work, the hidden trade has been viewed as a Hausa, a Nigerian, or perhaps a West African women's institution that serves the dual function of enhancing both their prestige and modesty and of providing them with some remuneration for their household labor.[3]

Inasmuch as the studies demonstrate the prevalence of the hidden trade among Hausa women, several questions about it warrant further attention. First, although there is general agreement among observers that the practice provides Muslim women with a measure of autonomy within the household, there is less said about whether it mainly serves economic ends, augmenting the Islamic obligatory contribution of husbands, or has sociocultural purposes, being reinvested primarily in the Islamic system of marriage. Second, while the prevalence and nature of the trade in Hausaland have become quite clear, comparatively little attention has been accorded to the region's groups or individuals who do not trade, in terms of the variables that may affect the broad patterns and individual choices. Finally, very little compatible information is available for non-Hausa women in northern Nigeria, who constitute a sizable percentage of the region's women, even in the cities that were studied.[4] Indeed, there appears to be a general assumption in the literature that all northern Nigerian Muslim women, given the right incentives (e.g., economic) and conditions, would choose to become active traders. In short, further research and analysis are necessary on the hidden trade, beyond the available case studies of Hausa women, to broaden the perspectives on the practice or more comprehensively cover ethnically heterogeneous communities dominated by either Hausa or other Muslim ethnic groups. Moreover, in view of Nigeria's current economic crisis and the government's designation of "women-in-development" activities as one way of alleviating its peoples' hardships, it is timely to determine exactly how widespread the institution actually is and whether this is an "economic" venture that can be enhanced by future development activities.

With these questions in mind, the following is a comparative study of Muslim women's trade in northern Nigeria, based on a review of the available relevant literature and on my own research in an ethnically heterogeneous northern Nigerian city, Yola, in which Hausa are numerically and economically significant yet are out numbered by the Fulbe and members of other ethnic groups.[5] The analysis first comparatively summarizes the data on Hausaland, discussing the factors that condition the women's roles and their decision to trade and the variations that obtain within Hausaland. The intensive, comparative study of Yola women will show that because of relatively uniform regional historical trends, political and economic factors, and cultural tendencies, the hidden trade is indeed prevalent outside Hausaland. The Muslim women of Yola, having shared in the common northern Nigerian experience, now participate in and rely on the practice, although the custom has been adapted to conform to local conditions and traditions and therefore varies in many respects from that of Hausaland. I also attempt to explain why the dominant ethnic group of Yola, the Fulbe, have thus far been resisting full incorporation into this tradition, largely on what they term cultural grounds and assess the impact of these attitudes on Yola's informal trade and food industries and on its non-Fulbe societies in general. Finally, I conclude by noting the factors that seem to be most effective in the Yola women's economic decision making and by providing a few suggestions for the further incorporation of their activities into national women-in-development plans.

THE REGION: NORTHERN NIGERIA

Popularly known as the Muslim North, and at times erroneously as Hausaland, Northern Nigeria actually comprises a diversity of linguistic and cultural groups, both Muslim and Christian, although the Muslims dominate numerically. The British colonial administration designated the region to the north of the Niger and Benue rivers a discrete political entity (Northern Nigeria) within Nigeria and further divided it into provinces based roughly upon existing units, especially Islamic emirates. Much of the northern region and beyond had already achieved a large degree of unity during the early nineteenth-century *jihad* of the Fulbe mallam, Usman 'dan Fodio, in which he and his supporters succeeded in consolidating into the Sokoto Caliphate the autonomous, age-old, trade-oriented Hausa city-states, as well as several non-Hausa Muslim and non-Muslim emirates. Although some areas (e.g., Borno) were not included, the proselytizing goals of the Fulbe spread to nearly all areas of the north and even to some kingdoms in the south, thereby politically and culturally unifying many peoples under the brotherhood espoused by Islam. Moreover, trade and local industries dominated by Hausa merchants and artisans expanded and altered the composition of the region's local economies.[6] With expansion of the regional commercial system, the usage of the Hausa language has noticeably increased at a rapid pace, especially in urban centers, even among the politically dominant Fulbe of Hausaland. In some communities many non-Hausa individuals have been learning Hausa as their mother tongue. Since the granting of independence to Nigeria in 1960, the peoples of northern Nigeria, now comprising largely Muslims, have tended to act together to form one political unit, especially at election time. This was particularly the case in the 1979 and 1983 elections, in which the Muslim North, generally associated with NPN (National Party of Nigeria), was clearly dominant over the "Christian" South.[7] Such a dichotomy has also been apparent in subsequent military administrations.

Although these regional alignments persist, the populace of northern Nigeria now suffers greatly from the economic and political crises that face the nation as a whole. Following a brief, artificial prosperity from oil during the 1970s, since the 1980s a multitude of problems has become highly noticeable, such as economic decline, inflation, lack of development, weak institutions, corruption, and a host of others, resulting at least in poverty and social malaise among a significant proportion of Nigeria's citizens. In particular, northern Nigeria, despite its political dominance of the country, currently lags behind the south in industrial development and Western education, so that this region's peoples, especially the poor, are among the most greatly affected. Northern peoples' sentiments of deprivation have been expressed, for instance, in local ethnic and religious antagonisms along with popular, at times destructive movements such as the Maitatsine riots in the early and mid-1980s.[8]

MARGINALIZATION OF MUSLIM WOMEN'S ROLES
IN NORTHERN NIGERIA

The transformation of women's roles in northern Nigeria may be understood at least partly within the context of the broader changes that took place in the region, beginning primarily with the *jihad*. Historical evidence suggests that prior to the nineteenth century many rural women were involved directly in food production in the household and on the farm and that seclusion was primarily an urban phenomenon.[9] Beginning with the jihad in the early nineteenth century, which had wide-reaching social and economic effects, the contributions of Muslim women began to change, albeit gradually. In the societies most directly involved in the war and the consequent "purification of the Faith," the changes were more dramatic. First, the increased prevalence of slavery and slave farms (plantations) in the new Fulbe emirates enabled some families to forgo agriculture, partly or entirely, and some others did so in response to raiding in the countryside.[10] These economic and social changes, together with a return to a more fundamental attitude toward Islam and an increased concern with Islamic scholarship seem to have encouraged the interpretation of Islamic ideology in a way that promoted the formal seclusion of women; seclusion facilitated the preservation of women's modesty.[11] Correspondingly, men and women would have more time to devote to their religious obligations, especially praying and reading the Koran.

The trends begun in the nineteenth century continued during the colonial period. By the time slavery was abolished in the early colonial period, in some areas of the caliphate a stigma had been attached to farming, especially on the part of women. M. G. Smith, for instance, argues that when the emancipation of slaves left a gap in the labor force, women, who worked as farmers in pre-jihad times, still did not return to farming to avoid their families' association with slaves and to pursue productive activities in the compound.[12] Likewise, many female former slaves refrained from farming as an assertion of their legal status as free persons. Moreover, while seeking to preserve the region's existing Islamic and social order, which included concubinage, British colonial policy in effect reinforced women's subordinate and dependent status and further encouraged their seclusion.[13]

As the British colony of Nigeria became increasingly status and prestige oriented, the association between women's behavior and men's honor became even more pronounced, and the seclusion of one's wives continued as a means of increasing one's prestige.[14] Indeed, by this time, there had developed a clear association between women's work and their husband's honor: women's work as farmers might tarnish their image. Consequently, seclusion, previously an urban phenomenon, began to penetrate rural households, further altering the composition of the rural labor force. Some early twentieth-century fundamentalist movements in the rural areas also accelerated this process,[15] as have more recent Islamic revivalist movements in several Hausa cities.[16] It is thus reported that most of today's married urban and rural Hausa Muslim women in northern Nigeria, with the exception of those in remote hamlets, are in seclusion; and very few are at present engaged in work outside the household—largely as a manifestation of social status and religious devotion.[17]

The system of seclusion of women in northern Nigeria follows the general Islamic pattern; under which besides men's legitimate control over their wives' behavior, it is an imperative that women's modesty be stringently guarded, although the precise means of achieving this throughout the Muslim world is variable. In northern Nigeria, purdah (seclusion) exists as a viable institution in which married women, generally speaking, can leave the house only with due cause, such as to receive medical treatment, to attend marriages or funerals, to visit nearby relatives, or nowadays, to go to their places of work.[18] In most instances, women must seek their husbands' permission to leave the house. Violation of these regulations may result in such measures as the accusation of promiscuity by one's family or, in an extreme form, divorce.

Women's modesty is further enhanced by the use of the veil and in some instances by the use of escorts. In much of northern Nigeria, even at present, the purity of young Muslim girls is also preserved by early marriage, which tends to preclude their continuation of school beyond the primary level. A few husbands may allow their wives to continue their education, at times to the university level. But they usually limit their wives' choices of work to those with minimal direct male–female interaction, especially as schoolteachers and nurses. Moreover, many women believe it is not their duty to work, for their husbands are obligated under Islam to provide for them and their children.

Despite Muslim men's control over their wives' extradomestic activities, wives enjoy a good deal of freedom within their section of the compound, which is viewed as the women's domain; and they have a very rich social life among their peers, all within the confines of seclusion. At the same time, the clear separation of men's and women's domains has encouraged the women's elaboration of what one scholar has called a "world of their own," in which they are in many respects politically and economically autonomous.[19] With this freedom in the domestic domain, coupled with what some scholars see as women's inherent desire for prestige, it is not surprising that these women would develop activities that would enhance their income or status and provide them with an investment toward an uncertain marital future.[20]

Throughout the Muslim world, in fact, women have devised means of asserting their autonomy and enhancing their prestige while remaining in seclusion.[21] But unlike women in some Muslim areas, where more equitable treatment in family law and employment is sought,[22] most northern Nigerian Muslim women (and men) for various reasons are reluctant to seek change.[23] Thus, on the one hand, the rigid system of seclusion encourages the women to adopt measures to gain some autonomy, and on the other it provides sufficient benefits for most not to contemplate changing any aspects of the system. This attitude, in fact, is implicitly supported by the Nigerian federal government which, despite its economic predicaments, does little to cultivate or further the interests or achievements of women. Since 1987, a national development program for women (coordinated by the first lady of Nigeria and the governor's wives) has operated in Nigeria, but so far in the north it has mainly supported the elaboration of Muslim women's handicraft industries.[24]

THE HIDDEN TRADE IN HAUSALAND

Barkow suggests that one reason northern Nigerian women conform so readily to the rules of purdah is to enjoy much leisure time at home.[25] They need only to prepare food for the house and keep their surroundings tidy, while their husbands provide funds for their personal use and household maintenance. Studies argue, however, that most do not opt for a leisurely life; they essentially establish their own businesses. Indeed, all relevant studies undertaken in Hausaland found that at least two-thirds and as many as all of the secluded Hausa women surveyed engage in household trade, regardless of their family income or status. This normally begins with a woman's investing a small percentage of her dowry, or the funds provided by her husband for the household, or her personal use in the necessary items for her to start a small trading business. She may then package for sale such finished products as detergent, sugar, groundnuts, grain, cigarettes, candy, or soft drinks. She may process and sell such nonperishable cooking items as groundnut oil (*mai* or *nyebbam*) or locust bean paste (*daddawa*) or perishable foods, such as porridge (*kunu*) and bean cakes (*kosai*). In an extreme form, she may prepare entire meals for other households in the form of soup (*miya*) or starchy food (*tuwo*). Some also sell luxury items such as cloth, clothing, perfume, cosmetics, and jewelry or provide services such as weaving, sewing, and hair plaiting. Many in fact engage in multiple activities. For instance, one study in rural Hausaland found that secluded women engaged in the sale of 65 different wares or activities.[26]

Despite the prevalence of the activities, the women need not leave the house on account of trade. Some women market sell or give on credit these items from the house to their women friends or relatives who visit them. But in most Hausa locales, the women traders use or employ their own or others' children to act on their behalf to purchase the necessary cooking ingredients from the market or from other women, to sell the goods they produce on the street or in others' households, and to buy meals or snacks from other women traders. The children traders, in some instances, become full-time street hawkers, at times with their own incomes, who consequently cannot attend school.[27] Because the proceeds of trading (or any income they earn) belong to the women, husbands do not prohibit their wives' trading activities, provided they do not leave the house and food is available for meals at the prescribed times, regardless of who prepares it.

Though it has existed since at least the nineteenth century, the hidden trade has evidently gained popularity among Hausa women throughout northern Nigeria in recent years. In the rural areas this activity is viewed by women as less strenuous than farming, to the extent that some pagan women have become Muslims, largely in order to reap the "benefits" of seclusion.[28] In urban areas it has proliferated to assist the increasing number of wage laborers who cannot eat at home. It is also widespread in relatively new Hausa communities on the fringes of Hausaland[29] and among women of the Hausa diaspora in regions of Nigeria and other West African countries where the Hausa constitute a numerical minority and strive to retain their cultural traditions.[30]

THE VARIATIONS IN HAUSALAND

Despite the prevalence of the hidden trade throughout Hausaland and perhaps northern Nigeria, some variations in the form and meaning of the practice can be noted in such areas as the women's relative income and profits from trading, the kinds of commodities they produce and sell, and the use they make of the profits. Generally speaking, at least in Hausaland, the relative demand for the products in the communities, the communities' degree of economic heterogeneity, and to some extent, urbanization, are among the major variables that affect the form and meaning of trade.

The hidden trade is evidently most developed in communities manifesting a considerable diversity of economic activities, namely those with commercial or wage orientations. For instance, in the town of Batagarawa, near Katsina, women played a prominent marketing role from their households, selling grain and other commodities on behalf of either their husbands or middlemen. Hill argues that the hidden trade was so widespread (and cost-effective) at the time of her study that it served in place of a formal market in the town, thereby enabling women to increase the number of wares traded.[31] In a more dispersed rural community she studied where marketing was less developed, the hidden trade existed on a much smaller scale: a narrower range of wares was traded; revenues were lower; food was less commonly traded; and children were less often employed to assist their mothers.[32]

In Batagarawa, however, where marketing was a central feature of the town, many women's incomes were large enough for them to support their households. In another rural community, one incorporated into a river basin development program, the rise of wage labor, together with other factors, similarly increased the incidence of the trade.[33] Although planners had envisaged that the women would gain employment on the new farms, many opted instead for increased involvement in the trade and profited enormously. In the city of Kano, the marked demand for goods, snacks, and meals by other traders and men at their place of work, has led many Hausa women to abandon food preparation for their households entirely. They spend the entire day preparing food for sale and buy less expensive goods or meals for their houses, thus making profits.[34] Similarly, in Katsina it is usual for a family to buy food prepared for at least one meal or to supplement a meal with a snack.[35] The rural traders profit more than those in the wage-oriented urban areas, at least in a relative sense.

Operating within an ostensibly agrarian system of production, in which most men are farmers just above the subsistence level, many women obtain profits that may be regarded as relatively high, often surpassing those of their husbands.[36] While their husbands seek to provide staple food for the house along with some funds from the sale of their crops, many skillful rural women either provide the bulk of the basic necessities for household maintenance or invest the proceeds in land or cattle.[37] In the city, in contrast, where men's incomes from wage or salaried labor (i.e., as civil servants) or large-scale trade and business clearly surpass their wives', men remain the primary supporters of their households.[38]

But cultural factors also intervene, especially in the cities and some of their densely populated heterogenous rural environs. Here, devotion to Islam has traditionally been strong, and many women feel they need not give any part of their income to their husbands, whose duty it is under Islam to support their households.

For instance, in Kano and some of its rural environs, most women save the profits of their activities, not only to enhance their prestige and indulge their tastes in cloth and jewelry but also for their future marriages or their daughters' marriages.[39] They normally purchase enamel or brass bowls, cloth, and jewelry, much of which is not used but displayed in their rooms. Many women must save for several daughters' marriages, a practice they believe will broaden their marriage choices and provide them with comfortable lifestyles when married. Moreover, dowry may act as a buffer against divorce, which evidently is quite common and increasing in Hausaland, though some observers argue that this is usually not a primary consideration among women traders of these communities.[40]

In sum, whereas women in rural areas of Hausaland are likely to invest (indirectly) the profits of the household trade into household maintenance to supplement their husbands' contributions, many of those in the very heterogeneous wage-oriented communities ultimately invest them in the current system of marriage. In the latter instance in particular, the women affirm their dependence on men, who in turn retain control over them under Islam, while being obligated to provide full support. However, given the current economic crisis of Nigeria, in which many families no longer have sufficient funds to support their members, this practice may be undermined by more practical considerations of men and women, as found in a more recent study by Coles among the Hausa of Kaduna.[41]

YOLA, ADAMAWA EMIRATE

As the southernmost emirate of the Sokoto Caliphate, Adamawa (Fombina) has shared in the northern Nigerian regional experience, with some peculiarities of its own. Until post-independence times, the region was not greatly affected by the spread of the Hausa language and remained culturally diverse, with over 100 linguistic groups represented. Unlike Hausaland, where Hausa constitute the numerically dominant ethnic group and have incorporated many peoples into their identity, including Fulbe jihadists, Adamawa continues to be dominated by the Fulbe. Originally a pastoral people who migrated to the Boon area in the eighteenth and nineteenth centuries, the Fulbe were confronted in their new territory with what they perceived as various oppressive demands from the land's indigenous pagan populations.[42] Though most of the area's Fulbe were superficially Islamic at the time,[43] their leaders sought the advice and spiritual leadership of their kinsman, Usman 'dan Fodio. Their representative, Modibbo Adama, himself a devout Muslim, then received the flag of Islam to wage jihad in the region; and he subsequently gave the new emirate the name Adamawa, which retained its subsidiary, tributary position vis-à-vis Sokoto.

Because of their relative success at subjugating and later converting to Islam a sizable portion of the area's non-Fulbe population, many pastoral Fulbe settled there and began to concentrate not only on warfare but also on Islamic scholarship and administration, leaving agricultural and certain domestic work to their slaves.[44] Over time, they consequently absorbed many non-Fulbe (former slaves and Muslims of free status) into their identity, in a process known as Fulbeization, especially in urban areas.[45] This process continues at present, particularly in Yola, where the Fulbe are numerically dominant; and many non-Fulbe still seek to improve their status by becoming Fulbe.

Yola has maintained a marked division of labor largely along ethnic lines. As a result of their success in the jihad and their prominent role in the colonial administration and the Nigerian government until recently, many Fulbe have continued to hold key administrative, judicial, and religious posts.[46] In the mid-nineteenth century, Hausa, Kanuri, and Nupe, among others, began to arrive in Adamawa to develop and maintain the necessary trading activities the Fulbe had shunned,[47] and their presence has greatly altered economic life in the area. Following independence and the designation of Yola as the capital of Gongola State, with the consequent prospects of new employment, migrations to Yola have accelerated greatly. Various peoples, especially the Hausa, recently joined by Yoruba and Igbo from southern Nigeria, continue to dominate large- and small-scale trade industries, both in Yola and in many of its nearby towns. Finally, Hausa is beginning to replace Fulfulde as a lingua franca in many parts of the emirate. As with much of northern Nigeria, commerce and business (and, of course, government and military work), rather than industry, have become the most popular and profitable enterprises.

As a result of the proselytizing mission of the Fulbe during the jihad, Adamawa and Yola have assumed a distinctively Muslim character. Christian missionaries were effective only in some rural areas; and only recently have some Christians migrated to the Fulbe towns. In the traditional part of Yola (Yola Town), one mainly finds Fulbe (those with pure Fulbe ancestry and those incorporated into the Fulbe identity), with non-Fulbe nowadays settling on the town's fringes. In the *sabon gari* (Jimeta), which was established early this century for "strangers," reside Fulbe, Hausa, and Kanuri Muslims; Igbo and Bachama Christians; and Batta, Kilba, Verre, and Yoruba, along with individuals from about twenty other ethnic minority groups whose members are either Christian or Muslim. Among the Muslims, a brotherhood exists to promote some degree of harmony and a general uniformity of behavior. Thus, at particular times (e.g., elections), Muslims and Christians are most clearly opposed; and in other instances, many non-Fulbe, regardless of religion, have massed together in attempts to dilute the Fulbe element in Adamawa. Equally often, many Muslims seek the benefits of incorporation into the Fulbe identity.

MUSLIM WOMEN IN ADAMAWA

In this section we compare the economic activities of Muslim Yola women with those of Hausaland. Among the married women of the Yola area (Adamawa Emirate), there is a uniform prescription for seclusion as an expression of religious devotion and a means of preserving modesty. They tend to fare less favorably in education and the pursuit of careers than do Christians, who do not follow this practice. Like the Hausa, Yola's Muslim women have various means of offsetting their lack of activity or power outside their own domain, one of which is participation in the hidden trade. Generally speaking, this industry is most prevalent in Adamawa towns with large daily market operations or local government activities. In the smaller, less densely populated towns, the incidence of the trade is lower. Here we concentrate on the city of Yola.

About two-thirds of the secluded Muslim women (in my 1988 survey of 107 individuals) belonging to a variety of educational and socioeconomic backgrounds and age groups reported gaining an income from some form of trade.[48] Those from families of high standing tended to trade more expensive, less labor-intensive goods, such as jewelry, clothing, beverages, and cloth, although some wives of Islamic scholars tended to refrain from trading altogether. Other women most commonly traded such goods as groundnut oil (*nyebbam*), groundnut paste (*barkuru*), sugar, pepper, locust bean paste (*daddawa*), or detergent; and a few dealt in plaited hair. As Pitten found in Katsina, recently married women (in their early twenties) were not as active as those in their thirties and forties, most likely because of the time required to save capital to start a business and develop potential trading and credit networks.[49] Yola women bear most of their children during their twenties and simply do not have time for other activities. Not included in the discussion here are figures for widows and divorcees, who notably are more active traders than the secluded women and to whom the rules of purdah do not apply.[50]

Despite the overarching similarities in the nature of the hidden trade between Yola and the Hausa towns and cities, there are some fundamental differences. Here we will examine the mechanisms of trading, the magnitude and uses made of the revenues, and finally the relative involvement in the preparation of meals for sale. Moreover, in Yola we find the perhaps anomalous case of the Fulbe, who are only marginally involved in these activities as consumers.

The hidden trade of Yola may be described as a truly household industry, perhaps even more so than with Hausaland: most secluded Yola women trade from within their houses, without requiring much outside assistance. Although there are various means of selling goods, a majority of women in my survey from several ethnic groups simply stated, "I do it myself." They sell or give the goods to women friends or relatives or to children, who visit their compounds on behalf of their mothers. They occasionally sell the goods when they visit other houses. Over 60 percent of the women reported following this procedure, although many enlisted the help of their children or of nonsecluded women to purchase necessary cooking ingredients. About 25 percent used their own children to assist in the trading, and some of the wealthier traders were aided by their servants.

The results from Yola therefore contrast with those from Hausaland, where children have been central to the trading operations, often as a full-time venture, which some argue is threatened by the children's mandatory enrollment in school.[51] It is possible that in adhering to the current national goal of universal primary education (instituted in 1976) some Yola women have simply chosen not to involve their children in the activities; indeed, none report that their children miss school on the account of trading. But unlike the women of Hausaland who feared that school enrollment would negatively affect the trade, the Yola women contend instead that they can, if they so desire, enlist their children's assistance after school hours or during holidays. Most Yola primary school children now return from school by lunchtime. If the women's responses are accurate, Yola children's minimal participation in the hidden trade may be attributed to the following: (1) children are not needed to sell the particular commodities sold in Yola by the women traders; (2) the control of children is not a central aspect of the hidden trade;[52] or (3) the Yola trade is simply not large enough to necessitate the children's assistance. We address these points below.

Although many economic transactions are conducted within their houses by the Yola women themselves, the profits obtained are significant. Whereas some women do not trade at all, especially the Fulbe, those who do so generally extract a large profit. Most reported earning about 20 naira per week from it, and many others earned more, with a maximum of 400 naira per week. Thus, some earn as much as or more than their men, more than the average annual GNP per capita income of Nigeria, and in a few instances, more than the salaries of moderately paid civil servants. These figures are compatible with those from Hausa cities; and in both regions women in wards nearest the market or government offices made the largest profits.[53]

Another area of contrast is the women's uses of the revenues. As was not the case in several of the heterogeneous communities of Hausaland, where most women reported investing their profits in their own or their daughters' marriages in the form of dowries, the Yola women use the profits for various, often multiple uses which they see essentially as economic ventures because their husband's contributions are now insufficient to maintain their households. The most common use (among 53 percent of the traders) is simply for "one's self"—for personal use, such as buying clothing, jewelry, soap, cosmetics, and the like. Second, the traders (40 percent) purchase such goods for their children, especially their daughters; and at times they contribute toward their school fees. Some (25 percent) report saving the money for dowries, but substantially less than those who use the money for goods for themselves or their children. A small number (15 percent) also report using the profits for general household purposes (e.g., buying food), a few others give the profits as alms, but hardly any (8 percent) give them directly to their husbands. In fact, most argue that the latter is inappropriate, with some stating, "It is not my duty to give contributions to my husband, even if he is out of work." Finally, especially among the traders with the highest revenues, the profits are used for multiple purposes, often including dowries.

These figures on Yola women's uses of trade revenues lead to another tentative conclusion: that the hidden trade in Yola may be more of an economic venture than that in the Hausa cities. As emphasized by the Yola women, their revenues most commonly supplement their husbands' contributions, but they are seldom invested in dowries and the system of marriage; the monetary support of the household in the face of harsh economic times has become a greater priority. Moreover, the fact that in Yola the dowry (especially among the Fulbe) is usually the responsibility of a bride's friends and extended family, and not of the bride or her mother alone, may also contribute to the difference. We return to this point later. In some respects, we find greater similarities between Yola and the rural Hausa towns[54] than with the highly heterogeneous settlements or the cities;[55] here the Yola women stress the economic importance of their work. However, the imperatives of Islam remain clear in the Yola case: women still view the profits as their own and their husbands as the providers of basic household necessities. Men remain the economic and legal guardians of their wives.

Finally, unlike women in Hausaland, where the industry of meal preparation for sale from the households is expanding, Muslim Yola women refrain from this practice, except for some widows and divorcees who must do it to support themselves. Although a majority (about 70 percent) of the secluded women traders were heavily involved in the preparation and sale of cooking ingredients and finished products (such as cloth), considerably fewer (about 20 percent) engaged in the sale of snacks, such as fried bean cakes (*kosai, akara*); and hardly any (about 5 percent) engaged in the preparation of entire meals (*nyaamdu, nyiiri*). Very few report purchasing meals from other women. Most argue that selling food is simply unheard of in Yola, or that it is *woo'dai* (bad), often saying, "It is not our custom." The very few married women who sold food claimed they did so against their beliefs. This, we shall argue, correlates with conditions perhaps peculiar to Yola, a city dominated by a people with a strong aversion to buying, selling, and eating food in public.

VARIATIONS IN YOLA

Within Yola there are highly significant differences in Muslim women's involvement in the hidden trade, largely attributable to ethnic and cultural factors. Some women have become active and productive traders, some sell only small amounts, and others only purchase goods from other traders without actually producing goods for trade. Whereas women from all other ethnic groups were active traders (75 percent of them earned over 10 naira per week), a majority of Fulbe had little involvement in the trade. About 65 percent of the married Fulbe women in the survey did not trade at all; and another 15 percent did so very occasionally, selling or bartering the surplus of goods produced for the house, such as groundnut oil (*nyebbam*) or locust bean paste (*daddawa*), earning less than 10 naira per week, although many reported buying goods from other (e.g., Hausa) women.

Table 4.1 suggests a great disparity between the trading practices of the Fulbe and those of other ethnic groups. An explanation for this may be summarized as follows: Fulbe customs now include a strong aversion to direct involvement in these kinds of activities.[56] Unlike ethnic groups from around Yola or other regions of Nigeria where farming and more recently trading have been viable or preferable occupations for men and women, the Fulbe have traditionally avoided these occupations. As noted above, as the rulers of the new emirate, the Fulbe founders of Adamawa, who were predominantly pastoralists until the nineteenth century

Table 4.1
Married Women's Weekly Returns from Trade in Yola*

	Fulbe (n=67)	Non-Fulbe (n=40)
Did Not Trade	64.5%	12.5%
Under 10 Naira	15.0%	2.5%
11-20 Naira	7.5%	40.0%
21-50 Naira	4.5%	22.5%
Over 50 Naira	4.5%	12.5%
Gainfully Employed	3.0%	10.0%
TOTAL	99.0%**	100.0%

Note: In 1988, 7 Naira = 1 U.S. dollar; in 1993, 24 Naira = 1 U.S. dollar.
*N = 107. Although widows and divorcees were also interviewed, they are not included here.
**Less than 100% because of rounding.

jihad, were assisted by slaves in farming until early in this century. Work in religion, the judiciary, and administration have been the preferred occupations. Trading has "always" been the responsibility of other groups, to the extent that Fulbe leaders often invited traders, such as the Hausa or Kanuri, to develop this necessary activity in their communities.

This attitude toward trade and marketing stems not only from changing Fulbe economic orientations but also from their cultural beliefs, the roots of which are found among their pastoral counterparts. All Fulbe argue, quite adamantly, that spending unnecessary time in the market is shameful (*chemtu'dum*); that preparing food for sale is shameful; that eating in public is shameful; and that any overt public demonstration is indeed shameful.[57] This fear of shame is summarized in a proverb: *Pullo nastan luumo wade, ammanastatta luumo semteende*, which means, "It is better for a Pullo to die than be shamed in public." A Pullo Fulbe must show great discretion and reserve when interacting with others, especially in public, and ideally should avoid any behavior or scenarios (i.e., the market) in which he or she might be shamed. Indeed, Fulbe go to great lengths not to eat in public, and I personally was advised on many occasions by Fulbe associates in Adamawa not to purchase and eat food in public, lest they be shamed.

These restrictions also apply even more stringently to secluded Fulbe women than to men. Although the pastoral women must by necessity engage in the sale of milk,[58] the married Muslims are now prohibited by their relatively new religious obligations from producing goods, especially of processed foodstuff, for sale to the public.[59] Although this seems a contradiction, it appears that during the sedentarization and Islamization of the Fulbe, the notion of shame (*semteende*) was broadened to encompass women's modesty in dress and demeanor, so such trading activities are now viewed by most settled Fulbe women as shameful, violating their *pulaaku* (Fulbe-ness), as well as their religious obligations (*dina*). By exposing themselves and their families unnecessarily, they bring shame upon themselves and reduce their family honor (*daraja*). And trading simply is not necessary, they now argue, given men's Islamic obligation to support them. Although many Fulbe women regard the practice as a good thing and agree that they benefit enormously from the activities of other women, most state that they themselves cannot become traders.

Married Fulbe women's avoidance of active trade may also be regarded as a manifestation of the Fulbe desire to dominate their region politically and culturally. These women, rich and poor alike, take pride in their excessive sense of shame, which they believe is ostensibly lacking or minimal among other, non-Fulbe peoples. It is thus often said among Fulbe and their neighbors that a Pullo will die of his or her shame. This means both that the Fulbe sense of morality is so strong that some of them will literally die from it and that a Pullo would rather die than be shamed.[60] Fulbe women, who believe they naturally have more *semteende* than Fulbe men, therefore epitomize this ideal, bearing their people's burden of demonstrating *semteende* (shame) to other peoples. Although other peoples may have *semteende* (or *kunya* in Hausa), the Fulbe believe that only they have the necessary ingredient in the blood that enables them to be culturally and morally superior. Thus, despite the great differences in wealth that now exist among the Fulbe, some of whom even lack the resources to feed their families, the women's rejection of trading persists in order to maintain and enhance the *daraja* (prestige, honor) of their people as a whole. Consequently, most depend solely on their husbands' or families' contributions to maintain their houses; and a girl's dowry is also jointly the responsibility of her family and friends and not her mother or herself alone. Of the few Fulbe women who reported that they did trade, hardly any used their incomes for dowry.

In contrast to the Fulbe, Muslim women of other ethnic groups are generally very active in trade and find nothing at all shameful in it. As noted above, nearly all "non-Fulbe" in my survey engaged in some form of trade, averaging about 20 naira per week from the activities. As might be expected, the Hausa (both indigens and migrants to Yola) are the most active traders, averaging about 25 naira per week income. They are followed by the Kanuri (originally from Borno in the northeast) and finally other indigenous groups from the Yola area (e.g., Bata, Chamba, Verre, Kilba, Laka) most of whom are first- or second-generation migrants from agricultural communities.

Despite the prevalence of the trade in commodities and snacks, non-Fulbe (along with the Fulbe), oppose the sale of meals to individuals outside the house. They too regard it as shameful, reducing their family honor, which suggests that Fulbe culture, being thus far the dominant one in Yola, has shaped the city's food and trade industry. On the one hand, the Fulbe demand, as consumers for basic household necessities, has bolstered the support of other women's activities and of the hidden trade as a whole. But their taboos against the preparation of food for sale and eating in public appear to have negatively affected the development of an informal food industry in Yola, both in general demand and in attitude. Whereas one finds in Hausaland the full range of activities from children's selling meals for their mothers, to small bukateria-type restaurants, to formal catering restaurants, there are hardly any such enterprises in Yola Town and very few in Jimeta, the city's stranger quarter, with these providing a livelihood for Muslim widows, divorcees, or Christians. This may explain why children are not often involved in trade on behalf of their mothers: the kinds of commodities (usually nonperishable items) marketed by secluded women in Yola simply do not require the children's involvement.[61]

CONCLUSION

This chapter poses three questions about the economic activities of Muslim women in northern Nigeria. First, exactly how widespread is the practice of the "hidden trade" and can it be considered a northern Nigerian or regional institution? Second, is the practice relatively uniform in its occurrence, design, and meaning outside Hausaland? Finally, is this a truly economic venture that should be encouraged and monetarily supported by the Nigerian government or development agencies to improve the livelihood of Nigerian women? Let us now address these questions.

Despite certain limitations, the data suggest that the hidden trade is rather widespread throughout northern Nigeria, attributable in part to the common historical experience of the region's peoples. In particular, the unity instilled as a result of the Fulbe jihad has promoted cultural interchanges, individual migration, and the spread of the Hausa language beyond the boundaries of Hausaland. Moreover, the spread of the Hausa diaspora and its commercial orientation throughout the area discussed is surely a major factor contributing to the increased significance of the hidden trade. With today's economic crisis, it is also not surprising to find further similarities in the economic responses of the region's men and women, particularly in the informal sector; in particular, women are noticeably responsive to the challenges posed by Nigeria's economic difficulties.

Although there is comparatively little information for Nigerian Muslim women's trade for locales outside Hausaland or for non-Hausa peoples, it may not be surprising to discover that the hidden trade, perhaps originating with the trade-oriented Hausa peoples, has been adopted by women of nearly all Muslim groups of northern Nigeria, to the extent that it may indeed be considered a northern Nigerian women's institution. This is supported by the study of women in Yola of very diverse backgrounds who share the common northern Nigerian experience. The research shows that the hidden trade, having been adapted to and shaped by local conditions and traditions, has become a viable economic activity in Yola, even among those who do not produce goods for trade, particularly today, when most have difficulty managing on the incomes provided by their husbands. All its secluded women, regardless of their actual production of goods for sale, depend on the trade to facilitate their household activities, and many gain revenues with which to increase their autonomy in the domestic domain. Based on their culture and religion, Yola women would choose time and again not to compete on the increasingly limited market for formal labor, so that this is one way of abiding by their traditions while contributing to their families' well-being.

Beyond the similarities there are also significant differences between Yola and the Hausa communities, such as the extent to which children serve as traders; the kinds of commodities traded; and the uses made of the revenues. The review of the Hausa cases initially suggested that differences are attributable in part to the economic structure of the respective communities. Heterogeneity seems to promote the diversification of activities in the first two areas; that is, in the number and kinds of wares traded and the need for children to assist in the endeavors. In contrast, the use of revenues seems to vary inversely with the degree of heterogeneity in the communities. Until recently, in the most complex communities, particularly among the Hausa, the venture has assumed a largely sociocultural overtone in its close correlation with the institution of marriage. The discussion then showed that Yola does not seem to conform to this framework entirely; although it is a heterogeneous community and the wares sold are quite variable, its married Muslim women do not often invest the revenues of trade into their dowries; children rarely sell the goods on their behalf; and food is seldom traded. Such differences appear to be due to different economic exigencies obtaining at the time the various studies were undertaken and also to cultural and perhaps religious variations.

Besides the economic factors and exigencies within Yola itself, cultural-historical elements or traditions also condition the nature and extremity of the trade. Those who come from groups with a strong tradition of trading tend to be the most active (as evidenced by their income), those from groups which recently began trading show a moderate commitment to it, and those with a traditional aversion to trade have very little involvement. Because it is an ethnically heterogenous community, Yola is an ideal setting in which to observe this continuum. The findings also point to the urgent need for cross-cultural studies of this activity within the relevant economic and cultural contexts that will further illuminate and explain the variations.

The case of Yola is also revealing about the role a dominant ethnic group can play in setting the standards for other groups to follow, in both positive and negative senses. The Muslim Fulbe, undoubtedly one of few northern Nigerian groups with an aversion to active trade, and especially to the sale of cooked food, seem to have influenced the behavior of other women traders. In Yola, the household trade has become a truly household industry in which children are infrequently involved as sellers, and its informal food industry is practically nonexistent. This contrasts significantly with Hausaland, where the preparation of snacks and meals is the most lucrative form of the hidden trade and where children are central figures in the institution. Indeed, many of the differences between the hidden trade of Yola and that of Hausaland can be explained at least partially with reference to the cultural peculiarities of the Yola Fulbe. Nonetheless, as the influence of the Fulbe and the impact of Fulbeization continues to wane in the modern era and as the process of Hausaization continues to increase, we predict the expansion of this venture in Yola as a whole, even among the Fulbe. Considering the restructuring of traditions and the ever-increasing economic hardships in Nigeria, it is likely that Fulbe women will devise other means of expressing their modesty and their ethnic identity.

The data presented here may also indicate changes now occurring in other regions of northern Nigeria. As economic hardships are experienced ever more widely and acutely, secluded Muslim women will become even more sensitive to contributing to their households, albeit indirectly, rather than investing in their marriages. Their primary concern will be more with their families' survival in the present than with their personal investment in the future. Moreover, as more women receive formal education, it seems likely that the institution of dowry will decline in significance, as has already occurred in Yola. However, women will continue to regard direct contributions to the household as a violation of their customs and religious duties.

The case also suggests that the sociocultural considerations underlying trading, in which women ostensibly affirm their dependent status by investing in marriage, can be viewed in a different light.[62] The few who are now able to save tend to do so as insurance against any economic hardships for their families in general rather than for themselves in particular. Indeed, all are painfully aware of their country's economic crisis, and most realize that they must contribute to their families' survival. Moreover, the distinctions between cultural and pragmatic considerations are not readily made among these people.

In view of these patterns and changes, especially women's ever-increasing sensitivity to Nigeria's current crises and their role of assisting their families, the hidden trade seems a viable enterprise to be targeted by development planners, whose primary task will be to devise means of reaching the women in seclusion with their aid. Although the widening of women's occupational choices and opportunities is also desirable, major societal changes in this region, where resistance has been the norm, seem unlikely in the near future.

NOTES

1. Polly Hill, "Hidden Trade among the Hausa," *Man: The Journal of the Royal Anthropological Institute*, Vol. 4, 1969, pp. 392–409. However, Hausa women's economic activities were discussed in Michael Garfield Smith, *The Economy of Hausa Communities in Zaria* (London: Colonial Research Studies, Monographs, Vol. 16, 1955) and in Mary F. Smith, ed., *Baba of Karo: A Woman of the Muslim Hausa* (New Haven: Yale University Press, 1981).

2. See Jerome Barkow, "Hausa Women and Islam," *Canadian Journal of African Studies*,

Vol. 6, No. 2, 1972, pp. 318–328; Emily Simmons, "The Small Scale Rural Food Processing Industry in Northern Nigeria," *Food Research Institute Studies*, Stanford University, Vol. 45, 1975, pp. 147–161; Polly Hill, *Rural Hausa* (Cambridge: Cambridge University Press, 1972), and *Population, Prosperity and Poverty: Rural Kano 1900 and 1970* (Cambridge: Cambridge University Press, 1977); Richard Longhurst, "Resource Allocation and the Sexual Division of Labor: A Case Study of a Moslem Hausa Village in Northern Nigeria," in Women in *Development: The Sexual Division of Labor in Rural Societies*, edited by Lourdes Beneria (New York: Praeger, 1972), pp. 95–117; Enid Schildkrout, "Dependence and Autonomy: The Economic Activities of Hausa Women in Kano," in *Female and Male in West Africa*, edited by Christine Oppong (London: George Allen & Unwin, 1983), pp. 107–126; Barbara Callaway, *Muslim Hausa Women in Nigeria* (Syracuse: Syracuse University Press, 1987).

3. Schildkrout, "Dependence and Autonomy," p. 125.

4. Some exceptions to this include Ronald Cohen, *Dominance and Defiance: A Study of Marital Instability in an African Muslim Community* (Washington, D.C.: American Anthropological Association, Paper 6, 1971), on the Kanuri; Ronald Cohen, "Women's Status in High Office in African Polities," *Annals of Borno*, Vol. 2, 1985, pp. 181–201, on the Pabir-Bura peoples; and Mette Bovin, "Muslim Women in the Periphery: The West African Sahel," in *Women in Islamic Societies: Social Attitudes and Historical Perspectives*, edited by Bo Utas (Copenhagen: Scandinavian Institute of Asian Studies, 1983), pp. 66–103, on the Manga, though they emphasize women's cultural rather than economic responses to being in seclusion.

5. Research was undertaken while I was a lecturer at the University of Maiduguri (September 1983 to November 1986) and in December 1987 and August and September 1988. I used participant observation, a questionnaire, and case history methods, and research includes several locations in Adamawa Emirate, but the data discussed here come mainly from the city of Yola (population over 100,000). I thank the Center for Women's Studies, Ohio State University, for its support of the most recent phase of the research, and Mustapha Aliyu Girei for his comments on an earlier draft of this chapter.

6. Paul E. Lovejoy, "Plantations in the Economy of the Sokoto Caliphate," *Journal of African History*, Vol. 19, 1978, pp. 341–368.

7. In northern Nigeria, Muslims are clearly in the majority; and in southern Nigeria, Christians are more numerous. However, many Christians reside in the north; and the idea of its clear correspondence with the NPN is employed here in general terms.

8. For a historical overview of economic decline in northern Nigeria during the twentieth century, see Michael Watts, *Silent Violence: Food, Famine, and Peasantry in Northern Nigeria* (Berkeley: University of California Press, 1985). For an explanation of the Maitatsine riots, see Paul Lubeck, "Islamic Protest under Semi-Industrial Capitalism: 'Yan Tatsine Explained," *Africa*, Vol. 55, No. 4, 1985, pp. 369–389.

9. Smith, *The Economy of Hausa Communities*, p. 121; Catherine Coles and Beverly Mack, "Women in Twentieth Century Hausa Society," in *Hausa Women in the Twentieth Century*, edited by Catherine Coles and Beverly Mack (Madison: University of Wisconsin Press, 1991), p. 7.

10. Lovejoy, *Plantations*, p. 349.

11. Mervin Hiskett, *The Sword of Truth: The Life and Times of Usman 'dan Fodio* (New York: Oxford University Press, 1973), p. 8; Coles and Mack, *Hausa Women*, p. 609.

12. M. G. Smith, "Introduction," in *Baba of Karo*, edited by Mary F. Smith, pp. 11–34; "The Hausa System of Social Status," *Africa*, Vol. 29, 1959, pp. 239–252.

13. Paul E. Lovejoy, "Concubinage and the Status of Women Slaves in Early Colonial Northern Nigeria," *Journal of African History*, Vol. 29, No. 2, 1988, pp. 245–266, argues

that to concur with the wishes of the women former slaves, the British allowed the retention of concubines, thereby affirming the dependent position of women, free and slave alike.

14. Smith, *Hausa System*; Schildkrout, "Dependence and Autonomy," p. 107.

15. Cecile Jackson, *Kano River Irrigation Project* (West Hartford, Conn.: Kumarian Press, 1985).

16. John Paden, *Religion and Political Culture in Kano* (Berkeley: University of California Press, 1973).

17. Longhurst, *Resource Allocations*, p. 101; Callaway, *Muslim Hausa Women*, pp. 55–61.

18. The actual degree of seclusion is variable. Wives of Islamic scholars never go out. Others go out only with due cause or at night. Still others (especially the university educated) go out often but claim they are in seclusion. See Renee Pitten, "Documentation of Women's Work in Northern Nigeria: Problems and Solutions," in *Sex Roles, Population and Development in West Africa*, edited by Christine Oppong (London: J. Currey, 1987), pp. 25–44; moreover, in some regions (e.g., Borno) seclusion is not as strict, especially in rural areas (Cohen, *Dominance and Defiance*). For some hypotheses about how the Borno system arose historically, see Gina Porter, "A Note on Slavery, Seclusion, and Agrarian Change in Northern Nigeria," *Journal of African History*, Vol. 30, No. 3, 1989, pp. 487-491; Humphrey Fisher, "Slavery and Seclusion in Northern Nigeria: A Further Note," *Journal of African History*, Vol. 32, 1991, pp. 123–125.

19. Callaway, *Muslim Hausa Women*, pp. 55–84.

20. Schildkrout, "Dependence and Autonomy," p. 125.

21. Lois Beck and Nikki Keddie, eds., *Women in the Muslim World* (Cambridge: Cambridge University Press, 1978).

22. See, for instance, Amal Rassam, "Introduction: Arab Women: The Status of Research in the Social Sciences and the Status of Women," in *Social Science Research and Women in the Arab World* (Paris: UNESCO, 1984), pp. 1–13; Ivy Papps, "Women, Work and Well-Being in the Middle East: An Outline of the Relevant Literature," *Journal of Development Studies*, Vol. 28, No. 4, 1992, pp. 595–615.

23. There are, however, exceptions. For instance, some effort was made, especially in Kano, by the radical PRP (People's Redemption Party) during Nigeria's Second Republic (1979–1983) to place women on a more equal footing with men within an Islamic framework. But with the return to military government, and particularly with Nigeria's economic crisis, the trends seem to have slowed, Barbara Callaway, "The Role of Women in Kano City Politics," in *Hausa Women in the Twentieth Century*, edited by Catherine Coles and Beverly Mack (Madison: University of Wisconsin Press, 1991), pp. 145–150. See also Bilkisu Yusuf, "Nigerian Women in Politics," in *Nigerian Women Today*, Proceedings of the 1st Women in Nigeria Conference (London: Zed Books, 1985), pp. 212–216; Bilkisu Yusef, "Hausa-Fulani Women: The State of the Struggle," in *Hausa Women in the Twentieth Century*, pp. 90–106, on the goals and activities of Muslim Women's organizations; Carolyne Dennis, "Women and the State in Nigeria: The Case of the Federal Military Government, 1984–1985," in *Women, the State, and Ideology: Studies from Africa and Asia*, edited by Haleh Afshar (London: Macmillan Press, 1987), pp. 13–27 on confrontations between Nigerian women and the military, especially in northern Nigeria.

24. Known as the "Better Life for Women Program," tens of millions of *naira* (close to $1 million U.S.) have been funneled into planning conferences for wives of government officials, handicraft demonstrations, and, in some instances, food processing technology. In northern Nigeria, few Muslims can leave the house to participate in these activities. Though women's economic contributions have gained some recognition, the issues of their

status, legal rights, and formal economic opportunities have not been addressed. For a further discussion see Catherine VerEecke, "Better Life for Women in Nigeria: Problems and Prospects of a New National Women's Movement," *African Study Monographs* (Kyoto: Kyoto University), Vol. 14, No. 2, August 1993, pp. 79–85.

25. Barkow, *Hausa Women and Islam*, pp. 317–328.

26. Hill, *Hidden Trade*, pp. 392–409.

27. Schildkrout, "Dependence and Autonomy," p. 117.

28. Jackson, *Kano River Irrigation*.

29. Coles, *Hausa Women's Work*, pp. 163–191.

30. See Abner Cohen, *Custom and Politics in Urban Africa* (Berkeley: University of California Press, 1969) for a discussion of Hausa women in Yorubaland; Deborah Pellow, "Solidarity among Muslim Women in Accra, Ghana," *Anthropos*, Vol. 82, 1987, pp. 489–506, also a discussion of Hausa women.

31. Hill, "Hidden Trade," pp. 392–409.

32. Hill, *Population, Prosperity and Poverty*, pp. 178–179.

33. Jackson, *Kano River Irrigation*.

34. Schildkrout, "Dependence and Autonomy," pp. 115–116.

35. Callaway, *Muslim Hausa Women*.

36. Pitten, *Documentation*, p. 28.

37. Ibid., p. 30.

38. Schildkrout, "Dependence and Autonomy," pp. 112–117.

39. Ibid., pp. 121–123; Callaway, *Muslim Hausa Women*, pp. 218–219; Jackson, *Kano River Irrigation Project*, pp. 12–15.

40. Callaway, *Muslim Hausa Women*, p. 70.

41. Coles, *Hausa Women's Work*, pp. 163–191, interviewed the same women traders in 1981 and 1985 in the city of Kaduna and found that whereas they earlier had been able to use their revenues for luxury items, by the mid-1980s they were contributing (indirectly) to household maintenance and personal necessities for themselves and their children because of their families' economic difficulties.

42. Sa'ad Abubakar, *The Lami'be of Fombina* (Zaria, Nigeria: Oxford University Press, 1977), pp. 29–32.

43. P. F. Lacroix, "Islam among the Adamawa Fulbe," in *Islam in Tropical Africa*, edited by I. M. Lewis (Bloomington: University of Indiana Press, 1966), pp. 206–212.

44. Heinrich Barth, *Travels and Discoveries in North and Central Africa*, 3 vols. (London: Ward Lock, 1965 [1857–1858]); Victor Azarya, *Aristocrats Facing Change: The Fulbe of Guinea, Nigeria, and Cameroon* (Chicago: University of Chicago Press, 1978); Philip Burnham, "Raiders and Traders in Adamawa: Slavery as a Regional System," in *Asian and African Systems of Slavery*, edited by James L. Watson (London: 1980), p. 4172.

45. Emily Schultz, "From Pagan to Pullo: Ethnic Identity Change in Northern Cameroon," *Africa*, Vol. 54, No. 1, 1984, pp. 46–63.

46. A. H. M. Kirk-Greene, *Adamawa Past and Present* (London: Dawson, 1969). In my 1984 survey of over 500 household heads resident in Yola, the Fulbe showed a slightly greater percentage of higher paying positions (e.g., civil service and contracting). They also dominate the prestigious occupation of "Islamic teacher." As the indigens of the town, Fulbe are often at an advantage because many of the poorer families can benefit from a complex network of kin and patron–client relations among the large Fulbe families of Yola.

47. S. Passarge, "The German Expedition to Adamawa," *Geographical Journal*, Vol. 5, 1985, pp. 50–53.

48. Approximately 200 open-ended questionnaires were administered in Yola. The re-sults presented here are from two wards in Jimeta (Ajiya, Luggere) and from three small wards in Yola Town (Galadima, Toungo, and Lamdo Sanda). Not included are the results of questionnaires administered to two remote village wards of Yola outside the town that re-vealed very little trading.

49. Pitten, *Documentation*, pp. 24–30.

50. See Catherine VerEecke, *Cultural Construction of Women's Economic Marginality: The Fulbe of Northeastern Nigeria*, Women in Development Paper No. 195 (East Lansing: Michigan State University, 1988).

51. Schildkrout, "Dependence and Autonomy," pp. 117–123.

52. Ibid.

53. The Hausa figures from Kano (obtained during the late 1970s and early 1980s) are actually lower than those of Yola (obtained during 1988). This may be associated with the devaluation of the naira that began in 1985. Along with that has followed inflation and higher wages, so that the prices of many commodities (and trader's incomes) are likely to have doubled since the early 1980s. See Enid Schildkrout, "The Employment of Children in Kano," in *Child Work, Poverty, and Underdevelopment*, edited by G. Rogers and G. Stand-ing (Geneva: International Labour Organization, 1981), pp. 81–112.

54. Hill, "Hidden Trade," pp. 392-409.

55. Schildkrout, "Dependence and Autonomy," pp. 107–125; Jackson, *Kano River Irri-gation*.

56. As discussed in greater detail in VerEecke, *Cultural Construction*.

57. Paul Riesman, *Freedom in Fulani Social Life* (Chicago: University of Chicago Press, 1978).

58. Derrick Stenning, *Savannah Nomads* (Oxford: Oxford University Press, 1959), p. 188; Marguerite Dupire, "The Position of Women in a Pastoral Society," in *Women in Tropical Africa*, edited by Denise Paulme (Berkeley: University of California Press, 1966), p. 9.

59. See Catherine VerEecke, "From Pasture to Purdah: The Transformation of Women's Roles and Identity in among the Fulbe of Nigeria," *Ethnology*, Vol. 28, 1988, pp. 53–73.

60. F. W. de St. Croix, *The Fulani of Northern Nigeria*, p. 9.

61. Hill, *Population, Prosperity and Poverty*.

62. Schildkrout, "Dependence and Autonomy," pp. 107–126.

words, Kenyan trade is yet another area in which women have been "outgendered by men." However, things are beginning to change. Recent statistics indicate that by the late 1980s, approximately 74.8 percent of all Kenyan women engaged in small-scale urban enterprises were concentrated in the area of wholesale and retail trade.[6] Therefore, an analysis of the role of Kikuyu market women in economic development is of particular importance, especially now that Kenya is experiencing an economic crisis. Like many other countries in Africa, Kenya must now deal with decreasing amounts of foreign aid and declining access to international capital markets. Although the Kenyan economy grew at an annual rate of 6.4 percent from 1965 to 1980, during the next decade, the growth rate decreased to only 3.8 percent.[7]

The World Bank (WB) and International Monetary Fund (IMF) advocated the imposition of Structural Adjustment Programs (SAPs) as a panacea for Africa's ailing economies; and indeed, for more than a decade, many African states have adhered to these policies. The SAPs have placed emphasis on increasing producer incentives in the agricultural sector, restructuring government finance, increased privatization of public enterprises, economic liberalization measures, and decreasing government expenditures in employment and social services. The WB and IMF have pressured African states to comply in spite of a growing body of evidence that demonstrates the increasing ineffectiveness of these programs.[8]

For example, since Kenya implemented its SAP in the early 1980s, women and men have experienced a drastic decline in their standard of living. Moreover, implementation of SAPs has led to rising costs in food and to higher interest rates and unemployment levels. Budget reductions in the areas of health and education have disproportionately affected poor and female-headed households.[9] "As the economic crisis deepens and the formal job market shrinks, women are turning to the informal sector economy to earn a livelihood for themselves and their families."[10] The successes of market women as they participate within the informal sector and thus help both to stimulate employment and to enhance economic growth and development can have an enormous impact on the overall development of the country. More important, such a study can be particularly instructive to other developing African economies that are currently bearing the burden of structural adjustment.

This chapter provides a microanalysis of Kikuyu market women traders in the Mathare Valley in Nairobi. It examines the critical role of market women traders in economic development from the theoretical context of informal sector participation. The chapter also analyzes the potential of the informal sector to stimulate overall development in the country. The basic premise is that Kikuyu women's participation in trade has been influenced by a number of important variables, including historical experience, culture, and structural impediments, that continue to severely constrain and limit their access to capital and credit resources.

This chapter suggests that the informal sector plays an important role in empowering women, as well as contributing to economic development. Given the fact that the number of jobs at present being generated within the formal sector is much less than the number of new entrants seeking wage labor in Kenya, it is imperative that political leaders and officials understand how economic growth rates can be generated and sustained within the informal sector. How women participate and mutually coexist within this sector is the major focus of the chapter.

In my recent field work in Kenya, I focused on women's participation in economic and political affairs. The data indicated that women participate minimally in the urban work force where they comprise about 18 percent of all wage earners in Kenya.[11] Many jobs in the formal sector require a high level of educational training and skills. Because of women's low level of educational attainment vis-à-vis men, it is reasonable to assume that the largest number of women earn their livelihood through the informal sector. In fact, many of the Kikuyu women whom I interviewed in 1985 indicated that their main profession was trade.

Here we shall discuss the salient characteristics of the informal sector, noting the impact of history and culture on the Kikuyu, for these have influenced their participation in trade. Second, we shall examine and analyze women's market activities in the Mathare Valley, focusing attention on the constraints and barriers that have affected women's market activities. Third, we shall both analyze the critical role of women's organizations in Kenya in the promotion of economic empowerment strategies for women and offer some conclusions and a set of research and policy recommendations that may be germane in improving our understanding of women's involvement in trade.

THEORETICAL ISSUES:
TRADERS AND THE INFORMAL SECTOR

Although the informal sector has received an increasing degree of attention from a number of scholars, there appears to be no consensus in the literature about what the term actually denotes.[12] Initially, the term was defined simply as the "unenumerated sector," a term that did little to provide analytical understanding of the concept. The use of the term developed out of a general dissatisfaction with the modern–traditional sector dichotomy. In this dichotomy, the "modern sector" was characterized as being large scale, dynamic, and very productive. The "traditional sector," in vivid contrast, was described as small scale, isolated, and only minimally productive. The International Labor Organization (ILO) has delineated several criteria that must be met if the term is to be utilized. These include considerable ease of entry; emphasis on indigenous resources rather than foreign ones; family ownership as opposed to corporate ownership; small-scale, labor-intensive enterprises, as opposed to large-scale ones; labor-intensive enterprises in which technology is harnessed and skills are utilized that lie outside the formal educational process; and unregulated enterprises that usually employ less than nine individuals.[13]

Informal-sector operations are invariably smaller than formal ones. In addition, informal operators do not possess the same degree of access to credit facilities. Although most activities in the formal sector have been accorded a "legal status," many informal-sector activities may involve some degree of illegality or "extralegal status." Such illegal activities may include hawking without a proper license or rent facilities, prostitution, theft, pickpocketing, and burglary.[14] Another point of debate over the concept has been to determine whether these activities operate under the control of government regulations (i.e., minimum wage laws) and whether these entrepreneurs pay taxes.[15] Rob Davies has analyzed the informal sector by focusing on its structural relationship to the formal sector. For Davies, a major distinguishing criterion between the two sectors is that the formal sector represents a highly developed, socially productive force, whereas the informal sector does not. The basic mode of production of the informal sector, as well as its techniques of production, are non–capital intensive.[16]

According to Davies, the formal sector is also distinct because the means of production are privately owned and controlled by a small class of individuals, governments, or states and are worked on by employees for the benefit of the owners. In contrast, within the informal sector, the individuals who operate the production process also own the means of production. When analyzing the informal sector in Kenya, Kinuthia Macharia has posited that "informal sector activities conserve scarce foreign exchange, require very little capital to create jobs, rely primarily on family savings, provide their own training in useful skills at no public cost, and offer an arena for the first-hand acquisition of entrepreneurial attitudes and expertise."[17]

The Kenyan government discontinued its use of the term informal sector in government statistics in 1987 and currently uses the term "small scale enterprises." Frequent references are also made to the "*jua kali* sector," which means "hot sun" and refers to many activities performed on a small scale in the open air. World Bank data for 1985 estimated that total employment in the urban informal sector in Kenya was approximately 30 percent of all employment outside agriculture.[18] Some economists have argued, therefore, that any realistic plans to ameliorate poverty must include strategies to effectuate productivity and expansion in this area. This is particularly germane to this study because Kenya, like many other African states, is currently involved in the implementation of developmental strategies that are increasingly being directed by the IMF and the WB. Therefore, the development of realistic avenues for economic growth is imperative.[19] In this chapter, both the ILO definition and Macharia's of the informal sector are utilized.

HISTORY AND CULTURE

Kenya is characterized by ethnic pluralism. Of almost fifty ethnic groups, four (the Kikuyu, Luo, Luyia, and Kamba) have exercised dominant roles. Together, they comprise approximately 70 percent of the total population. On the whole, other than residing in urban centers such as Nairobi and Mombassa, they usually reside in separate rural areas. Market women in the largest of these cultural groups, the Kikuyu, are the subject of this chapter.

The Kikuyu, an ethnic group of more than two million people, are linguistically related to several other Bantu-speaking groups in the country, such as the Embu,

Mbere, Kamba, Tharaka, and Meru. These groups all trace their history to a proto-type population called Thagicu. The Thagicu migrated from the north and settled around Mount Kenya between the twelfth and fourteenth centuries.[20] The history of the Thagicu during the fifteenth and sixteenth centuries included splintering and intermarriage with other groups. The Kikuyu believe that their ancestry emanates from one of the splinter groups which settled around the convergence of the Thagana and Thika rivers.

The Kikuyu are polygamous, patrilineal, and in most cases, patrilocal. There are, however, a few instances of neolocal residence. The terms *neolocal* and *patrilocal* refer to patterns of residence utilized after couples are married. Neolocal indicates that when a couple marries, they set up an independent household separate from those of the parents of either marital partner. This pattern was fairly uncommon in traditional African culture, although in the post-independent era, more incidences of neolocal residence are noticeable. Patrilocal, the more common pattern, refers to a situation in which the wife moves in with the husband and his family unit in his village. Some anthropologists also use the term *virolocal* for this phenomenon.

Two important terms have been used to characterize the essence of Kikuyu culture—*patrilineal* and *horticultural*. Patrilineal refers to the fact that descent and inheritance take place through the male line. Horticultural refers to their historical participation in agriculture in which the hoe cultivation was used to promote productivity. One of the most important roles for the Kikuyu has been in agricultural production, and in this area women have played a dominant role.[21]

Throughout history, the Kikuyu and the Maasai have been linked together through trade relationships and cattle raiding. There was a great deal of intermarriage between the two groups, and at times conflicts developed. In general, most of their relations were harmonious. Trade has always existed between the two groups, and women were generally accorded the opportunity to move freely from one area to the other.[22]

Performing primarily as agriculturalists, the Kikuyu grew foodstuffs, such as maize, millet, sweet potatoes, cassava, and bananas. Kikuyu women were the cornerstone of the agricultural sector. The Kikuyu also raised livestock and participated in trade activities with neighboring communities. They owned many sheep, goats, and cattle. In fact, the standard value of these commodities was often decided in goats, even though ownership of cattle was deemed to be prestigious.[23]

For many years, a lively trade flourished among the Kikuyu. The ivory trade developed over a long period of time, and men were the dominant participants. Kikuyu men utilized their herds to purchase ivory, and some hunters with whom they traded refused to accept any other commodity in return or exchange for it. Therefore, man's wealth was inexorably linked with the acquisition of ivory.[24]

Large markets were an important aspect of the Kikuyu culture, except within the northern ethnic groups. Markets were often held in open spaces specifically selected in relation to the convenience of a scattered people. In more populated areas, they were usually situated not more than seven miles from each other. Markets were often open on these locations every fourth day. The days were selected in this manner so that they would not conflict with other types of functions in the area. Generally speaking, feuds and fighting stopped on market days, as the markets were patrolled by members of the warrior grade groups.[25] A number of products were included in the trade such as iron, iron objects, salt, ochre, pottery, and other types of goods. Other items included tobacco, fat, strings, beer, and foodstuffs. The Kikuyu also traded spears, swords, tobacco, gourds, honey, and ochre with the Maasai in return for livestock.

Kikuyu women participated in the development of trade; they often traveled to nearby pastoral areas to barter food and other products for livestock. Although men ultimately became the most numerous participants in trade, especially in ivory, women made notable contributions in other forms of trade.[26] As Patricia Stamp has recently noted, "Women's trading activities, along with their primary tasks of distributing food and beer, contributed substantially to the material resources of their families and to the enrichment of the web of social relations within their society and with neighboring groups."[27] John Middleton and Greet Kershaw have also noted that the Kikuyu women were allowed safe passage into the territory of other ethnic groups, even when wars were occurring. Thus, while men were involved in long-distance trade that was much more lucrative, women were limited to trade in food items in local markets.[28]

The existence of age grades and a sexual division of labor are also important aspects of Kikuyu culture. "From the homestead to the fields and to the tending of the domestic animals, every sphere of activity is clearly and systematically defined. Each member of the family unit knows perfectly well what task he or she is required to perform, in their economic productivity and distribution of the family resources, so as to ensure the material prosperity of the group."[29] Before the Europeans colonized Kenya, men were largely responsible for felling trees, hunting, and warfare. Among the Kikuyu in particular, men were responsible for physical labor in home building; cultivation of the fields; and tending cattle, sheep, and goats, as well as woodcarving and hunting. Both men and women contributed to the process of physical production, but women were responsible for nurturing individuals who would later contribute to production and reproduction. This means that one central role for women has been in the area of reproducing their ethnic group or clan.[30]

Culturally and historically, household work fell within the domain of women. They prepared food, brought water from rivers, cleaned utensils, and brought firewood from the forests. Most often, the loads of firewood were carried on their backs. Women were also assigned tasks in cutting and carrying grass, harvesting food, pounding sugar, weaving baskets, and making dresses. Both men and women planted and weeded crops. Men planted bananas, yams, sweet potato vines, tobacco, and sugar cane while women planted beans, millet, maize, and sweet potatoes. In these ways, women made significant contributions in agricultural production. They also brewed beer and participated in trade activities. But even in the area of trade, as stated earlier, the sexual division of labor was noticeable; men participated in long-distance trade, while women generally traded in foodstuffs in local markets.[31]

Kinship groups and clans controlled the use of land. Women did not own or inherit land. Men's direct control of the land was predicated on their membership in the patrilineage, the basic land-holding unit in precolonial societies. Among the Kikuyu, land tenure was essentially clan tenure. Land belonged to the *m'bari* (clan), and the right to use it was provided to members of the clan.[32]

In societies that are predominantly patrilineal such as that of Kenya, women do not generally inherit land or property and have limited access to other forms of self-support. Women were, however, granted the right to use various pieces of land which they cultivated. Traditionally, within each lineage, the members of the extended family (either husband and wife or wives and children) were allotted a piece of land. In this way, members of the extended family network (which included grandparents, aunts, uncles, and cousins, as well as members of the clan more generally) jointly owned and exercised control over the allocation of land. Women worked on the land, which was provided to them for support of themselves and their children.[33]

Colonization affected the lives of all Africans, most particularly through the introduction of wage labor and cash crops and the development of urban centers, medicine, and education. In Kenya, colonialism involved the alienation of land occupied by white settlers. Kikuyu nationalists played a prominent role in the Mau Mau struggle, a violent movement against the white settlers to get back their lands, which had so forcibly been expropriated by the Europeans. It was also a reassertion of Kikuyu rights to maintain their own cultural identity, which clashed with the Western ideology.

KIKUYU MARKET WOMEN TRADERS
IN THE MATHARE VALLEY AND THE STRUGGLE
FOR ECONOMIC EMPOWERMENT

The Mathare Valley is considered to be a poor squatter community that consists of approximately one-fifth of the population of the city of Nairobi. The inhabitants of the Mathare Valley tend to be fairly young, and the origin of the community can be traced to the end of the Mau Mau emergency in 1960. Between 60,000 and 70,000 citizens currently live in the community of mud and wattle houses with cardboard roofs or wooden block houses with tin roofs on the outskirts of downtown Nairobi. Some are owners of their units, while others are renters. In general, the inhabitants tend to have very little education or training and to be predominantly from the Kikuyu ethnic group.[34]

According to Nici Nelson, about 80 percent of all citizens who reside in the area and 90 percent of the women derive their livelihood from some form of participation in the informal sector. Market women in Kenya can be characterized as petty traders, distinguished by the fact that they do not own or lease permanent facilities. Rather, they usually sell their goods and products from a streetside table or a temporary stall which is often considered by the Kenyan government to be illegal. Usually they are able to control a rather limited, specific inventory of goods, which they acquire daily. These they sell in small quantities for low rates of profit because of intensive competition. Because these activities necessitate little capital or special skills and knowledge, persons desirous of acquiring supplementary or subsistence-level incomes can easily be accommodated and usually undertake them.[35]

More than 65 percent of the vegetable sellers in the Mathare Valley are Kikuyu women. Other than beer brewing, prostitution, and wholesaling maize flour, vegetable selling involves more female participants than male. Sellers of vegetables utilize very basic establishments. In some cases, this may involve the use of a table or market stall with a piece of awning over the merchandise. In others, the merchandise may be placed on a plastic sheet on the ground. On the whole, this activity does not generate much profit.[36]

A typical day for a Kenyan market woman in this trade would start with a very early trip to the municipal or city market to purchase vegetables from licensed dealers. Because the goods themselves are perishable, they must be purchased daily. Vegetable sellers sometimes must pay more for their vegetables than the licensed vegetable vendors. In some cases, they face the possibility of selling at cost in order to get rid of goods they will not be able to sell the next day. These forms of trade are considered illegal, and the policemen of Nairobi pressure market women to reduce or eliminate their activities. Vegetable sellers, on the whole, are considered to be the "least permanent" entrepreneurs operating in Nairobi.[37]

For most market women, the ideal place to market their products is inside the Nairobi City Market. However, many women cannot afford stalls. Consequently, they are forced to set up illegal food stalls on the side of the road. Sometimes, these locations are unsafe, but they do provide women with the opportunity to sell fruits and vegetables.[38]

One persistent complaint of women is their inability to expand their trade, but they are unable to do so because of lack of resources. Thus, most market women operate at subsistence levels, usually purchasing their wares on a daily basis. Sometimes, they receive orders for a larger sale but are unable to accommodate them because of inadequate funds to build up their inventories and stocks of goods.[39]

Some market women in the Mathare Valley also sell charcoal. Like vegetable sellers, they utilize basic facilities with awnings to cover the charcoal during the rainy season. Charcoal is usually purchased from the lorries that reach Nairobi from the rural areas where charcoal is prepared. The charcoal is often purchased in large burlap bags, and is later sold in a large tin bowl called a *kurai*. In vivid contradistinction to women engaged in vegetable selling, women who sell charcoal are usually able to generate substantial profits.[40]

Women usually pay the rural wholesaler approximately 7.50 to 11.00 Kenyan shillings for one bag of charcoal. This bag will yield approximately 36 *kurais*, which can be sold for as much as 1 shilling each. Therefore, market women make 25 to 28.50 shillings in profit for each bag. Many sellers of charcoal sell about one bag per day, yielding 680 shillings per month. Several factors make the sale of charcoal a viable endeavor, including the fact that rental costs are low and many sellers keep the coal in their rooms and use a plastic cover each day on the ground, often near a busy street.[41]

Although the capital investment and level of skills necessary for the sale of charcoal are fairly low, fewer Kikuyu women sell charcoal than sell vegetables. The reasons for this are enigmatic and unclear, particularly since Kenyan women have traditionally had a strong attachment to fuel and made sure it was available for use by individual households. Also, the profit from charcoal is potentially much greater than that from vegetables.

From a cultural and historical perspective, the traditional role of Kikuyu women has always been associated with their central roles in agricultural production and provisioning of fuel. This explains why many Kikuyu women in the Mathare Valley are currently involved in vegetable selling and in the sale of charcoal, although a smaller number are concentrated in the latter area.[42] Thus aspects of traditional Kikuyu culture clearly affect the extent of their participation in the sale of vegetables and charcoal in the Mathare Valley. "In any given cultural situation, women will be found clustered in certain types of activities, and most of these relate to women's roles as providers of food, beer, childcare, and sex companionship."[43]

A large number of women in the Mathare Valley also brew maize beer. In fact, beer brewing to a large extent is considered to be a "woman's activity," and very few men participate in this area. Women usually brew the beer in the rooms where they live. Women have been attracted to this enterprise for several reasons. First, the few wage jobs easily accessible to women are those in which they serve as house servants or barmaids. These jobs of necessity require many hours—in some cases, ten hours per day for six days a week. Second, the wages for such arduous labor are usually minimal, in some cases, only about 100 shillings per month. Third, brewing beer permits women to work in their own rooms where they can take care of their children at the same time. Fourth, it requires little formal education, provides a reasonable return on their initial investment, and involves little capital investment. For example, for a few shillings, a woman can purchase the brew, arrange to borrow the necessary equipment, purchase oil tins to serve the beer, and pay for the room from which she operates.[44]

Unfortunately, brewing and selling beer is illegal, and women are sometimes arrested. They have, however, been able to establish cooperative networks over the years (with patron-clients, neighbors, and friends), which have helped them to deal with police action. In some cases, when the police raids have become too frequent, some brewers have taken up vegetable selling. Many women have found it quite easy to do this because the latter does not require permanent facilities, large amounts of capital, or a formal network of contracts. In 1974, women reportedly earned 250 to 400 shillings monthly from beer brewing. During this time period, the minimum wage was 200 shillings in the country overall. Clearly some market women were doing much better than workers in the formal sector.[45]

A number of *dukas* also exist in the Mathare Valley. *Dukas* are converted rooms that usually have a large front window and counter space. Usually, they are fairly small; but they are used to offer a number of food items to customers, including beans, rice, sugar, tea, flour, cocoa, cooking fat, salt, chili, curry powder, milk, and eggs. People in the Mathare Valley usually purchase their food items in fairly small amounts. Hence, dukas usually remain open for trade for ten or twelve hours per day. Although some women own dukas, the vast majority are owned by men. In such cases, however, their wives usually operate them.[46]

A large number of women in the Mathare Valley also sell various ingredients for beer brewing. These include maize flour and *kimera* (sorghum flour). In order to make a single brew of beer, 45 pounds of maize and 10 pounds of kimera are usually needed. Some women have found the sale of flour to be a very lucrative profession. Hence, more than half of all the kimera and maize flour sellers in the Mathare Valley are women. Invariably, the largest group are older women who have earlier made money in brewing. Often, at this stage of their lives, they are desirous of changing to a business that has less risk.[47]

A critical question to be addressed in this chapter is to what extent Kikuyu women have been empowered as a result of their involvement in trade. Empowerment, in this context, is defined as the extent to which women have enhanced their overall status in the society. Very few cultures remain static, and Kenya is no exception. A number of changes in traditional culture and the rural basis of community life have affected women's status and roles. This includes a decrease in the number of polygamous marriages and the availability of land, as well as an increasing number of divorces and increased premarital sexual activities and pregnancies. Many urban Kikuyu women do not have access to land in the rural areas, and hence they do not receive direct economic support from these areas. Besides, many are widowed, divorced, single, or separated from their husbands.[48]

These changes have led to a concomitant loss of status for many women in the traditional rural milieu. Consequently, the urban centers serve as a magnet for many women because of opportunities available in the formal and informal sectors. For a large number of women who possess limited educational training and skills, the opportunities available in the formal sector remain minimal. Thus, many women are drawn to the informal sector where they engage in various types of occupations. These include market trading, brewing and selling beer, preparing and selling cooked food, dressmaking, hairdressing, and prostitution. In this way, many poor, uneducated women with few marketable skills have been able to secure livelihoods. Many unmarried women with children find that they must bring up their children alone. Hence, participation in trade has provided several advantages. First, it has provided them with economic means to raise their families. Kamuti Kiteme has suggested that Kenyan women's commercial activities enable them to provide for the education of their children, family clothing, improvement of family housing facilities, and payment of taxes.[49] Second, through participation in trade, women have also been able to acquire economic independence and control over family assets. In some cases, such control has enabled them to further expand their market activities.[50]

FACTORS THAT AFFECT WOMEN'S INVOLVEMENT IN TRADE

The decision to engage in trade is obviously an important one for African women. Many factors and issues promote women's involvement in trade, however, just as other factors constrain and limit their participation. Several scholars have demonstrated that trading is a very important occupation, particularly for West African women. It is an important aspect of their culture, as Ekechi demonstrates in this volume. Audrey Wipper has also argued that trading is the major occupation for West African women. Her study indicated that 80 percent of all women are traders in Southern Ghana and among the Yoruba, 50 percent in Eastern Nigeria, and 60 percent in the Dakar region of Senegal.[51]

In many cases, of course, cultural beliefs influence action; hence cultural factors are important in studies of women's trade. In fact, they served as constraints to Kenyan women's participation in trade. For example, some men have adamantly opposed their wives' entrepreneurial and trading activities and argued that the most important contribution women can make to the development of the country is directing their talents toward taking care of their homes and families.[52] Even when Kikuyu women do trade, culture seems to be an important determinant of the products or goods they utilize. As indicated earlier, many Kikuyu women currently trade in vegetables or charcoal or brew beer. These are activities in which they have traditionally been involved, even in the precolonial era.

Also, their inability to secure capital and acquire access to credit has exerted severe and negative repercussions on Kenyan women's commercial activities. At present, there are no laws that specifically bar or restrict women from utilizing credit facilities in either public or private institutions; but a number of problems have developed. One of the most persistent is that loan institutions often demand collateral, high social status, title deeds, as well as proof of consent from husbands (if the women are married). Although both men and women must meet criteria set by lending institutions, the data indicate that women are doubly disadvantaged because men continue to control property to an overwhelming degree. Women can, however, purchase property, if they are economically able to do so.[53]

Because of the strict manner in which loans are made accessible to women, few women have been able to come up with the necessary collateral to secure them. As Maria Nzomo has argued,

The fact that women do not own landed property also means that they cannot acquire, *as easily as men*, businesses and real estate forms of property. Again the major constraint is the collateral required. In Kenya, for example, both public and private lending agencies such as DFCK (Development Finance Corporation of Kenya) and ICDC (Industrial and Commercial Development Corporation), look into such factors as land title deeds, liquidity, and social status of the applicant. Consequently, many women do not qualify as applicants in their own right, as they have no land title deeds and very few possess jobs that give them the kind of liquidity and social status required [italics added].[54]

Third, a report advanced by the Kenyan Women's Trust Fund indicated that many conditions attached to the process of lending by many Kenyan banks are particularly restrictive. The result of these policies is that in some cases women have been excluded. Some requirements necessary even to open a bank account, as well as land to be used for security, are stringent; and few women indeed can meet even the most minimal.[55]

Economic circumstance is clearly an important factor. In Kenya, a woman may enter the trading profession because her husband is an inadequate provider. Once she begins to trade, her husband may reduce the amount of material support he provides to the family. In other words, the husband may seek to influence or constrain the scale at which a woman can trade by altering responsibilities in response to her trading income. This stands in vivid contrast to customs in West Africa, where a woman is rewarded by her husband through his assistance in her ventures. For example, among the Yoruba and Igbo ethnic groups, a man often provides the trading capital for his wife after a marriage appears to be stable. A stable and secure marriage, therefore, affords a woman the opportunity and capital to enter into large-scale trading enterprises.[56]

Kenyan women's organizations have played a vital role in the process of economic development and empowering women. It is estimated that at present about 16,000 women's organizations exist and operate in Kenya. *Maendaleo Ya Wanawake* (Women's Progress), founded during the 1950s, is the largest such organization in the country and the only one with a countrywide group of clubs under its purview. One of its most important accomplishments to date has been its ability to lobby the government on behalf of women. In doing so, it has been able to develop a cohesive power base that has focused on issues relevant to gender and underdevelopment. *Maendaleo* has also been concerned about assisting women to secure credit in order to enhance their entrepreneurial activities.[57]

The Kenyan Women's Finance Trust (KWFT), an affiliate of Women's World Banking and an outgrowth of the World Plan of Action (1975), has played a key economic role by assisting Kenyan women to become traders and entrepreneurs. Some of its accomplishments have included providing training to women, particularly rural women, to help them to manage their own businesses and developing strategies to facilitate access to economic institutions. Thus far, KWFT has provided loans to Kenyan women to enable them to operate small businesses and engage in trade. Women's World Banking guarantees 50 percent of the loan amount, KWFT guarantees 25 percent, and the local bank guarantees 25 percent. The KWFT has been important for women because local banks often refuse to take risks with them.[58]

Credit rotation organizations and savings clubs are based on the principle that through collective efforts all members can participate and derive financial assistance. The number of participants is different from organization to organization, as well as the rotational cycles and amount of funds dispersed and made available. In Nairobi, large segments of the informal sector also utilize industrywide associations. Individuals who sell fruits and vegetables are able to join a general traders' union that represents them in negotiations with the municipal government. Unions generally focus on many policy issues, including discussions on how market stalls should be allocated and how police patrols interact with traders.[59]

Although important changes are occurring in the roles of Kenyan women, a number of problems remain. Most Kenyan women still reside in the rural areas, and most women attain less educational training than men and usually remain under the authority of their husbands and fathers. Traditionally, only males were allowed to inherit property among the Kikuyu and other ethnic groups. Although land reform programs have been introduced, they have usually paid only scant attention to women. Land reform programs have virtually ignored women's rights and established a situation of almost exclusive male ownership.[60] As Lisa Cubbins has noted,

Since the 1950's, land reforms have been put into place through registration programs to transfer land ownership from the extended family to individual holdings. Kenya has continued to pursue land reforms since independence and despite some resistance to land registration, registration has led to individual land holdings of five acres or less. . . . Since the land reforms, it is unusual for women to be given ownership and control of land.[61]

The Law of Succession Act, passed in 1972, for the first time advocated that both male and female heirs should be treated equally in matters of inheritance when a husband or father died without leaving a will. This law, which was put in effect in 1981, affects inheritance and property rights in Kenya by treating males and females as equal heirs in inheritance issues, by limiting the power of individuals to disinherit their dependents through their wills, by increasing the rights of illegitimate children to inherit from their natural parents, and by allowing a widow to inherit portions of her husband's property even if customary law does not so specify.[62] This law provides Kenyan women with property rights they can use when operating their businesses and obtaining credit.

The United Nations Decade for Women (1975–1985) served as a catalyst for a rejuvenation of the issue of the role of women in the development process. It also led to a situation where, it was argued, the law could be utilized by women in the Third World as a political tool to enhance their status if it were properly understood. However, as Margaret Schuler has so skillfully reminded us,

Essentially, the law regulates access to economic and social resources, such as land, jobs, credit, and other goods and services, and to political power, that is, control over the allocation or administration of these resources. This regulation is accomplished through one or a combination of the following mechanisms: the formulation of laws and policies that are skewed toward the benefit of some and the burden of others; the arbitrary or selective application of laws or policies; attitudes and behaviors that reinforce and condone the existence of inequitable laws and inconsistent application of the law.[63]

CONCLUSION

This chapter focuses primary attention on Kikuyu women's participation in trade activities in the Mathare Valley as an avenue through which they have been able to achieve some degree of self-empowerment. Central to the argument is an analysis of the importance of history, culture, and structural factors that have limited women's access to capital and credit resources.

Although Kenyan women were historically "outgendered" in the area of trade, they are continuing to challenge the current economic status quo and hence are creating new strategic locations and spaces for themselves within the informal sector. Kenyan women's participation in trade, however, must also be juxtaposed within the much larger context of changes taking place in the broader political economy. A host of external factors and conditions accompanying the imposition of structural adjustment policies is also evident and is affecting men and women at all levels of society. However, women and the poor, already economically vulnerable, have become increasingly more marginalized as they have disproportionately borne the burden of SAPs. Hence, women are moving into the informal sector now more than ever before. Within this context, women's participation in trade can be understood as a means through which they have become more independent or self-sufficient. Thus, Kenyan women's organizations have played a particularly significant role on several levels: (1) as a vehicle or avenue of resistance to the status quo, in which women have been rendered subordinate in the economic, political, and social areas or affairs of society; (2) as entities that have provided alternate strategies to assist women in the acquisition of credit and other critical resources in order to enhance their trade activities. Through the current processes under way in Kenya, which seek to "degender strategic economic terrain," women's participation in the informal sector is particularly noteworthy.

To this end, the informal sector is particularly deserving of attention because of its ability to spur economic growth and national development. More studies need to be performed by government leaders and policymakers on the future potential of this sector. Second, efforts must also be made by the government to make participation in this sector legal, rather than extralegal. Market women traders and others are often harassed by police, and consequently are unable to secure proper licenses to trade their goods. Current lending policies of financial institutions should also be scrutinized and revised so that opportunities for capital are provided to deserving women.

NOTES

1. Kamuti Kiteme, "The Socioeconomic Impact of the African Market Women Trade in Rural Kenya," *Journal of Black Studies*, Vol. 23, No. 1, Sept. 1992, p. 136.

2. See, for example, Ester Boserup, *Woman's Role in Economic Development* (London: George Allen & Unwin, 1970), pp. 1–50; Bessie House-Midamba, *Class Development and Gender Inequality in Kenya, 1963–1990* (Lewiston, N.Y.: Edwin Mellen Press, 1990), pp. 1–

30; Bessie House-Midamba, "The United Nations Decade: Political Empowerment or Increased Marginalization for Kenyan Women?" *Africa Today*, Vol. 37, No. 1, March 1990, pp. 37–48; Margaret Jean Hay and Sharon Stichter, eds., *African Women South of the Sahara* (London: Longman, 1984), pp. 17–23; Claire Robertson, *Sharing the Same Bowl: A Socioeconomic History of Women and Class in Accra, Ghana* (Bloomington: Indiana University Press, 1984), pp. 1–30; R. E. Porter, "Perspectives on Trade, Mobility, and Gender in a Rural Market System: Borno, North East Nigeria," *Economy of Social Geography*, Vol. 79, No. 2, 1988, pp. 82–91; Kiteme, "Socioeconomic Impact," pp. 135–137; Per Kongstad and Mette Monsted, *Family Labour and Trade in Western Kenya* (Uppsala, Sweden: Scandinavian Institute of African Studies, 1980), pp. 1–30; Cheryl Johnson, "Class and Gender: A Consideration of Yoruba Women during the Colonial Period," in *Women and Class in Africa*, edited by Claire Robertson and Iris Berger (New York: Africana Publishing Company, 1986), pp. 237–253; Barbara Lewis, "The Limitations of Group Action among Entrepreneurs: The Market Women of Abidjan, Ivory Coast," in *Women in Africa: Studies in Social and Economic Change*, edited by Nancy Hafkin and Edna Bay (Stanford: Stanford University Press, 1976), pp. 135–136.

3. Basil Davison, *Africa in History: Themes and Outlines* (London: Macmillan, 1968), p. 61; Richard Gray and David Birmingham, eds., *Pre-Colonial African Trade: Essays on Trade in Central and Eastern Africa before 1900* (New York: Oxford University Press, 1970), pp. 1–40; George E. Brooks, "African 'Landlords' and European 'Strangers': African-European Relations to 1870," in *Africa*, edited by Phyllis M. Martin and Patrick O'Meara (Bloomington: Indiana University Press, 1986), pp. 104–105.

4. Kiteme, "Socioeconomic Impact," p. 136; Kongstad and Monsted, *Family, Labour and Trade*, pp. 1–50; Richard Sandbrook, *The Politics of Basic Needs: Urban Aspects of Assaulting Poverty in Africa* (Toronto: University of Toronto Press, 1982), pp. 147–148; Niara Sudarkasa, "The Status of Women in Indigenous African Societies," *Feminist Studies*, Vol. 12, No. 1, Spring 1986, pp. 1–2; Ronald J. Lesthaeghe, *Reproduction and Social Organization in Sub-Saharan Africa* (Berkeley: University of California Press, 1989), p. 492.

5. Diane Kayongo-Male and Philista Onyango, *The Sociology of the African Family* (London: Longman, 1984), pp. 40–43.

6. Ian Livingstone, "A Reassessment of Kenya's Rural and Urban Informal Sector," *World Development*, Vol. 19, 1991, p. 656.

7. Barbara P. Thomas-Slayter, "Class, Ethnicity, and the Kenyan State: Community Mobilization in the Context of Global Politics," *International Journal of Politics, Culture and Society*, Vol. 4, No. 3, 1991, pp. 303–305.

8. Ibid.; see also Maria Nzomo, "The Gender Dimension of Democratization in Kenya: Some International Linkages," *Alternatives*, Vol. 18, No. 1, Winter 1993, pp. 69–71.

9. Nzomo, "Gender Dimension of Democratization," p. 70.

10. Ibid.

11. House-Midamba, *Class Development and Gender Inequality*, p. 58.

12. Rob Davies, "Informal Sector or Subordinate Mode of Production? A Model," in *Casual Work and Poverty in Third World Cities*, edited by Ray Bromley and Chris Gerry (New York: John Wiley and Sons, 1979), pp. 81–97; Sandbrook, *Politics of Basic Needs*, pp. 150–175; Jennifer Widner, "Interest Group Structure and Organization in Kenya's Informal Sector: Cultural Despair or a Politics of Multiple Allegiances?" *Comparative Studies*, Vol. 24, No. 1, 1991, pp. 33–35; William J. House, "Nairobi's Informal Sector: Dynamic Entrepreneurs or Surplus Labor?" *Economic Development and Cultural Change*, Vol. 32, No. 2, 1984, p. 270; Richard W. Hosier, "The Informal Sector in Kenya: Spatial Valuation and Development Alternatives," *The Journal of Developing Areas*, Vol. 21, July 1987, pp. 383–

390; Ian Livingstone, "A Reassessment," pp. 651–653.

13. House, "Nairobi's Informal Sector," p. 270; Sandbrook, *Politics of Basic Needs*, p. 61; Widner, "Interest Group Structure," p. 33.

14. Davies, "Informal Sector," pp. 81–97; Livingstone, "A Reassessment," pp. 652–653.

15. Livingstone, "A Reassessment," pp. 652–653.

16. Davies, "Informal Sector," pp. 81–97.

17. Kinuthia Macharia, "Slum Clearance and the Informal Economy in Nairobi," *The Journal of Modern African Studies*, Vol. 30, No. 2, June 1992, pp. 232–233.

18. Livingstone, "A Reassessment," pp. 652–653.

19. Ibid., pp. 651–652.

20. Jean Davison, *Voices from Mutira: Lives of Rural Kikuyu Women* (Boulder: Lynne Rienner, 1989), p. 13; Patricia Stamp, "Kikuyu Women's Self-Help Groups: Toward an Understanding of the Relation between Sex-Gender System and Mode of Production in Africa," in *Women and Class in Africa*, edited by Claire Robertson and Iris Berger (New York: Africana Publishing Company, 1986), p. 28.

21. Nici Nelson, "How Women and Men Get By: The Sexual Division of Labour in the Informal Sector of a Nairobi Squatter Settlement," in *Casual Work and Poverty in Third World Cities*, edited by Ray Bromley and Chris Gerry (New York: John Wiley & Sons, 1979), p. 87.

22. John Middleton and Greet Kershaw, *The Kikuyu and Kamba of Kenya* (London: International African Institute, 1965), pp. 18–25.

23. Ibid.; see Nici Nelson, "Female-Centered Families: Changing Patterns of Marriage and Family among the Buzaa Brewers of Mathare Valley," *African Urban Studies*, Vol. 3, Winter 1978–79, p. 87.

24. Stamp, "Kikuyu Women's Self-Help Groups," pp. 33–35; see also Penelope Ciancelli, "Exchange, Reproduction and Sex Subordination among the Kikuyu of East Africa," *Review of Radical Political Economics*, Vol. 12, No. 2, Summer 1980, p. 28.

25. Middleton and Kershaw, *The Kikuyu and the Kamba*, pp. 18–25.

26. Stamp, "Kikuyu Women's Self-Help Groups," pp. 34–35.

27. Ibid., p. 35.

28. Middleton and Kershaw, *The Kikuyu and Kamba*, pp. 18–40; Nici Nelson, "Female-Centered Families."

29. Jomo Kenyatta, *Facing Mount Kenya: The Tribal Life of the Gikuyu* (New York: Vintage, 1965), p. 52.

30. Stamp, "Kikuyu Women's Self-Help Groups," pp. 34–35; see also Kenyatta, *Facing Mount Kenya*, pp. 53–55.

31. Kenyatta, *Facing Mount Kenya*, pp. 53–55.

32. Ciancanelli, "Exchange, Reproduction and Sex Subordination," p. 26.

33. Ibid.

34. Nelson, "How Women and Men Get By," pp. 283–285.

35. Ibid., p. 285.

36. Ibid., pp. 293–294.

37. Ibid., p. 293; "Where Credit is Due," Video Documentary, Indiana University Press, 1984.

38. Nelson, "How Women and Men Get By," pp. 292–293.

39. "Where Credit is Due"; see also Nelson, "How Women and Men Get By," pp. 290–295.

40. Ibid.

41. Ibid.

42. Ibid., pp. 292–293.

43. Ibid.

44. Ibid., pp. 286–287.

45. Ibid., p. 286.

46. Ibid., p. 291.

47. Ibid., p. 294.

48. Ibid.

49. Kiteme, "Socioeconomic Impact," p. 136.

50. Nelson, "How Women and Men Get By," p. 294; see also Rosemary Awino Kaduru, "Kenya: Legal Services for Rural Women," in *Empowerment and the Law: Strategies of Third World Women*, edited by Margaret Schuler (Washington, D.C.: Overseas Education Fund International, 1986), p. 236; Efua Graham and Wendy Davies, "Women in Africa," in *Handbook to the Modern World Africa*, vol. 2, edited by Sean Moroney, (New York: Facts on File, 1989), p. 1045.

51. Audrey Wipper, "Women's Voluntary Associations," in *African Women South of the Sahara*, edited by Margaret Jean Hay and Sharon Stichter (London: Longman, 1984), p. 79.

52. Stamp, "Kikuyu Women's Self-Help Groups," pp. 41–42.

53. House-Midamba, *Class Development and Gender Inequality*, pp. 89–98.

54. Maria Nzomo, "Women, Democracy and Development in Africa," in *Democratic Theory and Practice in Africa*, edited by Walter O. Oyugi, Atieno Adhiambo, Michael Chege, and Afrifa K. Gitonga (Portsmouth, N.H.: Heinemann, 1988), p. 145.

55. House-Midamba, *Class Development and Gender Inequality*, pp. 101–102.

56. Felix K. Ekechi, p. 42; Kayongo-Male and Onyango, *Sociology of the African Family*, pp. 40–44.

57. Monica Udvardy, "Women's Groups Near the Coast: Patron Clientship in the Development Arena," in *Anthropology of Development and Change in East Africa*, edited by David W. Brokensha and Peter O. Little (Boulder: Westview Press, 1988), p. 221; Maria Nzomo, "The Impact of the Women's Decade on Politics, Programs and Empowerment of Women in Kenya," *Issue: A Journal of Opinion*, Vol. 17, No. 2, Summer 1989, pp. 9–17; Audrey Wipper, "The Maendaleo ya Wanawake Organization: The Co-optation of Leadership," *African Studies Review*, Vol. 18, No. 3, Dec. 1975, pp. 99–108; Bessie House-Midamba, "The United Nations Decade: Political Empowerment or Increased Marginalization for Kenyan Women?" *Africa Today*, Vol. 37, No. 1, March 1990, pp. 42–43; Lesthaeghe, *Reproduction and Social Organization*, p. 495.

58. "Where Credit is Due."

59. Widner, "Interest, Group Structure and Organization," p. 37.

60. Graham and Davies, "Women in Africa," pp. 1044–1055.

61. Lisa A. Cubbins, "Women, Men, and the Division of Power: A Study of Gender Stratification in Kenya," *Social Forces*, Vol. 69, No. 4, 1991, p. 1068.

62. S. B. O. Gutto, "Some Legal Rights and Obligations of Women in Kenya: A Lay Person Language Approach," Working Paper No. 367, Institute for Development Studies, University of Nairobi, 1980, p. 17; House-Midamba, *Class Development and Gender Inequality*, p. 88.

63. Margaret Schuler, "Women and the Law," in *The Women and Development Manual*, vol. 1, edited by Rita S. Gallin, Marilyn Aronoff, and Anne Ferguson (Boulder: Westview Press, 1989), p. 155.

Chapter 6

Comparative Advantage: Women in Trade in Accra, Ghana, and Nairobi, Kenya

Claire Robertson

The involvement of African women in trade has deep roots and important consequences. Having had the privilege of working with small-scale women traders in
both Ghana and Kenya, I attempt here to make some comparisons drawn from
these experiences.[1] The chapter considers both the causes and consequences of
women's trade for the societies involved. It is divided into three sections: (1) the
contrasting historical and cultural backgrounds of Kenya and Ghana, Accra and
Nairobi, and their peoples, (2) the role of governments regarding women traders,
British colonial administration and independence, and (3) the relationship of trade
to socioeconomic structures, especially regarding the contemporary situation.

Because of the broad level of comparison, the chapter is more general than my
usual work. For more detailed consideration of the evolution and conditions of
women's trade in Accra and Nairobi, readers are referred to *Sharing the Same
Bowl: A Socioeconomic History of Women and Class in Accra, Ghana*
(Bloomington: Indiana University Press, 1984) and to *Women, Men, and Trade in
the Nairobi Area, 1890 to 1990* (forthcoming). Here I would like to suggest that
there can be only limited grassroots economic development for African countries if
small-scale retail trade is ignored or persecuted along with the women who conduct
most of it. This point is significant because we already know that trickle-down theory,

which assumes that top-down development will benefit everyone, is neither efficacious, equitable, nor practical in the African context, especially now with the withdrawal of much foreign aid and investment from Africa. The businesses of women traders are, in effect, an extremely valuable, much ignored potential source for economic development in Africa and should be fostered, not persecuted along with their owners and employees.

I describe the differences between the experiences of Ga women traders in Accra, Ghana, and those of Kikuyu and Kamba women traders in Nairobi, Kenya. These differences are evident in the great impact of cultural and historical factors. However, there also seem to be growing similarities in which the decision to trade is increasingly related to negative economic circumstances caused by a failed "socialism," undermined by large-scale capitalism in Ghana, by increasing poverty under capitalism in Kenya, and by high population in both countries. Moreover, the Kenyan women's decision to trade and the resulting trading activities seem to be related to changes in women's marriage and residential patterns among the recently urbanized Kikuyu and Kamba. These changes tend to bring them closer to the long-urbanized Ga women of Ghana. There are, then, many complexities involved in the comparative advantage of trading for poor women. Women in both areas are struggling against formidable obstacles to carry out their family obligations through trade. The governments in both countries could, if they would, help their economies and their societies by helping such women.

Several years ago, I carried out research on women traders in Nairobi, Kenya, under the auspices of a Fulbright grant. How this happened has a great deal to do with the subject of this chapter. I had already done extensive research on Ghanaian women traders in the 1970s based on a great deal of reading in secondary sources. Later, I was able to go to Ghana and make a historical study of the Ga of Accra, Ghana, out of a number of disparate ethnographic studies done at approximately ten-year intervals beginning in the 1930s for the Ga of Accra, Ghana. But after mulling over these data intensively and publishing many of them in various forms, I then felt that I wanted to gain more perspective on women's trade by looking at it from a culture that was completely different. This time, instead of looking for a place where women's trade was known to be important and had been studied to some extent, I decided to research a relatively unknown situation insofar as literature was concerned.

My interest in Nairobi traders was provoked by a visit there for a conference in 1984 when I took a taxi tour of the city's open-air markets. These astonished me; I had been told that trading was not an important occupation for Nairobi women. Instead I discovered that there were many open-air markets, both legal and illegal, run by thousands of traders, the majority of them women. I then went home and started poking around in the literature to see what documentation was available about them and what their history was. This was not difficult, since there was almost none. A few late nineteenth-century explorers and soldiers had noted that, in the area where Nairobi now stands, their caravans stopped to be provisioned by the local people, in particular Kikuyu women carrying loads and loads of beans.

So extensive was this trade that tens of thousands of pounds of beans were regularly supplied to the caravans within a few weeks.[2] This, of course, excited my interest, especially in the bean trade. But then, with the advent of colonialism, the written record seemed to disappear—only in the 1980s did I find an effort to look at women's trade in and around Nairobi—one being a very small, unsystematic survey of periurban traders.[3] Because this was obviously a much-neglected historical subject, I set out to learn about the development of trade in and around Nairobi with particular attention to Kikuyu women and the bean trade.

Because of the relative lack of data compared to the Ghanaian situation, the research on the Kikuyu women's bean trade involved collecting basic information in a number of areas. For instance, even to begin a history of the bean trade it was necessary to investigate such topics as the development of the Nairobi area market system; the history of the introduction of various bean varieties and of government policy toward food production and marketing, including price controls; and the magnitude of present-day participation of women in trade. My method of proceeding was to spend some of my time doing archival research in libraries in Nairobi and the rest interviewing traders. I conducted three surveys of traders in sixteen Nairobi and area markets (see Map 6.1) located in a wedge from Shauri Moyo to the east in downtown Nairobi out to Kiambu town market to the northwest and Limuru market to the north-northwest of Nairobi, the total area covered being approximately 160 square miles (see Map 6.2). The markets included all kinds—from the largest Nairobi open-air market, Gikomba, to small rural markets like Gitaru, to medium-sized small-town markets like Kiambu and Limuru. Two illegal Nairobi markets were included—one on the street in a very tough neighborhood.

The sample included a rapidly growing squatters' market complemented by a moribund legal market with only a few traders. In the end I got census information—basic data—regarding some 6,000 women and men traders in fifteen markets. I also obtained marital information concerning a sample of over 1,000 traders in sixteen markets and life histories of some sixty traders. The census and the smaller sample included men also, but not the life histories. The proportion of women to men traders was exactly two to one, showing the female predominance among Nairobi-area market traders. There was a fair amount of information about decision making with regard to trade; much of it had the predictable effect of overturning some of my notions regarding women's trade derived from my research with the Ga in the 1970s. This comparison, however, is also tempered by the different time frame of research; the decade of difference between Ghana in the late 1970s and Kenya in the late 1980s should not be forgotten.

HISTORICAL AND CULTURAL BACKGROUNDS

One goal of selecting a completely different culture was to develop an appreciation for the impact of cultural differences on women's trading activities. I hoped to keep the kind of population studied—urban traders—constant in order to appreci-

Map 6.1
Markets in Nairobi

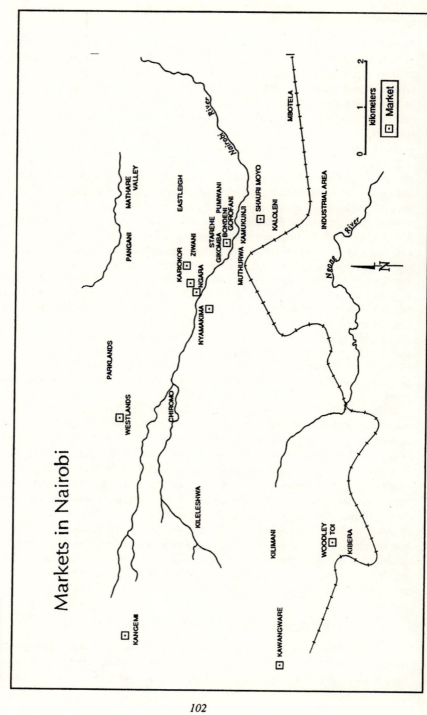

Markets in Nairobi

Map 6.2
Kiambu District

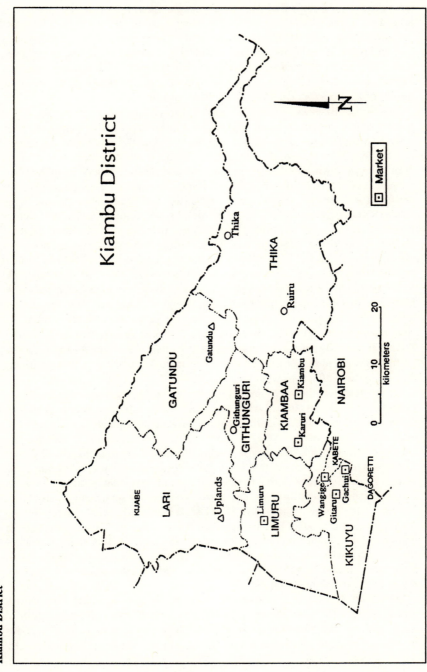

ate more fully the impact of the socioeconomic variables, including differences arising out of the social structure. In this chapter, I attempt to draw the outlines of major differences between the Kikuyu and the Ga women's experiences in trade deriving from different cultural and historical variables. The particular variables considered are marital and residential patterns and the differences in the historical development of the cities of Accra and Nairobi. I pay particular attention to the impact of these factors on women's decision making.

First, some discussion is needed about the historical setting and its impact. Accra and Nairobi at present are somewhat over a million in population, and both were selected by the British to be colonial capitals—of Gold Coast (Ghana) and Kenya, respectively. They are also similar in that the majority of their population consists of migrants to town, many of whom live in sprawling suburban slums with few or no amenities. There are also large elegant suburbs with well-guarded compounds housing the wealthy. Here the crude similarities end. While Nairobi now is the cosmopolitan East African headquarters for most corporations and many international agencies, Accra has fallen on hard times with the vicissitudes of Ghana's economy. The World Bank–imposed restructuring of the 1980s had not yet taken effect in the 1970s but also had worsened the plight of poor people in Ghana, among whom are traders. In Nairobi, a somewhat successful effort has been made to keep up the infrastructure, and phones usually work, although recent economic problems, including massive government corruption, have begun to degrade the infrastructure significantly. In Accra signs of decay are pervasively evident despite recent attempts to conform to IMF conditions so as to revive the economy. Phones in town may work, but many rural areas lack even basic amenities, a disparity also evident in Kenya. Rural transport in both countries is often a problem that particularly affects traders.

Most striking are the very great differences in the historical development of the two cities. Accra is an old city, with origins in the sixteenth century or even earlier. It was an early port for Africans and Europeans, and its population was very early on involved in the coastal West African trade. Its coastal location contributed to a cosmopolitan outlook and to extensive intermarriage with surrounding ethnic groups of the indigenous Ga population. As a nexus for both coastal and interior trade, Accra provided an ideal setting for the extensive involvement of women in trade. My research was done in the oldest areas of Accra—Asere, Sempe, and Nlesi (called Ussher Town by the British after Ussher Fort on the coast there)—among the Ga, centering around the oldest market, Salaga Market. This neighborhood is composed of a number of quarters, each with associated patrilineal clans containing the clan houses, or *wekusia*, to which all Ga trace their ancestry. In the 1970s it was a highly stable, relatively homogeneous, and settled population with a long tradition of involvement in trade.

In contrast, Nairobi is a relatively new city, its foundation dating from British efforts in 1895–1899 to build the East African railway. Located centrally in Kenya, it was selected as a prime site for the capital. There was no permanent indigenous population on most of the site; the location lay in an area sparsely populated by pastoral Maasai and agricultural Kikuyu peoples at the intersection of two ecological zones. There was much intermarriage between Maasai and Kikuyu in the area, as well as the interweaving of economies, with many practicing agriculture and pastoralism. This location attracted traders from Maasai, Kikuyu, and the Kamba peoples, who exchanged commodities coming from the two zones. And there was a small incursion of Swahili caravan trade, later joined by the Europeans in the late nineteenth century.

The Kikuyu were and still are notable farmers, especially the women, who do most of the agricultural labor and heavy hauling in rural areas. (In town markets, men are paid to carry heavy loads). They supplied quite a bit of surplus of goods to the nineteenth-century trade. Precolonial Kikuyu trade with the British was successful; but the colonial policy of favoring European businesses and East Indian traders, both in town and in the reserves, as well as the preferential pricing of European-grown maize, had a progressively negative effect on Kikuyu trade, as did land alienation.

In the Nairobi area, one section, Kiambu, was fairly densely populated by the time the British were permanently establishing themselves, and notions of private property had arisen, which then came into conflict with British efforts to alienate the Highlands to white settlers. Much of the most fertile Kikuyu land was alienated, as well as much of the Maasai land. The Highlands, because of their altitude, have a rather temperate climate compared to most of sub-Saharan Africa and therefore attracted European settlers. In West Africa, the epidemiological factor also militated against white settlement. Until the twentieth century, most Europeans living in West Africa died within six months of malaria or yellow fever.

Also in West Africa, the relatively small Lebanese population never seems to have achieved the officially sanctioned status and preference shown to East African Indians in Kenya, possibly because the influence of South African white settlers was absent, and South Africa was not used as a model for race relations, as happened in Kenya. There are, therefore, many more factors than the length and nature of settlement in Accra and Nairobi; there were in fact two very different colonial experiences under the British—one with white settlers, large land alienation, and attempts at racial and cultural segregation, and the other without. These factors played themselves out in obvious ways when governments dealt with small-scale traders.

Regarding social structure, there were also similarities and differences. Both the Ga and the Kikuyu trace descent patrilineally with extended clans tracing descent from a single ancestor. Both stress generational differences, with naming patterns in which children get grandparents' names; the Kikuyu had age sets and initiation rites involving circumcision for boys and clitoridectomy for girls. Ga puberty rites for boys and girls did not involve circumcision (boys had it done earlier) or clitoridectomy and had largely disappeared in Accra by the 1940s.[4] Because of clitoridectomy, Kikuyu girls' initiation rites became a subject of controversy among missionaries in the 1920s and feminists in the 1970s. Today, the practice is diminishing rapidly,[5] and boys' initiation rites and age sets have largely disappeared.

The Kikuyu, in addition to losing land to the Europeans and being confined to the reserves, suffered the additional disruptive impact of the Mau Mau freedom struggle of the 1950s, which split the community between those loyal to the British government and those seeking land and independence. The tactics employed by the British may have provided a model for those used later in Vietnam by the United States. The Kikuyu population, which had dominated African trade, was expelled from Nairobi, along with Embu and Meru, approximately 37,000 people.[6] Loyalists were given land confiscated from freedom fighters. With the beginning of the land registration program to make private landownership universal, suspected Mau Mau were confined to camps surrounded by barbed wire in various parts of the country. This net was cast very widely so that it included all kinds of people on whom reeducation efforts were concentrated. After the end of the emergency in 1960, many people never returned home—the population was in effect scrambled. Also, overpopulation in many Kikuyu areas encouraged colonization movements into the Rift Valley and even to the coast after independence in 1963. By the 1980s the Kikuyu had undergone considerable population mobility, both voluntary and forced.

Nevertheless, the Kikuyu remain ideologically focused on landownership and devoted to farming; indeed it was land hunger that induced much of their mobility after the emergency with the removal of restrictions on movement and land ownership. Perhaps because their urban residence has been, until recently, rather unstable; perhaps because of land deprivation; perhaps because of the potential wealth of their land, even wealthy, educated, urban Kikuyu count land ownership as a key indicator of wealth. In contrast, the Ga, whose land was concentrated around Accra and included a far smaller area than that of the Kikuyu, are progressively urbanized without the preoccupation with farming. Kikuyu and Ga women both did and still do much of the farm labor. In the precolonial period, Kikuyu men in the Nairobi area were often involved in pastoralism like the Maasai, grazing cattle, which could involve leaving home for some period of time. Urban Ga men involved in canoe fishing were more likely to be home each evening. Under colonialism, urban Kikuyu men also moved, like the Ga, into wage labor early on or into self-employment in starting businesses to serve African urban residents. Unlike the Ga, Kikuyu men and women were pressed into plantation labor on European-owned farms with taxation policy aimed specifically at providing sufficient labor for white settlers. Thus, government labor policy was always a critical issue for the Kikuyu.

Inheritance rights among the Ga were traced bilaterally; men passed property to sons and women to daughters, although both might cross gender lines on occasion. In precolonial days, women could own property and make contracts independently of men. The Kikuyu, on the other hand, passed property patrilineally to brothers and sons only. Only sons inherited land rights. Women gained use rights to land only through a husband or his father. As with the Ga, there is a sparse record of wealthy influential Kikuyu women traders, in either oral or written sources, although we know that women served as guides and traders in Kikuyu caravans sent to trade with the Maasai.[7]

Polygyny (polygamy) was also a factor in wealth accumulation for both the Ga and the Kikuyu, but not practiced by most people. Neither the Ga nor the Kikuyu had centralized governments with great concentrations of wealth among the politically powerful, although over the centuries as the involvement of the Ga in trade grew, so did the material wealth of some urban dwellers. Chiefship with the Ga developed out of intensified contact with Europeans on the coast and pressure from their aggressive neighbors, whereas for the Kikuyu it was a product of colonialism. Nevertheless, like the Kikuyu, the Ga did not have strongly elaborated traditions of pictorial or scriptural art. Rather, the Ga seem to have learned some woodcarving from the Akan, while the Kikuyu acquired beadwork from the Maasai.

Although both were doing metalwork early on, neither used wheels or draught animals. Precolonial trade was carried out by head-loading sixty to a hundred pounds per individual, sometimes over quite long distances. The Kikuyu women, as is common in hilly terrain, used tump lines, while Ga women balanced baskets on their heads. However, in the twentieth century, the Kikuyu began using donkeys and oxen successfully and, despite tse-tse fly problems, the Ga have been raising some cattle on the Accra Plains. In the twentieth century, the areas around Accra and Nairobi have been increasingly well served by roads and motorized transport compared to much of the rest of the country.

A last facet of difference needs mentioning. While the Ga occupy a low coastal plain with savannah-type vegetation, Kikuyuland is divided into forested (now farmed) ridges, sometimes with very steep hillsides. The topographical ridges sometimes serve as boundaries for clan lands, with rivalries between ridges. The ridges are easily defendable, and warfare was confined to counter-raiding among and between Kikuyu and other groups. The Accra area, however, became an attractive target for surrounding kingdoms in the seventeenth century with increasing trade opportunities; the Akwamu fought with and subdued the Ga into tributary status, imposing more centralized rule. As a result of their contrasting historical experiences and topography, then, I would say as a subjective judgment that the Ga, a small ethnic group with many cross-cultural contacts historically and a multilingual tradition, are cosmopolitan and rather open. The Kikuyu, on the other hand, the dominant ethnic group numerically in Kenya, are more defensive and suspicious of outsiders. Kikuyu contacts with Europeans, in particular, have had a negative impact on them for the most part and bred justifiable skepticism.

GOVERNMENT POLICY AND WOMEN TRADERS

Perhaps the best way to begin a comparison of trade among the Ga and the Kikuyu is to contrast two markets and how they developed. For this purpose, I have chosen Salaga Market in Accra, the oldest market at the heart of the oldest neighborhood, and Kariokor Market in Nairobi, which holds an analogous position. Salaga Market's origins lie buried in history—it probably originated in the late seventeenth century with the expansion of Accra and its increasing involvement in trade to the north brought about by the Akwamu subjugation. Indeed, its name, Salaga ("Swalaaba" in Ga dialect) seems to have arisen from the famous town in the interior to the north-northeast, an entrepôt for trade coming down from the Sahara.[8]

Salaga Market began as an open-air market with no fixed infrastructure in approximately its present location. The British claimed Accra as part of the Gold Coast colony in 1874 and eventually provided some market infrastructure—first a paved surface and then a building to house fish sellers after World War II. No sanitation facilities were provided, and open sewers carried both fecal matter and vegetable garbage through the market. Post-independence Ghanaian governments have not made major improvements; while they collect substantial taxes from the traders, they do not usually reinvest them in improvements for the market. Salaga Market is in an advanced state of decay; the sole building has had to be evacuated for lack of maintenance; chunks of broken cement and ordure litter the aisles outside. The sole improvement is a long, open-roofed shed built in the 1970s to shade the fish sellers. Salaga is one of only a very few legal markets in Accra; street trading is more pervasive and often tolerated by the authorities.

Kariokor Market, on the other hand, is the oldest specifically African legal market in Nairobi (the oldest official market is City Market, which was originally designated to be used only by Europeans and Indians). It began as an informal market serving the first substantial legal African population of Nairobi—the World War I recruits into the Carrier Corps, hence its name. The oldest government-built African housing was built there in the 1930s, and eventually an official market was added in the 1950s, with tile-roofed stalls and a wall; and rent was to be paid to the Nairobi City Council by stall holders. The British colonial government made strong efforts to confine African trade to this and other official markets until 1961. Kariokor's infrastructure and that of the other legal markets were, and still are, kept up fairly well by the colonial and independent governments. Traders operating inside such markets (there are over thirty of these legal markets in Nairobi, some in operation, others effectively defunct) tend to be the elite among traders; they have more capital and are able to afford the rents.

Nairobi also has many illegal outdoor markets, including its largest market, Gikomba, in which less-well-off traders do business. Trading here is accompanied by intermittent persecution from the Nairobi City Council police. The even poorer traders who sell on the streets of Nairobi are subject to a great deal of persecution, a tradition begun by the British. The British tolerated peddling in Nairobi until 1940 since they themselves bought most of their fresh vegetables in this way. During and after World War II, they attempted to eradicate it, even more so during the emergency of the 1950s, when traders were thought to be an uncontrolled source of help for urban dissidents. Only toward the end of colonialism, from 1961 to 1963, did the British begin to acknowledge the need for more extensive markets and relent somewhat in their persecution of street traders.

Since independence, the Kenya government has continued the persecution of unlicensed traders, especially those on the streets, to such effect that relatively few people routinely trade on the street—mainly the licensed newspaper and book sellers. In December 1987, I witnessed the partial destruction of a small street market by the police, encouraged by the competing shop owners in nearby stores. In October 1990, intensified persecution of traders escalated into the destruction of much of Gikomba Market by the Nairobi City Council police. Running battles between police and hawkers were not only a feature of 1961 but also had become the characteristic of 1990. These actions fall into a long and constant tradition of persecution of traders, then, compared to the 1978–1979 attacks on traders by the Rawlings government soldiers in Ghana, which were unprecedented and therefore all the more shocking. The largest Accra market, Makola Number One, was destroyed and replaced by a car park.

In comparison, then, the Kenyan government has been much more dominant than the Gold Coast or Ghana governments in regulating trade in a situation where there were few indigenous markets to build on. The consequence for Nairobi has been a much more structured marketing system and more definitive differences between "inside" and "outside" traders. In Accra, by way of contrast, some of the most successful traders are kiosk owners who sell at strategic locations on the street (in Nairobi kiosk owners have been embroiled in a long fight to maintain their right to operate their kiosks).

When the Ghanaian government attempts to regulate trading, such regulations are more often than not ignored and go unenforced, whereas the Kenyan government makes strong efforts at enforcement which have often negatively affected traders. In general, the Kenyan government was more concerned with regulations, a possible legacy of a white settler colonialism that adopted many of the same measures to control population movement for Africans developed in South Africa. For instance, anyone can be stopped by the police and asked to show a passbook at any time. There were obvious negative consequences for poorer traders arising from this tradition. In Ghana I never observed or experienced anything of this sort.

If the different colonial systems had certain consequences for the development of markets, they also affected women's decision making as traders. For instance, to be really successful in retail selling, it is better to be selling legally, to have sufficient capital and influence to get a market stall in either Accra or Nairobi. But few women in Nairobi fall into this category. There is more competition from men, who tend to have more access to capital and more collateral for loans. So women must seek illegal selling space, which is also very crowded in the semicondoned, illegal markets, where less formal internal market structures determine access to selling space. For those new to town with very little capital, street selling may be the only option, but it is very risky; one may end in jail or, at the very least, experience the loss of one's commodities. The choice of a selling space, then, is not a free one for many women; their resources do not allow it.

In Accra there is more flexibility although market stalls are scarcer, most desirable, and difficult to come by. But the tolerance of street selling allows more choice, and there are many variations in selling spaces. It is not so easy to distinguish between market and street sellers in terms of resources and income, but there is more latitude for innovations. The traders' individual choices play a larger role.

If government policy affects trading location, it also has a determining effect on supply in both Kenya and Ghana. To make a large subject manageable in a confined space, I confine myself here to two examples. Marketing dried staples like maize has been subject to both colonial and independent governments' regulations—price controls, movement controls, and the like. The consequence has been that only persons with strong, influential government connections can conduct large-scale trade in controlled commodities. Small traders are restricted by law to a maximum number of bags that can be sold. In Kenya this was largely enforced until 1992; in Ghana a large black market flourished for years in all controlled commodities. In contrast, the marketing of fresh produce is not controlled and forms an area of potential expansion. In Kenya market gardening for urban areas and for European export is a fast-growing industry, but it is increasingly controlled by multinational corporations. In Ghana, transport and soil are generally poorer, the former a result of British quashing of local efforts in order to keep control and of the lack of concern about it in the absence of white settlers. Thus, market gardening is generally smaller in scale and intended mainly for local consumption. The consequences for trade are that men are increasingly involved in the Kenyan fresh vegetable commerce, while women in Ghana maintain their dominance in a setting of small producers but also of small profits.

WOMEN'S TRADE IN RELATIONSHIP TO SOCIOECONOMIC STRUCTURE

Sociocultural factors also play an important role in women's decision making regarding trade; but the effects are reciprocal—the societies have also changed because of involvement in trade. It is logical to begin this analysis with Ga women traders, who have a long and intensive involvement with trade. For urban Ga women I do not think that for a long time there was a conscious decision whether or not to trade. It was a universal occupation. Women were expected not only to feed their families but also to sell their husbands' or male relatives' fish. Women carried out the marketing of all kinds of produce as early as the sixteenth century.[9] When I began my initial field research in 1971, I was intent on doing a social survey to discover what occupations women engaged in. In a house-to-house survey of over 200 compounds, I found that all the older women were or had been trading. Market trade then assumed an important role in my study because it was so critical to the women's experiences. When I asked these women why they traded, they looked at me in disbelief that I should ask such a stupid question. Virtually all able-bodied women thirty years of age and over were trading or had traded, and 99 percent of the traders in Salaga Market were female.

Not only did economic imperatives and a lack of other opportunities make women's trade necessary, but it was a cultural tradition. Mothers, sisters, and daughters were in business together, planning to pass the businesses on to their daughters, as they had been passed to them. Daughters served apprenticeships under their mothers; often the businesses were passed to the eldest daughters, who were not sent to school. In one family where this had happened, five generations of women were engaged in the bead and cloth trade. The fifth generation consisted of an illiterate old woman who no longer traded and her younger sister who had been sent to school. The sister was a member of the British peerage by virtue of the fact that her husband was the first Ghanaian legislative assembly leader, posing quite a contrast in social status within one family.

Passing businesses from mother to daughter was widespread and had many effects. From my point of view as a historical researcher, it was a tremendous boon. Women had collective memories, as it were, not only of their own experiences but of those of their mothers and grandmothers. Unlike Ga men, whose relatively early induction into Western education and wage jobs broke with tradition, Ga women had become the repositories of tradition. The wisest Ga man I knew, who had extensive knowledge of the old customs, told me that this was because, unlike his brothers, he had sat at the feet of his mother and grandmother and absorbed what they told him.

For young people, however, the situation was changing in many ways. Beginning in the 1960s, most children of both sexes in Accra attended primary school. This meant that fewer girls were doing market apprenticeships to learn trade. While in the 1970s most girls attended primary and some middle school, it did not give them sufficient skills to get clerical jobs in competition with better-educated boys, but it raised their aspirations enough to make market trading unattractive. Market trading is stereotyped as something illiterate women do in Ghana; the vast majority of traders earn only enough for subsistence needs, and this aspect of trade also does not appeal to those with education. Thus, such minimally educated girls are more likely to become seamstresses or hairdressers, if they have capital for training, or one of a variety of types of prostitutes, dependent on men for their earnings. For a few, government employment as cleaners or petty clerks may serve. Therefore, they will not preserve the collective memory, or the reality, of trading.

The residential system of old Accra lends itself so well to women's trading partnerships that it is possible that it developed in response to those needs. Marriage for the urban Central Accra Ga did not involve a change of residence for either spouse; each stayed in the family compound in the company of matrilateral or patrilateral relatives of the same sex, so that mothers, daughters, and granddaughters lived together in the same compound; and fathers, sons, and grandsons in separate compounds. Small children stayed with their mothers until, in theory at age six or up, sons were sent to join their fathers. (In practice sons usually joined fathers as teenagers, when at least partially self-supporting, or not at all when the parents were divorced, a common phenomenon.) Husbands' and wives' compounds were not usually more than a mile or so apart in the crowded quarters; women did the cooking and laundry, sending food and clean clothes to their men via one of the children.

In rural areas, the predominant pattern was neolocal and nuclear, husbands and wives farming together. The urban pattern probably evolved out of a situation in which men and women members of a patrilineage had different sections of a clan house. As time went on, the male section was sometimes left to women when upwardly mobile men moved out to the suburbs. The ideal became for men to establish neolocal households; men were also moving out of collective enterprises like fishing, which were enabled by the residential system. In towns, husbands were traditionally more likely to become fishermen, nowadays to be wage work-ers—petty clerks, artisans, drivers, carpenters—having profited from relatively early and extensive missionary-style European education. Until the 1960s, women's collective enterprises remained and expanded: communal manufacture of prepared foods and trade in various commodities. Thus, women's decision to perpetuate the old residential system can be viewed as influenced by the imperatives of trading. Young women who do not trade are far more likely to live neolocally.

Another facet of Ghanaian women's decision making in trade has to do with economic autonomy. Women saw the advantages of autonomy from males in their residential system, zealously guarding information about profits from husbands, while men did the same regarding their earnings. Although men were in theory expected to support children and contribute to wives' support, they often could or did not do so. They knew that women would still feed and support their children. For their part, women felt that if men knew how much they earned they would use that knowledge as an excuse not to contribute anything. Women's economic au-tonomy also takes advantage of their extremely important customary right to make contracts independent of men; in fact, the right may have evolved out of their participation in trade. So, women pursue and preserve their economic autonomy; it is essential to their trade activities.

This autonomy also extends to marital relations not only in spouses' main-taining separate residences and property but also in the stress on marriage as an economic relationship lacking effective ties in many cases. It was common for marriages to dissolve when men stopped contributing "chop money"—a sum set at the beginning of the marriage which symbolized the man's contribution to the household. Women's judgments of husbands as good or bad depended largely on their economic contributions to the household. A common sentiment expressed was that it was better not to depend on husbands too much since marriage is a fragile thing. The strongest links between men and women involved siblings, rather, and mothers and sons. But even these were being negatively affected by the in-creasing segregation of men and women by education and occupation. Thus, trade for illiterate women loomed ever larger as a survival strategy; regular economic dependence on particular men was not a choice. Most felt that, given their train-ing, it was the only occupation available to them. Moreover, they like being self-employed and formed tight networks with their cohorts in the market. So, both by inclination and by necessity market trade suited Accra Ga women with little or no education; there were, in fact, few options for them.

Turning to Nairobi market women, it is in the area of sociocultural factors that the most significant differences are evident. Kikuyu women's involvement in trade can be traced back to at least the mid-nineteenth century, but there is no certain evidence for earlier times. It is certain, however, that their involvement was a logical extension of their primary role as farmers; their trade was largely in staple foodstuffs, mainly beans, and then maize and vegetables when Nairobi began growing. When I went to Accra to study wives, I found traders; when I went to Nairobi to study traders, I discovered farmers. Farming is still the chief occupation for most Kikuyu and Kamba women, who composed the chief population in my surveys. However, urban trade is a growing necessity for many Kikuyu and Kamba women as a result of landlessness in Kikuyuland and drought in the Kamba Machakos area (called Masaku by the Kamba). Thus, trade for these women is clearly a response to crisis. Even among elderly traders, very few had trading histories stretching back more than twenty-five years, and fewer than 1 percent had ever traded with their mothers. Most older traders began trading only after menopause, but there are also young traders who are school leavers, none of these with the lifelong trade histories common to Ghanaian traders.

The residential system of the Kikuyu did not facilitate mother–daughter or sibling partnerships. The Kikuyu are normally virilocal in rural areas, wives moving to join husbands on dispersed compounds in separate huts on the husbands' fathers' lands. In Kiambu, near where Nairobi is now, there was considerable intermarriage with the pastoral Maasai—raiding back and forth which often involved snatching women and incorporating them into lineages as junior wives. There were no substantial concentrations of population prior to the colonial era and thus no indigenous development of specifically urban residential patterns. As Nairobi developed, the British changed their ideas about African housing. To begin with, laws ordained that Africans should stay in rural areas, in barracks provided for soldiers or railway workers (men only), or in servants' housing behind colonial houses. In the 1930s and after World War II, the colonial government provided some dormitory-style African housing, while the Africans themselves constructed housing illegally, much of which became boarding houses. There was always a severe shortage in Nairobi causing housing to be expensive, a situation exacerbated by the government's periodic destruction of illegal housing. It is difficult to say, then, that there was one urban residential pattern for Kikuyu—rather the situation varied widely and tended to be very fluid, with lots of geographical mobility from rural to urban areas and vice versa, and considerable government intervention in housing efforts.

This contrasts sharply with the settled Central Accra population, which had a history of permanence, although there was plenty of flexibility in temporary living arrangements when necessary and a fair amount of geographical mobility in order to meet trading needs. The colonial government never questioned Africans' rights to live in and around Accra; but in Kenya the government was very stringent regarding African urban residence in Nairobi. One outstanding difference caused by differing colonial policy and historical experience was that in Nairobi the sex ratio always showed a preponderance of men, while in Accra this was true only for areas of new expansion, old areas like Central Accra had the more balanced sex ratio associated with long-settled populations. The exception was the greater tendency for older men to move out and begin neolocal households, leaving Central Accra with more older women.

The dominant older rural Kikuyu residential pattern did not lend itself to women helping each other to trade easily. Women knew that daughters would leave and sisters would separate. The dispersed rural residential pattern made cooperation of female blood kin difficult. There is some evidence, however, that co-wives traded together with the permission of their husband, but this cooperation did not represent a pooling of resources. Rather, each wife sold her own produce, often turning profits over to her husband. The presumption that the land belonged to male patrilineage members made women's rights to the profits of selling its produce a contested area. Restricted land rights for women fed into reduced possibilities for Kikuyu women's autonomous trading ventures.

Both precolonially and in the present, women's accumulation of capital has been discouraged by more restricted property rights than Ga women enjoyed. Women did not have independent rights to the most significant resource, land; the prevailing ideology gave them only such rights as their husbands chose to acknowledge. Women could not make independent contracts and had so little property acknowledged as theirs that independent rights to transmit property were a moot point.[10] Their disabilities in property rights were also echoed by a lesser capability of recruiting labor than Ga women had. Thus, their scope for independent economic action seems to have been limited even in precolonial days.

Under colonialism, male control of women's actions weakened. In Kiambu, men tried to keep women from going to Nairobi to trade and failed until 1940 because the British wanted the products brought by the women. But increased concern about controlling population movement during World War II and under the emergency caused the British to reverse their policy and put stringent controls on traders coming to Nairobi. A black market arose as a result, but most traders seem to have stopped coming to Nairobi. Thus, the oldest still active traders I encountered, those who began coming to Nairobi to trade in the 1940s, usually had not done so from 1952 to 1960 for the duration of the emergency. Many were interned elsewhere, including one who was active in the Mau Mau resistance. From most traders I could get no information about Nairobi trade before the *1970s*, and many Kamba traders, in particular, began coming to Nairobi only after the 1984 drought. So, there was, for many reasons, no collective memory of trading activities going back beyond those of the present participants or retired traders.

It is nevertheless clear that the decision for Kamba and Kikuyu women, as well as many others, to trade is increasingly necessary and common. Women are turning to urban trade in ever-growing numbers as a survival strategy in the face of increasing landlessness caused both by population growth and by a higher divorce rate. Not only is there more landlessness, but marriage is becoming less stable—and for women, divorce or male desertion means landlessness. That trade is an answer to economic crisis was abundantly clear among most of the thousands of traders we surveyed.

There were many stories of immediate crises like drought, but the marital histories of traders also showed that many were widowed, divorced, or unwed mothers.

Many were widowed mothers and grandmothers coming to town to sell, leaving unwed daughters with children to farm in the rural areas. Some widows had sons whose youth at the time of their fathers' deaths made them vulnerable to the loss of their land to their father's brothers. Widows were supposed to have rights to use some of their husbands' land until or unless they remarried, the strongest position being insured by levirate marriage. But the ongoing struggle for land in Kiambu and Murang'a is often ruthless; and such rights were ignored, while many women were not interested in a polygynous levirate marriage in which they became a junior wife. Some simply packed up their meager possessions when their husbands died and went to Nairobi.

From some of the Kamba women came many of the most touching stories. During the 1984 drought, the fields dried up; they could not feed their children. One trader told me that she was sitting at home in despair wondering what to do when her neighbor came and said, "Come to Nairobi with me and I'll teach you how to trade. You can't sit here and starve anymore." Leaving the children with her farmer husband and using as starting capital a small loan from the neighbor, she went— and kept going and fed her children as a result. She and her neighbor frequented a small Nairobi neighborhood market where the solidarity and warmth between the sellers was noteworthy.

The increasing involvement of women with little or no education in market trade in the Nairobi area seems, then, to be having an impact on the socioeconomic structure. Such women are gaining more economic autonomy by earning a living independently of men. Moreover, their residential system is evolving in a direction similar to that of the Ga in Central Accra—multiple generations of women living in one household with men present as sons or brothers but not as husbands and fathers. This should facilitate women's expansion of their businesses in blood kin partnerships, but it is not clear that it will do so. While Accra traders assumed that their eldest daughters would help them and ultimately take over the business, Kikuyu and Kamba traders wanted their daughters to stay home in rural areas in order not to be corrupted by big city ways, or at least not to present more competition for them in the market. "If she comes here to trade," said one women, "she should go over to the other side of the market."

Urban resident traders wanted their daughters to go to school and get better jobs. Young traders often viewed trade as a temporary or part-time occupation, not as a career. Thus, many traders were not concerned about investing in a business for the sake of posterity or about improving skills useful for trade. Their daughters were not serving, nor had they ever served, apprenticeships, as had been the case in Accra in the 1970s when such apprenticeships were still common. Nairobi women traders' ambitions centered around educating their children and buying land, which women have had the right to own in Kenya since 1985. While traders' rotating savings associations in Accra were aimed mainly at securing capital for trade, in Kenya the profits were more likely to be used for buying land or roofing rural homes, although Kiambu women's groups are increasingly becoming involved in commercial ventures. Meanwhile, from the 1970s on, most young girls in Kenya have been sent to school and have acquired ambitions similar to those of Ghanaian girls. Trade again is something seen as only for illiterates, despite the fact that there were sizable members of middle school dropouts in the markets. They usually did not *want* to be there, however.

So, while women's market trade provided a satisfactory low-level income for many women in Accra and Nairobi, contemporary trends are undermining it in both areas. Increasing competition in Nairobi, supply difficulties in Accra, government prosecution of traders in both cities,[11] as well as status considerations, have made trading an undesirable occupation. The decision to trade is therefore becoming increasingly a solution of desperation in both areas. Both the failure of governments to grasp the positive potential involved in fostering such trade rather than discouraging it and the participants' suffering from government persecution and neglect combine to depress trade as a strategy for development.

The Kenyan government, influenced by economic considerations and the well-known 1972 International Labour Organization report, which established the respectability and prospects for the informal sector, has taken measures to promote small manufacturing, overwhelmingly dominated by men,[12] but it has neglected and persecuted Nairobi retail sellers, who are usually women, as in the Gikomba destruction. But with increasing desperation, more people will trade anyway—with ever-lessening opportunities for earning decent incomes. Given that such a trade is ideally suited to the needs of most consumers in developing countries, the depressing of its potential has detrimental effects on much of the population.[13] It is hoped, then, that governments will appreciate the potential involved in petty trade and reverse their policies to foster it; it would be an act of enlightened self-interest.

CONCLUSION

To draw some implications from the findings here, trade and trading patterns are intimately related to cultural factors such as marriage and residential patterns. In both areas, there seems to be a reciprocal relationship in which marital instability creates more need for women to earn money to support their children. But this was less important for the Ga women, who appear historically to have had more independent ownership rights. African women in and around Nairobi and Accra, like most African women, have always been expected to feed their families. The reciprocity comes when increasing trade activities forced upon them by landlessness, divorce, or drought contribute to more economic autonomy and less dependence on men and therefore less willingness to subordinate themselves to men. Nairobi women are asserting the right both to control their own labor and bodies by rejecting clitoridectomy and using contraception and to control their trade and profits independent of men. In both cases, the steady impoverishment evolving out of the dependent neocolonial situation makes the economic "freedom" of women less viable. This, in turn, may lead them into more male-dependent occupations, such as prostitution among younger women. But Nairobi and Accra women are looking for ways to be autonomous, rejecting aspects of patriarchal marriage in favor of consensual unions, living in female-headed households, and struggling to feed their children.

The historical conflict between Kikuyu men and women over control of trade profits has been resolved to some extent in the contemporary era by the decline of legal customary marriage forms (the reduction in payment of bridewealth) in favor of women.[14] Their present autonomy is both achieved and enforced; it is, in essence, the freedom to be poor because women are increasingly cut off from the wealth circulating among the male-dominated elite both within Kenya and Ghana and internationally among multinational corporations. Marital forms and trade relations, then, are inextricably entwined in socioeconomic change.

In terms of residential patterns, reciprocal relations are again evident. Mother–daughter cooperation in trade, as with the Ga, or a division of labor favoring trade, as with the Kikuyu rural–urban split, is greatly facilitated by coresidence, which may have been maintained in Accra because of its convenience for carrying out trade activities and which Kiambu and Murang'a seem to have evolved out of a lowering marriage rate—men not marrying the women they impregnated. In addition, high unemployment and increasing landlessness among the Kenyan men make older women less willing to foster male relationships for the younger women, since they feel that they themselves will have to support the resulting grandchildren. For instance, one Kamba woman involved in a "woman-marriage" was most upset because her wife continued to produce children for her to support. She was trying to discourage the wife's male friend from coming around. Thus, trade serves as both cause and effect in changing social relationships, a reciprocity that will continue. It would be better, however, if trade formed a more viable method of earning a living, since any portion of a population that is forcibly dependent upon another is at risk; the lives of children are doubly dependent—first on women and then on men—and therefore most vulnerable.

Over the centuries, market trade in the Accra and Nairobi areas has grown tremendously, with dominant participation by women traders. It has proved to be a viable strategy for women in both areas to support their children and even their husbands on occasion, and it has had a strong impact on socioeconomic structure. Yet governments have routinely persecuted small-scale traders on various grounds to the extent of damaging their businesses and well-being substantially. In the evolution of contemporary capitalist economies of Ghana and Kenya, the skills and knowledge of the retail traders are ignored, subsumed into the voiceless, despite traders' protests and attempts to secure better treatment.[15] Confining women traders to low-profit enterprises for the most part, whose profits must overwhelmingly be devoted to family subsistence needs, is not a smart economic policy. Fostering small-scale retail trade is an appropriate, logical, and viable strategy for development. It is unfortunate that male desire to control women impedes rational policy in this area and that male-dominated government elites allow class considerations to obscure possible benefits for everyone, especially the poor. But whatever the policy, women will continue to trade; they must. Whether the governments maximize on this potential or try to destroy it (intentionally or unintentionally) may well be a critical determinant of the economic health of the two countries.

Moreover, fostering women's trade offers an unexplored vehicle for development ignored in the Western experience. It could form a unique African contribution to alternative methods of development. Such a policy would align governments with grassroots efforts that could be harmonized with those of big business, but only if governments are willing first to recognize the value of small-scale trade, second to promote it through appropriate methods and the abolition of discriminatory policies toward women, and third to abandon policies that solely benefit big business in favor of more balance.

Given the pressure of international politics, however, the lack of alternatives allowed by the overweening neocolonial influence of foreign governments and agencies, as well as the lack of will toward equality of the sexes among African policymakers, this scenario seems unlikely, especially when keeping the poor poor is in the direct interest of those who profit from a permanent low-wage labor pool. Only when the political and lifestyle consequences for the elite of progressive immiseration of an ever-growing proportion of the population become too threatening will some changes be made. Those are likely to be cosmetic only. If this seems an unduly pessimistic view, it is rooted in a fundamental appreciation of the struggles of women traders, whose efforts are not generally appreciated. To ask them to add the burden of saving the whole economy to their already overladen shoulders is too much; to ask governments to treat them fairly and foster their efforts is very little and can only help in opening up new and optimistic possibilities.

NOTES

1. The fieldwork was done in Ghana in 1971–72 and 1977–78 and in Kenya in 1987–88.

2. Peter Rogers, "The British and the Kikuyu 1890–1905," *Journal of African History*, Vol. 10, No. 2, 1979, p. 262.

3. Kavetsa Adagala and Patricia Bifani, *Self-Employed Women in the Peri-Urban Setting: Petty Traders in Nairobi* (Nairobi: Derika Associates, 1985).

4. M̦. J. Field, *Religion and Medicine of the Ga People* (Oxford: Oxford University Press, 1961 [reprint of 1937 edition]), p. 176.

5. Claire Robertson, *Women, Men and Trade in the Nairobi Area, 1890 to 1990* (forthcoming), Chap. 8.

6. Andrew Hake, *African Metropolis, Nairobi's Self-Help City* (New York: St. Martin's, 1977), p. 61.

7. Godfrey Muriuki, *The History of the Kikuyu 1500–1900* (Nairobi: Oxford University Press, 1974).

8. Marion Johnson, "The Slaves of Salaga," *Journal of African History*, Vol. 27, No. 2, 1986, pp. 341–362.

9. Peter de Marees, "A Description and Historical Declaration of the Golden Kingdome of Guinea . . . ," in *Hakluytus Posthumus or Purchase His Pilgrimes*, vol. 6, translated by G. A. Dantisc (New York: AMS Press, 1965), pp. 286–287.

10. This may have been less true in Nyeri than in Kiambu.

11. Claire Robertson, "The Death of Makola and Other Tragedies," *Canadian Journal of African Studies*, Vol. 17, No. 3, 1983, pp. 469–495, details the Ghanaian government's persecutions of traders, especially under the Rawlings regime.

12. Dorothy McCormick, "Small Manufacturing Enterprise in Nairobi: Golden Opportunity or Dead End?" Ph.D. dissertation, Department of Economics, Johns Hopkins University, 1988; Robertson, *Women*, Chap. 8.

13. Robertson, "Death," p. 477.

14. Robertson, *Women*, Chap. 6.

15. Claire Robertson, "Traders and Urban Struggles: The Creation of a Militant Female Underclass in Nairobi, 1960 to 1990," *Journal of Women's History*, Vol. 4, No. 3, Winter 1993, pp. 9–42.

Chapter 7

Baganda Women's Night Market Activities

Nakanyike B. Musisi

The night markets that have proliferated recently on the streets of suburban Kampala are an important component of the informal economy that emerged in response to the economic crises in Uganda since the early 1970s.[1] These markets are invigorated primarily by women vendors who offer their customers a wide selection of foods, from quick snacks to full meals. The term applied to these markets in the Luganda language—*toninyira mukange* (TM), translated into English as "don't step in mine"—encapsulates the aggressive minicapitalist ethic that motivates vendors to participate. This chapter examines women's significant contributions to the informal economy through their night market activities. The central argument of the chapter is that women, as revealed in their contribution to night market activities, have made and continue to make a significant contribution to economic life in Uganda.

The chapter is divided into three parts. Part one presents a review of the literature about Uganda's economic crisis. It argues that male bias is pervasive in this literature, which has paid little attention to women's contributions to the economy.

This chapter was written in collaboration with Jane Turrittin. It reports on preliminary work of a larger research project now in progress. I am also very grateful to several Ugandan research assistants, headed by Fred Bukulu of Makerere University in Uganda, who administered a preliminary survey in Kampala between December 1992 and August 1993.

This male bias is not unique but originates in colonial-period literature, which overlooked women's participation in cash crop production.

Part two traces the historical background of the "eating out" industry in Kampala. It argues that the origins of the night market activities are closely related to the crisis in the restaurant industry and hence should be traced historically. The data present a structural analysis that includes consideration of sex, race, class, and rural–urban dynamics.

Empirical data on women's participation in night markets are presented in part three. The main thesis is that the economic transformation Uganda has experienced since the early 1970s (economic mismanagement under Idi Amin and subsequent governments, civil war, and most recently, structural adjustment programs) has affected both men and women. The main burden of the economic crisis has affected women more heavily than men, however, because women have been the primary producers and distributors of food.

MALE BIAS IN THE ECONOMIC LITERATURE ON UGANDA

The male bias characteristic of scholars who study the more recent Ugandan economy is revealed in the writings of Marxists and non-Marxists alike (Lateef, Ochieng, Jamal, Loxley, Mamdani, Banugire, and others). For example, in his brief description of the economy prior to 1972, Vali Jamal, a senior research economist with the International Labour Organization (ILO), states that there were "huge inequalities along racial, occupational and geographical lines" but makes no reference to gender inequalities.[2] While Jamal presents detailed evidence showing the effect of economic changes on food consumption patterns and nutrition levels among various segments of the Ugandan population, he fails to give credit to women for their contribution to the maintenance of adequate subsistence food levels even during the period of economic and political crises. He leaves the reader with the erroneous impression that only men were farmers and wage workers in Uganda.[3] Jamal is also oblivious to the fact that expectations about what work is appropriate for men and women are culturally defined and that access to economic resources is constrained by cultural beliefs about sex roles. Jamal fails to analyze the differential effect of the astronomic decline in wages on men's and women's standards of living within the urban working class. Nor does he pay attention to sex as a factor that influences the responses of urban men and women in their efforts to make a living.

Firimooni Banugire, an economics professor at Makerere University, describes how the collapse of the modern formal sector of the economy resulted in the astronomical growth of the informal sector. He writes, "The inability of the majority of the working population to meet even five per cent of their basic needs requirements out of the formal wage incomes [forced them to] the perpetual search for 'informal' incomes to fill their yawning basic needs."[4] Banugire's work, which focuses on the social effects of Uganda's Structural Adjustment Program, is surprisingly gender blind.[5] Though Banugire documents the decline in social services since the 1970s, he makes no mention of the fact that the decline affects men and women differently.

While giving greater emphasis to ethnic dynamics as they affected economic policy than Jamal or Banugire did, John Loxley at least shows sensitivity to the situation of women.[6] He argues:

Women were particularly hard hit by the crisis, often having to undertake petty trading as well as holding down a regular job, carrying the burden of the housework and dealing with the acute problem of shortages of goods and deterioration in health care and other social facilities.[7]

He describes how the Obote II regime, faced with the recession and severe balance-of-payments crisis, "turned to the international institutions and to bilateral donors for large-scale assistance" between 1981 and 1984.[8] As Mugyenyi describes the situation, the Obote II Agreement with these institutions was negotiated in a situation in which political factors were more salient than economic ones.[9] The agreement called for a massive devaluation of the Ugandan shilling from 8.4 to the U.S. dollar to 78. Loxley, Mugyenyi, and Jamal agree that these policies had a negative effect on the urban working class because the agreement "relied heavily on expensive, short-term IMF credits" to the extent that the debt-service ratio had jumped from under 20 percent in 1981 to 55 percent of export earnings by 1985.[10]

These policies were continued reluctantly by the National Resistance Movement (NRM) government, which has signed two major structural adjustment agreements, in 1987 and in 1990, with the World Bank and International Monetary Fund. Inflation remained high; and by July 1988 a second stabilization effort was put into place. According to a British scholar, Reginald Green, historically Western contact with African societies has had an uneven effect. Continuing his analysis to recent IMF and WB policies, Green writes, for "urban wage earners—formerly above the absolute poverty line—the real purchasing power of whose wages has fallen so sharply that it is clear both they *and other household members* have had to enter 'informal' sector activities to survive and that their living standards have nevertheless declined precipitously" (italics added).[11]

Diane Elson's explication of the IMF's and WB's strategies and priorities is useful with respect to understanding how the policies in place between 1981 and 1984, as well as those adopted by the NRM government in 1986 and 1987, affect women. Elson agrees with the analysts of Uganda's economy that "the important question is not whether to adjust but how to adjust."[12] Elson advocates changes in both policy objectives and areas of intervention. In her view, "Adjustment with (gender) Equity" would introduce changes that "encompass not just relations between the public and private sector control of resources, but between women's . . . and men's control of resources."[13]

On the other hand, Christine Obbo argues that the commoditization of food is affecting the health status of children, as women sell more nutritious foods, such as eggs, fruits, and vegetables, to generate incomes and then spend some of the money they earn on medical care for problems of malnutrition.[14] For Obbo, the real causes of poverty existed prior to the implementation of the SAPs, which only aggravated the situation of the vulnerable (women, children, and the elderly). If women's activities in the night market are viewed as taking place in Uganda's "second economy," Janet MacGaffey's suggestion that the second economy "exists for political as much as economic reasons" is vital to this chapter's argument. MacGaffey presents the following statement: "It is important to see them not simply as solutions to household survival or individual subsistence problems, but rather as political options, co-opted by political discourse."[15] MacGaffey strongly believes that the informal economy, which she prefers to call the "second economy," is "essentially a political phenomenon . . . empowering the unskilled or the semi-skilled."[16]

HISTORICAL BACKGROUND OF THE "EATING OUT" INDUSTRY

In Buganda, as in many precolonial African economies, much of the external trade was an activity of the state administration. Contact with Arab and Swahili traders and European explorers and missionaries led to trade becoming monopolized by Buganda's state bureaucracy. This gave rise in many areas to the growth of peripheral markets in which "the market place" was present but "the market principle" did not determine acquisition of subsistence or the location of resources and labor.[17] Paul Bohannan and George Dalton, who make the distinction between "the market place" and the "transactional mode of market exchange," write:

The market place is a specific site where a group of buyers and a group of sellers meet. The market . . . principle . . . entails the determination of labour, resources, and outputs by the forces of supply and demand regardless of the site of transactions. The market principle can and often does operate outside the market place, as when a business firm hires labour, land is sold in the real estate market, or grain is sold on the "world market."[18]

The colonization of Buganda brought tremendous institutional changes. First was the growth of economic activity organized on the market principle (market-dominated economy), with the concomitant attenuation of redistribution and reciprocity. Second were the social changes whereby labor, entering the market, moved geographically and occupationally in response to market demand.[19] Since then, commodification has become an integral part of the Ugandan economy as a whole. However, men and women did not become involved in market activity in the same ways. The growth of the market principle and the increasing participation and changing roles of women in market activity (predominately cooked food) must be examined in relation to broader aspects of the changing political economy in Uganda.

Because eating out is not traditional in Uganda, the first commercial eating places were associated with foreigners. These early eating facilities were established as transportation developed along the trade routes and as trading centers expanded. The completion of the Uganda railway in 1905 was a significant step in this process. It is important to note that the restaurant industry developed along racial lines. The elegant restaurant buildings that catered to the Europeans were often painted white, in contrast to the Indian restaurants, which were usually painted combinations of green, grey, red-brown, and white. African restaurants were housed in a range of structures—modest restaurants were built of mud brick and had cor-rugated iron or thatched roofs; more substantial African restaurants were in very elegant buildings similar to those owned by Indians. While the restaurant industry developed along racial (European, Asian, and African) and class lines in its forma-tive years, the Africans who patronized restaurants were predominately migrant workers and long-distance truck drivers hauling goods between the coast and the interior.

Despite efforts of the colonial administration to constrain urbanization, it was estimated that close to 100,000 Africans lived within a five-mile radius of Kampala by 1957. The Africanization of the administrative bureaucracy and the develop-ment of small industries, combined with the fact that African food was not packagable, attracted workers to eat out, although working-class people generally preferred home-cooked to restaurant food. Home-cooked food tasted better, por-tions were more generous, and such food was ethnically authentic.

Hence, there is ample evidence that by the 1960s hotels (restaurants) were kept by many Baganda and others, such as Arabs, Swahili, and Indians. These hotels varied in popularity, and their clients were mainly clerks whose homes were dis-tant and who bought lunch in town every day. The restaurants offered African, modified Indian, and Arab dishes ranging from cooked *matoke* (plantain) to milk.[20] A. B. Mukwaya's data indicate that as early as the 1940s a small number of women were engaged in hotel activities. Mukwaya notes that these women, who started their businesses with very meager resources, were "mostly single women moving out of childless marriages." Citing one such woman, who, "after noticing that many men in [her locale] had no women to cook for them [she] bought an old paraffin tin for fifty cents, three shillings worth of firewood and two shillings bunch of plan-tain."[21] Mukwaya's description of this woman's marketing activity after six in the evening indicates that the pioneers of what has become contemporary TM were active in the 1940s.

By the mid-1960s, Kampala's suburbs had become more metropolitan, and the population was large enough to support the restaurant industry.[22] Vali Jamal argues that by the late 1960s one could speak of urban wage earners as the "labour aris-tocracy." The minimum wage had been raised sixfold by 1970.[23] The increasing number of town dwellers divorced from the primary means of food production would have signaled positive growth for the food industry. However, a number of constraints operated against African town dwellers' full utilization of the industry. Christine Obbo suggests that many unskilled town dwellers were unemployed and lacked the basic means of survival.[24] Those who were employed were content to return to their homes at meal times. Those who could afford it would avail themselves of small snacks sold by local street vendors. The majority, however, went without lunch.[25]

Restaurant meals were always too expensive for those workers, who were part of the aspiring middle class. These workers gave high priority to providing their children with the best education possible and to purchasing modern material goods, such as china dishes, bicycles, gramophones, radios, clothing, and other items for their families. Because eating out was an expensive luxury, meals were usually prepared and served at home.

Home-prepared meals offered several advantages to the household head. First, they were the product of the unpaid domestic labor of women family members. Second, they had generous portions (a generous portion was guaranteed, always, to the household head—the *man*) compared to the portions served in restaurants. In addition, when the household head ate at home, he was served with due respect. Moreover, home-cooked meals were consumed in a familiar environment and an unrushed atmosphere. These factors, together with the economic disincentive, combined to make home-prepared-and-served meals preferable.

However, by the end of the 1960s, and against all odds, eating out had become more acceptable to the Baganda, particularly those of the lower middle class. To meet the food demands of this segment of the population, there was a proliferation of African restaurants offering full African meals as increasing numbers of working people found themselves away from home at lunch time. According to both Obbo and Jamal, these urbanites had to devise a means of survival in towns.[26]

The restaurant industry was beginning to boom at the time the Indians were expelled in 1972. Western-type fast-food restaurants, such as Wimpy's, Mona Lisa, Chez Joseph, and El Dorado, had opened in Kampala in addition to the formal hotel-based restaurants. The secretary general of the Hotel and Allied Workers' Union was among those who hoped the industry would gain by Idi Amin's coup.[27] However, Amin's ad hoc and unpopular economic and political policies resulted in a drop in local industrial production. The country's increasing isolation from the international economy resulted in the quick transformation of Uganda's economy into the *magendo* economy, characterized by hoarding practices, artificial commodity shortages, price inflation, and black-marketeering.[28] Many essential commodities, such as fuel (for both cooking and transportation), milk, sugar, and meat, were in short supply. Reginald Green suggests that by 1980, the black market (*magendo*) accounted for 51 percent of the country's GDP. Inflation was so high that the average income of city workers in 1980 was equivalent to only 6 percent of the 1972 rate.[29] However, Jamal presents a convincing argument that despite the gloomy trends in the modern sector and in the export crop sector, enough food was produced during this "lost decade" to meet the population's needs.[30]

The *magendo* economy was associated with the emergence of a new class in Uganda—the "get rich quick" people, locally known as *mafutamingi*.[31] For a variety of reasons, the *mafutamingi* patronized restaurants. First, restaurants provided a venue in which business transactions could be struck. Second, the *mafutamingi* had limited time to return home for meals. Many divided their time between bootlegging and several female consorts they were obliged to entertain. For many, beer drinking and late-night dancing became integral to their lifestyles. Being at home at mealtimes was no longer meaningful to them. In addition, because they had money and could give big tips, the quality and quantity of the service they received at these places was kingly. Their desire for deference, respect, and glorification was no longer dependent on the behavior of members of their households. Moreover, frequenting restaurants enabled them to show off their newly acquired wealth, especially to their consorts. Many innocent young women fell victim to these men through whom they had access to luxurious meals and lifestyles. Last, while there is no doubt that the *mafutamingis* could provide their families with essential commodities, the variety of meals prepared by the restaurants was more attractive to them. The high prices of these meals, however, were prohibitive for ordinary Kampala citizens.

The *magendo* economy during Amin's rule was also accompanied by a general state of lawlessness and civil disorder. In the face of not only perverted and corrupt law enforcement but also serious shortages of materials and buildings, the food industry searched for ways to meet town dwellers' increasing demand for cooked meals. The result was an upsurge in local roadside food vending,[32] an activity that continued into the night and came to be known popularly as *toninyira mukange* ("step not in mine"). During the day, some TM vendors would "invade" work sites for lunch. At night, the roadsides of suburban Kampala became the center of the TM vendors' aggressive minicapitalist ventures under paraffin candle lights.

During the 1970s, when the demand for restaurants was increasing, restaurant owners had difficulty supplying the materials to meet the expanding market demand. Capital and exotic commodities (including food and cooking equipment) became increasingly scarce and expensive.[33] Restaurant owners had little choice but to purchase materials they needed to meet the increasing demand on the black market. At this time, food vendors, as well as other types of vendors, were often harassed by the police and by military and prison wardens.[34]

The years 1980–1991 witnessed a rapid growth of the informal economy, during which roadside vendors not only increased in numbers but also gained sophistication with respect to the quality and quantity of the goods and services offered. A number of factors contributed to the upsurge in the development of the roadside food industry. First, after 1972, African entrepreneurs stepped in to fill the void left by the expulsion of the Indians. Because food vendors met the needs of an increasingly large working-class clientele, *toninyira mukange* continued to grow and attract people in the towns. Second, the growing population resulting from migration into Kampala and its neighborhoods guaranteed the industry a stable market. Third, increasing numbers of these urban dwellers were divorced from direct control of resources such as land and fuel. Whereas eating out had previously been viewed as convenient for those away from home at mealtimes or, as during the period of Amin's rule, as a way of showing off wealth, something new was now taking place. People were leaving home to purchase food from *toninyira mukange* because doing so was essential to their way of life.

THE DYNAMICS OF TM

Since the early 1980s, TM has grown steadily in suburban Kampala; and it has now spread to many other urban areas in Uganda. The steady success of TM raises a number of important historical and economic questions regarding the relationship between gender and market activities. Qualitative changes are occurring in the social and economic structures associated with the change in eating habits and market activities. These changes have been dictated by a number of factors, such as who has access to land, labor, and reliable sources of income and how urban space in suburban Kampala is used.

The following data are based on a preliminary survey of a larger research project we are undertaking to study TM activity in Kampala. A sample of 69 vendors and 31 regular customers in nine locations is represented in this preliminary sample.

The class base and function of TM are revealed by none other than the fact that TM vendors are found mainly along the roads in less affluent neighborhoods with low-rental properties in suburban Kampala. Many operate in crowded slum areas such as Mulago Hill, Kibuye, Kivulu, and Nakulabye, where as many as eight people live in a single room.[35] On certain roads, the TM vendors replace day vendors who deal in used clothes or raw foods. The markets are always overcrowded and noisy. The vendors, who are not licensed, tend to congregate where people pass, for example, along morning and evening work routes and at major road intersections, as well as gates and entrances of institutions such as schools, hospitals, or colleges. Other common sites include outside day markets, near bus and taxi parks, bars, post offices, banks, cinemas, factories, hair salons, nightclubs, and road junctions. They arrange themselves in lines and operate from makeshift tables or mats laid directly on the ground. Many vendors make use of locally made paraffin wick lamps (*munaku tadooba*—the meek does not suffer), while others rely only on light from shops or the streetlights. Some vendors who do not operate by candlelight (paraffin lamps) move their locations frequently. It is in these market activities that Bagandan women have become increasingly involved since the early 1980s. Small streets and poorer neighborhoods are served primarily by women vendors, while bigger intersections and better-off neighborhoods and ethnically mixed populations are served by both men and women.

Most TM women workers start operating after dusk; they may close as late as midnight. The first signs of activity in the night TM markets occur at about 5:15 P.M. At one market, for example, a woman selling fresh tomatoes, onions, and dried fish appeared. Shortly thereafter, vendors who sell roast maize (corn), cooked maize, and milk organize their affairs. Once they arrive at their vending locations, the vendors set up their businesses with the utmost speed. Toward 5:45 P.M., both male and female vendors who sell items such as fried cassava, liver, and chicken appear with their charcoal stoves; and by 6:00 P.M. those with other types of cooked food appear. Shortly thereafter, women and children carrying already cooked food on their heads appear with their benches. At around 7:30, the male vendors frying *emputa* (Nile perch) become very busy. Women selling fried foods such as Nile perch bring their wood. They have the fish already cut up into smaller pieces, ready to be barbecued or deep-fried. They are also equipped with water and soap for their customers to use after eating. The market becomes very active around 8:00 P.M. and does not slow down until after 11:00 P.M.

WOMEN AND THE TM TRADE

Most women involved in TM vending were forced to engage in this activity because of the economic changes in Uganda in the last thirty years. Many of these women's husbands or partners have no regular jobs. Others, dissatisfied with the poor village life, have migrated to Kampala. Some have been abandoned by careless husbands or partners or lost them in war or to AIDS. Still others have been separated from husbands or partners because of misunderstandings or other problems such as opposition to polygyny and poverty. TM has also attracted single mothers who dropped out of school and left home. Because of economic problems, these women have had to take major responsibility for their own and their dependents' support. Some women have been attracted and encouraged to join TM to support themselves. Lacking enough education to be gainfully employed and lacking access to land, these women have become the backbone of the night market. Although many admit that it is a difficult and tiring job, they accept or tolerate TM because they have no alternative way to earn a living.

There are interesting comparisons between men and women who engage in TM activities. On the one hand, the night market women range in age from fifteen to over seventy, while men are commonly no more than forty. Because far more women are illiterate in Uganda than men, women have fewer chances of employment in the formal economy. Though many night market women had acquired a little primary education, others have virtually no formal education; yet they are self-sustaining. One-third were either widows, orphans, or people who had been displaced either by the war of liberation or by AIDS. Another third had been separated or divorced from their partners. The remainder were either unmarried or refused to reveal their marital status. Many of those who considered themselves married had partners who did not stay with them permanently, because they either had jobs in far away places or were polygynous men.

The ways women are drawn into TM operation are equally revealing of gender disparity that has roots in the unequal access to resources and their distribution. Several women entered TM on their own, while others got involved after being employees of TM vendors. While many have never worked outside the household (some have worked as housegirls), others were involved in other businesses before joining TM. Some female TM vendors work with their male partners. More than 75 percent of all the women surveyed opened business with small amounts of capital; 37 percent had worked as porters or toiled at other low-status occupations before they managed to save enough capital to start their own businesses; 12 percent were financed by relatives, friends, husbands, or partners. A few inherited small amounts of money that they used to start TM. Fewer than 7 percent had borrowed the money to start the business. A smaller percentage of women have regular paying jobs; but because of high inflation rates, they must supplement their income through TM. Most of these women hire other women to buy the food, prepare it, and sell it. Four of the working-class women expressed their willingness to directly engage in TM themselves if they lost their jobs.

Most women engaged in TM are the sole supporters of their families. The married women are in most cases forced to participate in TM because their partners do not earn enough to sustain the family. TM vendors, whether men or women, either rent single rooms or share accommodations with husbands or partners, relatives, or friends. Asked whether they used family planning, 87 percent of the women said they did not. Renting single-room houses, maintaining a family, and paying school fees for the children are major problems for these women. The survival stress drives many of them to TM operation. While their children could be doing well at school, the stress and strain they live under because they try to help their mothers prepare the food or engage in direct sale in the night market tends to make them give up school early and thus end up in TM themselves. Of all the children engaged in TM, 62 percent had mothers or aunts who were TM operators. Young girls who become pregnant before finishing school also end up in TM. Our survey showed that this was the case for 40 percent of young girls who operated in TM.

On the other hand, men who engage in TM are mostly boys for whom no one has paid school fees or older men who have been frustrated by low-paying jobs and an urgent need for an independent income. Some of these men have regular 8:00 A.M. to 5:00 P.M. jobs in the low-paying sector—they work, for example, as street sweepers or slash the grass in the city; a few are office boys or clerks. Most men engaged in TM, nonetheless, depend on their female relatives to do the cooking. The few who do not (perhaps because they have none) deal in fried foods, for example, fish (the Nile perch and tilapia), meat, or chicken which they buy and fry, roast, or barbeque on the spot (*mucomo*).

At dusk, when the market activities begin, space is equally gendered. Well-lit streets tend to be served by women and children and a few men, while dangerous locations, which are characterized by less competition, tend to be served by men or male youths. To protect themselves from harassment or unnecessary exposure to undesirable people, or even rape, girls tend to carry out business near their mothers or other female relatives, while boys are seen alone.

The division of labor in the night markets reveals not only gender but ethnic identity. In Wandegeya market, for example, Baganda night market women tend to concentrate on typically Buganda traditional foods, while women from Toro specialize in roast chicken, and those from the north concentrate on cooked or roasted corn. Each woman vendor has a specialty. Some serve full meals such as a combination of plantain and beans, cassava and beans, fish, and a variety of greens. Others specialize in only one item, such as boiled eggs, *chapatti* (sort of a pita bread), peas, groundnut sauce, cooked cabbage, or just greens. Still others become known for different sauces they have improvised which add variety to ordinary dry foods such as cassava, yams, roasted potatoes, and bread. Many of these foods are also available in a precooked form. Some night market women specialize only in local drinks, such as banana and passionfruit juice. Sodas, fresh milk, varieties of teas, coffee, porridge, and local brews, including beer (*tonto*) and crude gin (*waragi*), are also available.

Much of the food sold by the night market women is purchased at the day markets or from neighboring villages, since very few TM vendors grow their own food (they do not own land). In addition to food items, about 2 percent of the TM women sell articles such as second-hand clothes, toothbrushes, toothpaste, books, soap, biscuits, matchboxes, saucepans, and a variety of household items needed for day-to-day use.

Our research significantly indicated that participation in TM is patterned by gender. Men are very active in trading in luxury goods, while the activity of women vendors is restricted to selling foodstuffs and other small commodities in the day markets and processed food in the night markets. Two-thirds of those who sold cooked food in TM were women. Information from men who sold cooked food revealed that it had in most cases been prepared by women and the men did only the marketing. In some cases, men sold manufactured goods in the night market. This division of labor reflects Baganda expectations with respect to gender hierarchy in which women are responsible for agriculture, cooking, and distribution of foodstuffs.

The survival role that TM is currently filling is exhibited not only by the class of the vendors and the areas they operate from but also by the variety of people TM serves. Customers include people of all classes, from professionals and factory workers to peasants and slum dwellers; adult men and women, as well as children, and people of different occupations. For example, there are office employees, taxi drivers, day vendors, family people, and single men and women who return late from their jobs. Many are working men who do such jobs as building or hawking; others are civil servants; and others are self-employed—shopkeepers, mechanics, and even prostitutes. Most live in the area of the TM night market women they patronize. The fact that today people of different occupational backgrounds utilize TM is an indication that the need for survival is currently felt by all.

While the age of the customers varies in relation to the space or street of operation, bachelors respond to TM in large numbers. Since they view cooking as a woman's task but do not have enough money to marry, they maintain relationships with female partners or hire cooks. In general, customers have unstable low incomes based on daily remuneration and prefer TM to the inconvenience of buying charcoal or paraffin and taking time to prepare food themselves. In some places, boys thirteen years old or younger eat in TM. Such youths have dropped out of school for one reason or the other and lack parental control. They do all sorts of odd jobs during the day, such as working in quarries breaking stones, playing cards, or even stealing. Others, such as university and boarding school students who live in hostels, patronize TM to supplement their inadequate school diets. A small number of people with kin in hospitals, as well as household heads (men or women) who bring in money late at night, find TM convenient. Selfish men, acting secretly so that they are not recognized by people who might know them, buy either corn, corn-flour, or cassava and beans (poor foods) for their families and more nutritious foods, such as fish, chicken, fried rice, greens, barbecued beef or chicken, and vegetables, for themselves.

Consumption is patterned by sex, age, and ethnicity. Men usually eat the most nutritious foods, such as meat or roast chicken, during or after drinking in a nearby bar. Such men often send barmaids to fetch meat from a vendor. Youths may stop to eat inexpensive food. Many of those who buy roasted or cooked corn are schoolboys or girls or university students who cannot afford the expense of full meals. Customers prefer to buy from the night market women who speak their own language.

Twenty-one of the customers in our study prefer not to eat in TM but do so out of necessity. Some of these carry their food home in containers after purchasing it from TM night market women. These women often make special appeals to their customers, who are shy, encouraging them to try TM meals by reducing prices. In the TM market at Owino, the main streetlight was disconnected because shy customers were afraid of being seen. Most customers eat in silence and bend closely over their plates so that they cannot be identified by passers-by or other vendors. This behavior violates Baganda norms of food consumption and etiquette, but it illustrates the discomfort felt by some customers who feel that eating in TM is below them (class or culture consciousness).

Answers to a question about why most TM vendors are women revealed a stunning gender bias prevalent in Kampala. Among the many reasons given were that women have traditionally been responsible for cooking "good" food, that women have mastered the soft persuasive language to lure customers, and that women are endowed with more patience than men. Betraying their sexism, informants who believed that the marketplace was not a proper space for women stated that women with weak morals use TM as a venue to acquire male lovers so that they can "retire from poverty."[36] Despite the fact that they must put up with the distrust of such customers, many women involved in TM have developed good relations with their customers and have acquired genuine friends who can back them up economically.

TM market activity has given rise to a special culture and language that separates the TM population from the general population. Night market women have developed a special language, not understood by customers, which they use when quarreling, discussing prices, and assessing customers, particularly those they believe will not pay or whom they view as worthless or potentially dangerous. This language includes terms that indicate the value of money. For example, *ekida*, indicates 10,000 Ugandan shillings (UgShs; about U.S. $10); *ekida piece*, 15,000 UgShs; *ekidashini*, 100,000 UgShs; *ekitiyondosi*, 1,000 UgShs; *Pajero*, 500 UgShs; *ekigana*, 100 UgShs; and *ekyamusi*, 50 UgShs. These are not Luganda words, nor do they belong to any particular language, but they are specific to TM.

On the other hand, night market women also use a number of slang words and expressions familiar to customers to advertise their goods. For their part, the customers have developed slang to let market women know their financial difficulties.[37] When customers want a good meal for less money or want to eat on credit or want to warn the vendor not to cheat them, they use kinship terms such as aunt, mother, uncle, child, or in-law in an effort to establish a fictitious kin relationship. Similarly, night market women resort to terms of respect such as "my boss," "elder," "my master" to put themselves in a humble position vis-à-vis customers.

Examples of the slangs vendors use among themselves are given below:

Step not in my throat (Do not take away my customer)

They are passing by you (You are being cheated)

That one is from the red tiles (The customer is a policeman or woman, has no money; reduce the price)

That one needs to be jump-started (That customer needs encouraging words to persuade her or him to purchase)

He or she is a judge or doctor (She or he has no money or is very opinionated)

Blow the smoke (Such and such a person is engaged in witchcraft so watch out)

Do not make me a driver (Please do not turn me into a slave)

Examples of the slang between customers and night market women include

My sibling or my mother! (Please, I have no money, but offer me something free)
That one is a charcoal stove (She or he is impertinent)
I have unloaded (I have finished selling for the night)

The women concurrently carry on their gender politics on the spot in the process of luring customers. For example, if a customer is male, the women may remind him of his obligations to his family by saying, "Sir, sir, take some food to your children," or "Your wife will love this yam," and so on. As one woman who identified herself as Nakato said, women "adequately know that men tend to think about themselves first before their families." Newcomers to TM activity who have not served an apprenticeship and thus have not fully acquired the language, culture, or aggressive behavior characteristics of TM activity are not likely to be successful.

TM women experience a number of work-related problems. First, TM activity is a tiring job which many women combine with other responsibilities, including domestic tasks, such as laundry and cleaning and childcare. Many women start work early in the morning when they purchase food items and return home very late after selling everything. Preparing meals is time consuming. Some women start cooking around noon so that they can be ready by about 4:00 P.M., when they eat lunch to be ready to take up their positions in the market by 6:30. Other night market women take their suppers in the night market while engaged in TM since they return to their homes very late. Because most do not have time to care for their children, they either employ maids or leave the children with a relative or older children. Some of these women operate in both the day and evening markets, selling whatever remains from their daymarket activity in TM.

Second, prices in TM markets are not formally regulated, but they are not determined haphazardly. Because competition is tough, prices in TM markets tend to be lower than those in the day markets. When setting their prices, however, women must take several factors into consideration: the cost of the foods they purchased, fuel costs, and the cost of utensils. For fear of chasing customers away, prices must not be set too high (prices are sometimes set in accordance to customers' looks). Most TM women discount their own labor, which, as in their homes, is not paid for. Experienced night market women tactfully reduce the quantity of food served to customers. Male vendors who sell fried food tend to benefit more from TM than vendors who sell meals that require lengthy preparation, as the former do the frying on the street itself and incur little waste. Envy and fear of witchcraft, which some vendors believe is used to make their businesses fail, is sometimes experienced by night market women who sell the same types of foods.

Third, proximity to the road makes for unhealthy conditions. Because these women operate without shelter, they must cope with the vagaries of the weather. Each season brings its particular problems. During the wet seasons, night market women work in great discomfort; some, including those with babies, brave the rain, cold, and mud for four to six hours. Those without hot charcoal stoves have a particularly rough time. Moreover, when it rains unexpectedly during their active hours, it is difficult for TM women to budget for a day's work. During the dry season, dust from the roads often gets mixed into the food forcing the women to reduce prices so that customers will still buy from them. Moreover, nights during the dry seasons tend to be cold.

Fourth, at certain locations, near the Owino market, for example, TM women and their daughters operate in conditions of insecurity. Not only do customers run off with their plates, but homeless boys and girls steal their food and other property and beat customers up. Lacking protection, customers and marketers alike face this insecurity and the threat of being robbed; at times serious injuries have occurred. TM women operators in Owino and Nakulabye markets have begun to organize in an attempt to solve this problem. One strategy is to hire storage space for their property during nonbusiness hours. In some places, these women have engaged the militia of the local resistance councils to patrol the market.

Because most of the streets and areas where TM women operate are poorly lit, most of them use paraffin candles. However, lights installed in the Nakulabye and Wandegeya markets for purposes of security were deliberately switched off to ensure anonymity since some customers do not want to be identified. Moreover, balancing a charcoal stove or hot food on one's head is potentially dangerous. A slight mistake while walking can cause one to stumble and lead to serious bodily harm. Several women have suffered serious burns in this way.

Equally important, many night market women incur losses because they have no way to preserve unsold food. This problem has forced some of them to close their operations. Some give leftover food away because they do not want it to go to waste. Others take leftovers home as a late supper or breakfast by household members. Because of lack of adequate storage facilities, most vendors purchase food in small quantities in daily use for fear of losing their base capital or their profit.

The structure of TM as a business venture gives rise to potential conflict between night market women and customers. For example, a night market woman who establishes regular customers faces the problem of extending credit. A customer may pay at first but disappear after getting credit, thus causing losses to the vendor. Night market women need to be paid daily for the food they sell because the money they earn is essential to their own subsistence; moreover, they need a daily turnover to stay in business. If a customer pays only after eating a meal, the woman is at a disadvantage because the customer can claim that the food was not good and thus offer a low price. Most operators have resorted to a system of "pay and get served," even though this may reduce the number of potential customers. Haggling over the price exposes these women to insults and abuse from customers, who sometimes use shameful words. Experienced night market women claim they have learned to cope with such insults by paying little or no attention to abusive customers and not reacting in the expected manner.

In the majority of TM markets, activity takes place outside official government control; and in some locations, it is even difficult to identify the market authorities. Thus far, it is not necessary to have a government permit to operate TM; and except for Owino market where the city council has attempted to intervene on several occasions, the government has not put any systematic policy in place that would either encourage or stop TM activity. In Owino, some vendors either pay 100 Uganda shillings (10 U.S cents) per night or obtain a permanent place for 5,000 shillings (U.S. $5) from the market authorities. Policies with respect to the operation of the Owino market were created after local restaurants and day market vendors complained that night vendors were taking their business away.[38] The same incident happened at the Nakulabye TM, which used to be along the main road to Wandegeya near the day market. It was removed by the city council after complaints from the day market vendors charged that "customers were no longer buying from the main market as TM offered competitive prices."[39]

Most urbanites want TM activity to be maintained and encouraged rather than abolished. In support of this view, they argue that night market women are helpless people who have no other way to earn a living and that women engaged in TM are able to pay school fees for their children who, in turn, will help them in their old age. Supporters also state that they believe customers need the services offered by those who make candlelight roadside dinners and that only the night market women have been able to fill the demand for inexpensive cooked food. Night market women themselves, however, are divided about whether they favor or oppose government intervention. Because of the disorganized and, at times, unhealthy conditions characteristic of TM markets, some of these women argue that the government or city council should provide proper places from which they can operate, as well as basic amenities such as stalls and streetlights. They also want some provision to regulate prices. Others, however, argue that if they are forced to carry out their TM business off the roadsides they will not be able to attract enough customers. In addition, they fear that government intervention will lead to taxation, which they do not want.

Despite such problems, many vendors evaluate their TM activity favorably because it provides them with incomes with which they can support themselves and their families. Some women state that TM activity has freed them from reliance on men for basic survival and that they are now free to choose their lovers not because they need economic support but because their economic autonomy gives them greater control in their relationships. Moreover, TM has helped them meet the obligation imposed on all citizens to pay a graduated tax and thus assist in the development of the country.

Most night market women have high expectations about what TM will enable them to do in the future. Some believe it will enable them to experience upward mobility and hope to get enough money to move into more lucrative businesses within the informal economy. Many, for example, want to sell hand clothing (*mivumbo*). Others hope to return to the rural areas from which they came. They continue with TM, however, because they have no alternative source of income. Most women hope their TM activities will enable them to survive in a hostile economic environment, educate their children, buy land in the rural area, eventually move to a bigger business, and thus achieve economic independence. Some, who have become outspoken on this issue, have millennial expectations and believe that they will be rewarded with a better life in the future.

There is no question that TM has enabled some women to achieve some semblance of freedom from dependence on male relatives. In this way, it has liberated them from some of the unnecessary social controls that emerge from economic dependence. In most cases, these women vendors control the profits they make from TM activity, although in situations in which women work with male partners or are employed by other women, the profits are controlled by the partners or employers. These women use what they earn to cover day-to-day household expenses, such as buying soap, food, paraffin, and other commodities, and to pay children's school fees, purchase children's clothing, and secure health care. Some of them use the proceeds to support dependent family members, such as elderly parents.

TM is a very empowering experience for the women who participate in it. The fact that researchers found female vendors to be "very aggressive and very money minded" indicates the emergence of a minicapitalist spirit in these women. Four out of the six research assistants reported that many of the female vendors "behave as if they were men, they are very aggressive [and] cannot be easily threatened like women in the old days." This observation suggests that aggressive behavior is not a characteristic of males only, underlining that aggressiveness is a learned trait rather than an inherited one. The women are challenging and breaking down (though with difficulty) the social construction of female and male gender characteristics.

CONCLUSION

The political and economic crises in Uganda since independence have dramatically transformed the lives of Baganda women. These women have been pulled into the informal sector of the economy more than at any other time in their history. The Ugandan case illustrates that women collectively have had less access to the civil service jobs or the lucrative trades in the formal sector than men. Nonetheless, some women have profited from their participation in the informal sector as candlelight dinner providers. Their trading roles have been and continue to be essential for the development of Kampala and its suburbs. Women cater to, and maintain the resurgent process of, urbanization by their participation in food production in the rural areas and the sale of processed foods in TM.

The social organization through which cooked meals are produced by the night market candlelight women vendors and consumed by the customers reveals important social networks, class relationships, and linkages between the formal and informal sectors of the economy. In many ways, the contemporary manifestations of capitalism drew upon and transformed existing cultures and social relations, including gender relationships. This study has shown that the capitalist social relations can be modified and reinforced within the indigenous social, cultural, political, and economic arenas.

Candlelight dinners on Kampala's suburban streets not only illustrate the integration of Baganda women into market activities but also demonstrate how a social activity that was once limited to the household has become a business activity. The problems these women face are dictated by forces outside of their control. Moreover, the restructuring of choices available to consumers is being dictated by the rising food and fuel costs brought about by the changes in the economic structure. Thus, emerging patterns through which cooked food is provided and consumed relate to the changing patterns in the levels of public and private expenditure. These same patterns indicate a need for the rise of a fast-food industry, as women start with small-scale self-employment for basic survival in a hostile economic environment.

Toninyira mukange offers on-site meal consumption or "take-away" options at prices that are very attractive and comparable to those of raw food. The "menu" at the sites offers a variety of attractive foods all cooked in the traditional way. Customers, apart from those who take the food home, do not have to wash dishes or follow certain customary eating rituals. Moreover, they are not rushed. Nor do they share in the work. Another advantage to the vendor is that there is no prior direct commercial advertising. Instead, advertising is done on site by direct inspection of already prepared food, and thus luring potential buyers; the competition between vendors is a real drama. Most important, the meals are affordable, delicious, and ethnically authentic and acceptable.

A systematic study of the changes currently under way in Kampala and its suburbs, involving the activities of these night market women food vendors, is needed to further look into the composition of the labor force outside the household, changes in the financial contribution of women and men to the domestic unit, and the social networks through which TM participants are linked to the street and neighborhood cultures and to the wider economy and society.

NOTES

1. The kingdom is called *Buganda*; the people, *Baganda*; the language, *Luganda*; the culture, *Kiganda;* and the country, *Uganda*.

2. Vali Jamal, "The Agrarian Context of the Uganda Crisis," in *Changing Uganda*, edited by Holger Bernt Hansen and Michael Twaddle (London: James Currey, 1991), p. 81.

3. Ibid.; Vali Jamal, "Coping under Crisis in Uganda," *International Labour Review*, Vol. 127, No. 6, 1988, pp. 679–701.

4. Jamal, "Agrarian Context," p. 95.

5. "Employment, Incomes, Basic Needs and Structural Adjustment Policy in Uganda, 1980–87," in *The IMF, the World Bank and the African Debt*, vol. 2, edited by Bade Onimade (London: Zed Books, 1989), p. 101.

6. Loxley acted as an economic advisor to the Ugandan government when President Museveni engaged the services of a Canadian government research agency (IDRC) about economic recovery plans (1988).

7. John Loxley, "The IMF, the World Bank and Reconstruction in Uganda," in *Structural Adjustment in Africa: Côte d'Ivoire, Cameroon, Ghana, Morocco, Madagascar, Tanzania, Uganda, Zimbabwe*, edited by Bonnie Campbell and John Loxley (London: Macmillan, 1989), p. 71.

8. Ibid., p. 72; see also, E. O. Ochieng, "Economic Adjustment Programmes in Uganda, 1985–88," in *Changing Uganda*, edited by Holger Bernt Hansen and Michael Twaddle (London: James Currey, 1991), p. 43.

9. Joshua B. Mugyenyi, "IMF Conditionality and Structural Adjustment under the National Resistance Movement," *Changing Uganda*, p. 63.

10. Ibid., p. 65.

11. Reginald Green, "The Broken Pot: The Social Fabric, Economic Disaster and Adjustment in Africa," in *The IMF, the World Bank and the African Debt*.

12. Diane Elson, "How is Structural Adjustment Affecting Women?" *Development*, Vol. 1, 1989, p. 60.

13. Ibid., p. 71.

14. Christine Obbo, "Women, Children and a Living Wage," *Changing Uganda*, p. 108.

15. Janet MacGaffey, with Vwakyanakazi Mukohya, Rukarangira wa Nkera, Brooke Grundfest Schoepf, Makwala ma Mavambu ye Beda, and Walu Engundu, *The Real Economy of Zaire* (London and Philadelphia: James Currey and University of Pennsylvania Press, 1991), p. 9.

16. "Initiatives from Below: Zaire's Other Path to Social and Economic Restructuring," in *Governance and Politics in Africa*, edited by Goran Hyden and Michael Bratton (Boulder, Colo.: Lynne Rienner Publishers, 1992), p. 243.

17. Paul Bohannan and George Dalton, *Markets in Africa: Eight Subsistence Economies in Transition* (Garden City, N.Y.: Doubleday & Company, 1965), p. 5.

18. Ibid., pp. 2–3.

19. Ibid., p. 25.

20. A. W. Southall and P. C. W. Gutkind, *Townsmen in the Making: Kampala and Its*

Suburbs, East African Studies No. 9 (Kampala: East African Institute of Social Research, 1957), p. 54.

21. A. B. Mukwaya, "The Marketing of Staple Foods in Kampala, Uganda," *Markets in Africa*, p. 56.

22. See Christine Obbo, *African Women: Their Struggle for Economic Independence* (London: Zed Press, 1980), Chap. 2.

23. Vali Jamal, "Uganda's Economic Crisis: Dimensions and Care," in *Beyond Crisis—Social Development in Uganda: Proceedings of the UNICEF-MSIR Conference, Mweya Lodge*, edited by Cole Dodge and Paul Wieke (New York: Pergamon Press, 1987), p. 126.

24. See Obbo, *African Women*, pp. 23–24.

25. Ibid., p. 22.

26. See Obbo, *African Women*; Jamal, "Uganda's Economic Crisis."

27. See Mahmood Mamdani, *Imperialism and Fascism in Uganda* (New York: Heinemann Educational Books, 1983), p. 37.

28. Ibid.; Banugire Firimooni, "The Political Economy of *Magendo* Society: The Case of Uganda," Makerere Institute of Social Research (MISR), Academic Forum, 1985; Banugire Firimooni, "Class Struggle, Clan Politics and the *Magendo* Economy," Fourth Mawazo Workshop, Makerere University, April 26–28, 1985; Banugire Firimooni, "Towards an Appropriate Policy Framework for a *Magendo* Economy," *Eastern Africa Social Science Research Review*, Vol. 2, No. 2, 1986; "Employment, Incomes, Basic Needs and Structural Adjustment Policy in Uganda, 1980–87," in *The IMF, the World Bank and the African Debt*, edited by Bade Onimade, pp. 95–110.

29. See Vali Jamal, "Coping under Crisis in Uganda," *International Labour Review*, Vol. 128, No. 6, 1988, p. 687.

30. Jamal, "Uganda's Economic Crisis," p. 123.

31. Mamdani, *Imperialism and Facism*, pp. 39, 53. Mamdani describes this new social group as "a class of persons for whom fascist terror provided a framework for quick enrichment. These were the main local beneficiaries of the Amin regime. [Their] investments were directed towards high-risk, quick-return activities. They preferred commerce to productive investments, and magendo to legal commerce." According to Mamdani, their lifestyle "was marked by incessant and conspicuous consumption. They lived like a declining nobility, determined to make as big a show of their wealth as possible. Each competed with the other to deck 'his' women with the most expensive jewelry. . . . Show-off, decadence and waste—these were the hall-marks of mafutamingi life" (p. 39).

32. Jamal, "Uganda's Economic Crisis," p. 129.

33. See Mamdani, *Imperialism and Fascism*, pp. 48–49.

34. *Munno*, April 25, 1974; *Voice*, April 25, 1974; see also Mamdani, *Imperialism and Fascism*, pp. 51–52.

35. Other locations where research is being undertaken include Kikoni, Najjanankumbi, Kalerwe, Wandegeya, Owino, and Katwe.

36. Research Notes, 1992.

37. The youths use special whistle sounds to warn each other and to communicate other messages. Research assistants gathered terminologies whose meanings are not yet clear to us.

38. Similar complaints led the city council to remove the Nakulabye TM, which was near the day market along the main road to Wandegeya. Vendors in the day market complained that night market vendors had taken away their business.

39. Research Notes, 1993.

Chapter 8

Women's Fresh Produce Marketing in Harare, Zimbabwe: Motivations for Women's Participation and Implications for Development

Nancy E. Horn

Throughout the developing world, women struggle daily to meet their family food-provisioning needs and to generate incomes. This chapter considers one subset of women—those in Harare, Zimbabwe—who have chosen to fulfill their goals in a particular way—by selling fresh produce from market stalls and streetside tables. The chapter, based on research conducted in Zimbabwe from September 1985 to December 1986 and in July 1993, answers two questions: (1) why do women elect to engage in fresh produce marketing enterprises in the so-called urban informal sector? and (2) how do these activities contribute to economic growth? The response to the first question is presented through an analysis of the sociohistorical parameters of the labor reserve economy that precipitated women's movement into Harare and their need to earn an income, the employment and sociopolitical constraints limiting their choices to earn an income, and state failure to recognize women's role in providing food security to economically vulnerable populations. The response to the second question is presented through an analysis of current development policies and initiatives aimed at assisting enterprises in the informal sector in Zimbabwe. The final section of the chapter discusses ways the state might be more supportive of women's efforts to provide food to the urban community and thus promote economic growth.

THE LABOR RESERVE ECONOMY AND WOMEN'S TRADE

Rural cultural practices of Shona-speaking people assign to women the responsibility for provisioning their families. To fulfill this role, women were given domain over a well-watered *vlei* or streambank plot to grow garden crops; they also labored in the rainfed fields of their husbands to cultivate staple crops for the family granary. Any surplus of women's *mawoko* (labor of the hands) could be traded with kin and nonkin in an exchange network that ensured rural food security.[1]

During the colonial era, which began with the arrival of the Pioneer Column from South Africa in 1890, fertile lands cultivated by Africans were appropriated by settlers. Reserves or Tribal Trust Lands in areas less suitable for farming were created for African habitation, thus limiting productivity. Hut taxes were imposed on Africans to induce them to work for commercial farms and mines established by the settlers.[2] Women attempted to stave off the need for tax-induced labor migration of their husbands by selling agricultural surpluses to settlers. Their attempts produced limited success but were attenuated by the enactment of laws curtailing the sale of food crops by Africans. Hence, in the long run, African men provided the labor needed for production in white-owned mines, cities, and commercial farms.[3]

As men migrated, women began exercising total domain over rural production, either *de jure* or *de facto*. Colonial policies necessitated that women be left behind on the farm to continue providing food to the family, members of which were both in the reserves and at the migrant worksites. The settlers used this as a rationale for keeping men's wages low.[4] On periodic visits to Harare, wives brought foodstuffs to their husbands residing in the barracks and dormitories near their workplaces; but most fresh produce could not be stored. Hence the daily need for fresh vegetables and fruits led to the development of markets at the migrant worksites.

Recognizing that a market existed in all migrant labor locations, African women in adjacent reserves began selling their surplus harvests.[5] Although strict urban-influx laws were promulgated to keep Africans, especially those unemployed, out of the city centers, African women traders were allowed access. Their marketing roles were viewed unofficially as an effective means of keeping Africans out of the city centers where shops that catered to a white clientele were located.[6]

During the 1950s, after the passage of the African Land Husbandry Act, male heads of households were classified *either* as urban migrant laborers, or as rural farmers. While there were many difficulties in enforcing this law, it required urban employers to construct family housing for their African laborers.[7] With the availability of family housing in the urban townships and with declining productivity in the Tribal Trust Lands, women also migrated to the capital city, Salisbury (later renamed Harare).

In town, women were beset with the problem of how to provision their families or to grow food crops without plots to cultivate. Where men were earning sufficiently, food provisions could be purchased. In most instances, however, artificially low wages necessitated a second income to maintain the household. How could women provide food to their families and generate cash to supplement their husbands' earnings? Many women followed the example set by women farmers in the neighboring reserves and adapted it to their own urban circumstances.

At first in a quasi-partnership, urban women "ordered" their needs from the rural women farmers who came to Harari township in Salisbury (later renamed Mbare) and resold their purchases at makeshift stands in their own communities. As townships expanded and the need for local trade increased, fresh produce market sites were constructed. Incorporation of such structures in township development plans was not necessarily motivated by colonial recognition of female economic roles but by the segregationist desire *not* to have Africans come into the white domain of the city center to purchase food.[8]

White settlers not interested in farming carved out an agricultural crop-trading niche primarily to satisfy the white settler palate. Through ethnic ties to kin in South Africa, many fresh produce and staple commodities were imported. Until settler farms were fully operational, traders also purchased or bartered with African growers for their surpluses.[9] With the Unilateral Declaration of Independence (UDI) in 1965 and the imposition of trading sanctions, traders were instrumental in the development of domestic horticultural crop production. Whites grew the crops; traders purchased them wholesale and then resold them to institutions such as hospitals, schools, or the military and to greengrocers seeking high-quality produce for resale in the white suburbs. Disposal of lesser grades was primarily through the African women vendors.

White commercial growers, as well as African reserve growers, came to the townships to sell their products. While many direct purchasers were African women vendors, sales were often cumbersome for growers because the amounts purchased were relatively small. To bridge the gap between growers and retailers, African men established wholesaling enterprises at *Mbare musika* (market).

In this bifucarated marketing system, white commercial growers traded their product with white wholesalers, who in turn distributed the commodities to institutions and white greengrocers. African growers, on the other hand, traded their product largely at Mbare either to African wholesalers or vendors or to consumers directly. White growers also disposed of their produce at Mbare, but only those grades that did not meet the quality demands of their clientele. After independence in 1980, African growers, who were able to grow a high-quality product, traded with white wholesalers.[10]

As a consequence of colonialism, the creation of the labor reserve economy, and the establishment of reserves, many men and women migrated to Harare and sought to make economic sense out of their alien work environment. Without the means to maintain their families and unable to find adequately compensated work, women adopted trading strategies to earn an income. Despite the racially bifurcated marketing channels directing the distribution of food commodities, African women developed strategies to overcome constraints in order to generate incomes to supplement their husbands' wages or to become individually self-sufficient. Women's work ethic, self-reliance, and tenacity were thus major contributing factors to the development of urban food security.

Why was produce vending, as an income-earning activity, so attractive to so many women? It can be argued that economic need and cultural role ascription brought women to this occupation. The knowledge they acquired in the rural cultivation of horticultural crops, however, provided a particular impetus. At this juncture, I advance an argument that might provide an underlying rationale for the establishment of fresh produce microenterprises.

Sahlins draws an analytical distinction between production for use and production for exchange in precapitalist, nonmarket economies.[11] His theories can be illustrated by examining Malinowski's work in the western Pacific, which found that the islanders produced certain commodities for home consumption but certain others, such as armbands, for exchange with people on the other islands.[12] Exchange served two purposes, one practical and the other symbolic. Practically, many of the items exchanged were foodstuffs needed for survival; symbolically, the size and pedigree of the armbands and other items exchanged represented the cosmological and political status of the person exchanging them. That is, the inherent value of the items exchanged was the acknowledgment and enhancement of the political status of the individuals involved in the trade.

This analysis can be applied to women in Zimbabwe. In the rural areas, women produced horticultural crops to serve two functions, one practical and the other symbolic. Practically, women's harvests fed their families; symbolically, their production indicated acceptance by their husbands' patrilineal ancestors. An extension of this symbolic value was the exchange relationships facilitated by surplus harvests. Hence, acceptance by the ancestors enabled women to produce surpluses to feed their immediate families, other members of the patrilineage, and potentially members of adjacent communities.

In establishing fresh produce microenterprises, women were able to adapt and transform their rural skills to meet the economic needs of an urban environment. Selling horticultural crops can be viewed similarly to rural production. Purchasing wholesale quantities of a commodity enables a vendor to recoup her initial expenditure, as well as make a profit and feed her family. Concretely, this trade allows women to fulfill their traditional provisioning roles in the city where they have little or no chance to cultivate gardens. Symbolically, the customers vendors cultivate indicate a congruence with the ancestors. If customers do not come to a particular stall, it is assumed the vendor has done something to violate ancestral trust. That trust must be reestablished in order that good business can resume.[13] Concerning trade, women also serve a practical and symbolic function. Practically, they provide the city with fresh produce; symbolically, their trade confers status on the community of strangers and helps them to make sense of a chaotic city. Fresh produce mediates relationships with non-kin friends and strangers. Through fair trade with customers, vendors also establish a public reputation for being upright citizens in the community.

The sale of foodstuffs in the city thus entails both use and exchange value. Functionally, they serve to identify women as not only family but also community provisioners. Furthermore, women's trading networks enhance their status. Symbolically, success implies ancestral blessings, required in both rural and urban settings—in the former to cultivate crops, in the latter to cultivate customers.

The knowledge system developed by women in garden crops provided them with skills they could adapt to other areas. When marketing opportunities were presented (i.e., first the settlers and then the migrant laborers), women created a niche for themselves that allowed them not only to continue feeding their families without the direct means to grow crops but also to generate incomes in an environment that offered very limited employment options. Fresh produce vending, for many urban women, was an optimal choice.

SOCIOECONOMIC CONSTRAINTS
AND SURVIVAL STRATEGIES

The urban environment presents a number of economic challenges to household viability and creates the need for a cash flow that is not easily generated by one individual alone. Low wages, especially those paid to unskilled workers, necessitate supplemental earnings to cover rising housing, transportation, and food costs. Complicating their coping strategies are the broader economic stresses brought about by poverty, the parameters of urban development, and the recently imposed Economic Structural Adjustment Program (ESAP). What many urban women, living on the brink of poverty, seek are reliable income-generating activities that will provide the means to meet family survival expenditures. Given the limited range of employment opportunities open to women, many establish enterprises in the informal sector.

The following analysis, discussing many of the reasons women have elected to establish fresh produce marketing enterprises, utilizes data collected during focal group and individual interviews conducted with approximately 3,400 vendors in Harare, Zimbabwe, from September 1986 to December 1987 and during July 1993. The analysis considers aspects of the broader political economy of the city, as well as individual motivations for entering the fresh produce trade.

City life requires daily expenditures for food and transportation. If an individual is employed, wages—usually paid at the end of the month—generally cannot be stretched to meet all household needs. Thus, to prevent end-of-the-month stress, many women seek income-generating activities that provide daily cash.[14]

According to the 1982 census, 18.5 percent of the adult labor force was unemployed. For males, the inability to find work is directly related to levels of education achieved; for females, unemployment rates are higher regardless of years of education.[15] In my survey of fresh produce vendors, 19.7 percent (47) of those married reported that their husbands were unemployed, 1.2 percent higher than the national average, despite the educational levels that they had achieved (see Table 8.1). The average age of spouses, 42, may be related to unemployment figures. At an earlier point in Zimbabwean history, the completion of primary school would have provided more than enough skills needed to find employment, but independence and the imposition of ESAP have changed the nature of the demand to better educated and more highly skilled individuals. These factors have created the "bumping" phenomenon (older, less educated employees are being replaced by younger, more educated recruits). As a result of male unemployment and low wages, females must find employment.

For many urban women, the range of employment opportunities is limited because of their education. As a result of the availability of very few formal-sector jobs for uneducated women, many establish microenterprises in the informal sector, and some in fresh produce trade (see Table 8.2).

The age of the vendor relates to the amount of education received: the younger the vendor, the more education she has received. Years in school, however, cannot be directly correlated with employment. After their arrival in Harare, some vendors reported they had sought and found work in a number of enterprises: 22.5 percent (73) had been employed as domestics; of the remaining 35 who reported working for a salary, formal activities included working as a shopgirl; in a creche or nursery school if they had received training; making greeting cards; sewing in a clothing factory; cleaning in a hotel, hospital, or office building; and as casual laborers in the tobacco industry. Most of these jobs were not compatible with women's domestic responsibilities and could not be sustained over the long term.

Lack of adequate education and formal-sector employment opportunity, as well

Table 8.1
Educational Levels of Husbands of Female Fresh Produce Vendors in Harare, 1985–1987

Educational Level	Percentage	Number*
None	18.9	45
Grade 1-3	8.4	20
Grade 4-5	13.9	33
Grade 6-7	26.5	63
Form 1-2	24.8	59
Form 3-4	3.8	9
> Form 4	3.8	9

* N = 238.

Table 8.2
Educational Levels of Female Fresh Produce Vendors in Harare, 1985–1987

Educational Level	Percentage	Number*
None	18.8	60
Grade 1-3	14.4	46
Grade 4-5	21.9	70
Grade 6-7	27.2	87
Form 1-2	15.0	48
Form 3-4	2.5	8
> Form 4	.3	1

* N = 320.

as compatibility of work with childcare, have guided women into "informal" economic activities, including buying and selling clothing, knitting and selling sweaters, operating a tuckshop (kiosk), hairdressing, catering, and crocheting tablecloths and articles of clothing for sale.[16] While many of these enterprises are lucrative, they generate cash only periodically and rely upon a market highly dependent on disposable income. Fresh produce vending seems to be more attractive since daily purchasing yields daily cash.

The impact of rising unemployment rates has exacerbated social problems, giving rise to a greater probability of marital dissolution and the rising incidence of children born to single women. If spousal support has been discontinued, women must provide for their children alone. Moreover, if education has limited female income-generating choices, the presence of small children limits it further. Formal-sector workplaces do not provide daycare, and the economics of urban life militate against the probability of having a responsible caregiver continuously present in the home. While many vendors indicated the presence of other adults in their homes, the large numbers of small children in the marketplace attested to the absence of other caregivers. Thus, women must identify an income-generating activity that is compatible with childcare. The informal marketplace offers that opportunity.

It is assumed that members of a household (those who can) contribute financial resources to meet the expenditures incurred for their benefit. This assumption needs reexamination. African women living in the high-density suburbs of Harare appear to be in a constant struggle to earn an income regardless of their marital status. Among fresh produce retailers, 73.3 percent reported being married (see Table 8.3), but a smaller percentage reported a resource-sharing ethic in their households.

Table 8.3
Marital Status of Female Fresh Produce Vendors in Harare, 1985–1987

Status	Perentage	Number*
Married	60.9	192
Divorced/Remarried	4.4	14
Widowed/Remarried	1.9	6
Married/Polygynous		
One other wife	5.7	18
> One other wife	0.3	1
TOTAL MARRIED	73.3	231
Divorced	14.0	44
Widowed	11.7	37
Single	1.0	3
TOTAL NOT MARRIED	26.7	84

* N = 315.

Of the total number of women who reported they had spouses, 76.6 percent (177) indicated their husbands were working, but that only 71.7 percent (165) of the total number were earning salaries. Only 46 percent (106) knew their husbands' earnings, and they reported that incomes ranged between Z$30 and Z$1,500 per month, with the mean of Z$172.73. Despite marital status and husbands' income levels, out of the total number of married women, only 34 percent (79) reported that their husbands share their earnings in helping to pay for household expenses, school fees, health care, and the like.[17] As an alternative to providing financial support, I thought men might contribute foodstuffs and other household items they had purchased themselves. I found that only 1.3 percent (3) of husbands reportedly provide these inputs.

Analysis of these data implies that household pooling of resources may be non-existent in many cases. A more appropriate analysis of income and expenditure in the urban household may reflect a "separate purse" or gender-based division of financial responsibilities in which women and men are responsible for providing separate resources to the family. Historically, in the rural areas women generally provided all manner of cultivated foodstuffs, whereas men provided meat and other family necessities. In urban areas, women continued to be responsible for feeding their families, but the lack of land to cultivate required that most foodstuffs be purchased. House rents, utility bills, clothing expenses, and school fees, all of which require cash, became the responsibility of men who were earning incomes.[18] As a consequence of changes in the urban family, however, women now either share or assume total financial responsibility (especially in the case of single female parents) for food, clothing, housing, and educating their children. Fulfilling these responsibilities is both a motivation for and a consequence of their ability to generate an income.

Selling fresh produce as an income-generating activity also satisfies other needs. As discussed earlier, African women are responsible for family food provisioning. Urban living, however, does not afford them the wherewithal to grow crops. Housing plots do not have adequate garden space, and the cost of real estate is prohibitive, necessitating temporary lodging in other people's houses.[19] Consequently, urban dwellers, for the most part, must purchase their food.[20] This means that some cost-efficient methods must be employed to maintain a household. In this case, fruit and vegetable vending is cost efficient; wholesale expenditures are recouped in a portion of retail sales, families can eat any remainder, and a profit can still be realized. Thus, a cultural role is fulfilled in the process of meeting economic objectives.

The economic contributions women make to rural households are facilitated by their work in and domain over gardens. In the urban areas, women must carve out an economic domain. The challenge they face is how to adapt their skills to a different environment in order to continue fulfilling their gender-based roles. An urban area parallel to their rural garden domain must be established.[21] Fresh produce vending for many has become that substitute. Similar to the pride women take in their horticultural crop harvests (indicating ancestral blessing), vendors exhibit a "pride of professionalism" in their urban businesses. Women are not only able to feed their families from their professional activities but also to establish public reputations for serving the community by keeping food costs low.

This pride of professionalism was incorporated in women's business operations. Vendors hand-picked their wholesale purchases because they know their customers' needs. Although group purchasing might have reduced wholesale cost, it might also have reduced the number of vendor "regulars" (customers). Just as a rural woman might hand-pick crops to feed her family, so too urban vendors carefully choose stocks to sell to their customers. Consequently, women provision their communities much as they provision their families; the urban community has become a substitute for their rural kin.

On the household level, if a woman marries, bears children, divorces, and subsequently remarries, the second husband usually refuses to support the children of the previous marriage if the wife has custody. Custody of children will reside in women if bridewealth has not been paid,[22] if the families of widows do not want the financial burden of the children, or if the husband refuses to take them after divorce. Thus, if a woman wants the children of her first marriage to be educated, she must develop her own financial means.[23] Through vending food crops in daily demand and utilizing the opportunities daily cash intake affords in accessing other funds, women can pay for their children's education.

Data collected on vendor cash intake revealed weekly gross incomes of anywhere between Z$1.81 and Z$242.08. Low income necessitates access to other resources. In establishing cash fluidity, vendors can participate in daily revolving credit and savings societies. Of the 325 vendors interviewed, 56.9 percent (185) indicated they belong to these societies and that they contributed between Z$0.10 and Z$10.00 per day. Although a daily outlay is required, a vendor could receive a sizable lump sum at stated intervals depending on the number of participants. Those amounts could pay for school fees,[24] funerals, larger household purchases or could be used to purchase larger stocks at the end of the month when salaries are paid out or at Christmas bonus time when urban dwellers purchase gifts of food for rural kin.

The professional bonding generated in sharing space over time has promoted an intervendor reliability such that when one must be absent another can sell for her. Some 36.9 percent (120) indicated that in their absence another vendor sells for them. Bonding has its limitations, however. The remaining vendors indicated that a relative or their children would come to sell for them, the reason being that in matters involving finances coworkers cannot always be trusted.

The motivations just discussed serve both a practical and a symbolic function. Practically, vendors overcome the challenge of fulfilling their provisioning roles in an urban environment without the means to cultivate. In doing so, they also find the means to adapt their skills to support their families and send their children to school. Symbolically, vendors maintain the pride they feel in trading a surplus with kin and non-kin by supplying their communities with daily food. Pride and practicality are both served in gaining access to other financial resources made possible by daily cash intakes.

STATE OVERSIGHT AND NEGLECT

The entrepreneurial behavior of fresh produce market women in Harare is an outgrowth of historical circumstances, cultural work ethics, and individual resiliency in adapting skills honed in the rural areas to fit the parameters of urban areas. Incomes generated from the sale of horticultural commodities have been used to educate several generations, purchase housing, clothe families, and maintain rural kin. A direct outcome of women's behavior has been the citywide distribution of fresh produce at prices affordable even to the most vulnerable groups. Despite these development outcomes, market women must maintain their enterprises in a policy context that is blind to their efforts. Lack of recognition of women's efforts can be viewed from at least two perspectives (i.e., gender and the commodities of their trade).

Although the precolonial economic division of labor relied upon and recognized women for their contributions to the maintenance of their households, the imposition of the labor-reserve economy relegated women to subservient spousal supporters. The orientation of colonists toward women and their economic activities was that any amounts they could generate would be redistributed by the family patriarch. Many misassumptions about African society on the part of the colonial government led to failure to consider women's economic activities as anything more than trivial. When women began selling fresh produce in the urban townships, the incomes they generated were not considered meaningful. A similar mindset influences urban policy and development efforts today.

In the design of markets in the high-density suburbs (the former townships) where the majority of Africans live, as many as 105 stalls have been constructed in one location to accommodate vendors. When conducting my research, I saw at once that creating a regular clientele that would yield livable incomes was impossible; there was simply too much competition. Little, if any, attention was paid to the needs of the vendors. I view this policy failure as the direct result of planners' views of women and of the commodities in which they trade. Planners do not recognize that market women are conducting legitimate businesses; nor do they take into account women's activities in the urban distribution of food commodities, thus serving as the end transaction point in a production–marketing chain of perishable commodities.

Lack of state recognition has translated into hardships for market women, made even more onerous by urban policies. These include bus routes that make transporting purchases from wholesale to retail markets very cumbersome and costly, lack of security at each market to prevent theft and harassment, relaxation of zoning laws to allow ad hoc vending throughout the city, and increased rents for stall space decreasing profit margins.

While market women and their fresh produce form an integral part of the urban landscape, plans to improve agricultural marketing fail to take them into account. Hence, in 1986 when the European Economic Community (EEC) developed a plan to assist African producers to be more efficient in horticultural crop production and to upgrade the facilities at *Mbare musika*, no provision was made to alleviate the distribution and marketing constraints women must overcome to get their products to consumers. When I revisited Zimbabwe in 1993, I found that the male wholesalers at *Mbare musika* were able to prevent the implementation of the EEC plan by formally protesting to the city council. As a result, the market was improved, but not in the way envisioned by the EEC. In the adjacent market, where approximately 1,200 women sell fruits and vegetables retail, no improvements were made; and women must continue to construct their own stall shelters. The same is true in many high-density suburban locations where permanent markets have not been constructed.

City council and urban planners' neglect of market women's needs has meant that fresh produce vendors bear many expenses that are not readily passed on to their customers. Supermarkets and greengrocers in the low-density suburbs have their fresh produce delivered by wholesalers; vendors must take daily bus transport to the wholesalers and "emergency taxis" (Peugeot 404 station wagons) or lorries to their retail sites, thus incurring expenditures in both directions. Wholesalers catering to the needs of low-density suburban clientele obtain all the commodities needed by a customer, even if it means contacting another wholesaler; market women must go to *Mbare musika* first to see if the commodities they need are there, and then take several buses to other wholesale markets to obtain what they need. Supermarkets and greengrocers pay for their commodities monthly; vendors must pay daily and are not extended credit. When wholesale prices rise seasonally, supermarkets and greengrocers increase the prices of commodities; vendors absorb seasonal cost increases to maintain their customers. Supermarkets and greengrocers can store any unsold perishables in coolers to prolong freshness; most vendors do not have any storage space at their stalls and must head-carry to their homes what they have not sold.

Despite state neglect of market women's activities, more than half the vendors I interviewed have maintained their enterprises for more than twenty years. They have indeed contributed to the welfare of their families and enhanced urban food security for many economically vulnerable groups.[25] What could the state do to "legitimize" market women's operations and alleviate their constraints?

The need to provision the city with fresh produce is juxtaposed against the lack of resources available to do so with greater efficiency. Entrepreneurs must rely on their own resources to expand their operations. If market women's activities are acknowledged as integral to the development of the agricultural sector and supported by appropriate government institutions, resources to expand or develop individual enterprises would be available. What is needed first, I believe, is formal (i.e., government) recognition of vendors' operations as the final link in a production–distribution chain of horticultural commodities. Formally incorporated into the agricultural sector, as are the activities of low-density suburban greengrocers, market women would be empowered to insist on the placement of markets, to advise city planners on the optimum number of stalls to allow healthy competition, to lobby for rerouting of city transport, to access any wholesale market in the city, to purchase wholesale commodities on credit, and to develop innovative marketing strategies that would enhance their income-earning abilities.

Failure by government to recognize market women's activities as legitimate long-term businesses has led to malinformed ESAP policies detrimental to vendors. Because of the relaxation of vending-site regulations, unemployed school dropouts and individuals whose employment has been retrenched and are unable to find other jobs have developed ad hoc trading sites throughout the city, especially at bus stops. Other ESAP policies have increased the cost of all food commodities through devaluation and deregulation. The resulting impoverishment has limited the quantity of food a family can purchase. Consequently, vendors are not able to conduct the same volume of trade they once did or experience the same level of profit. In effect, failure to recognize the integral urban food distribution roles vendors play has precipitated their decline.

ESAP has focused government attention on the informal sector as a locus to instigate growth and development. Among those concerned with the reduction of government expenditure and expanding the capabilities of the private sector, the informal sector is now viewed as an untapped resource. Funding is being made available to microentrepreneurs to develop products needed by formal-sector enterprises. Together, it is envisioned, productivity partnerships will be established to provide training to microentrepreneurs while at the same time satisfying the needs of value-added production businesses. Marketing enterprises, unfortunately, are not a part of this plan. Market women must therefore continue taking risks and incur a range of expenditures in order to remain in business.

The impact of market women's income-earning activities must also be viewed as integral to urban development. When I asked vendors in both focal-group and individual interviews why they sold vegetables, the second most important reason was to send their children to school (the first was to feed their families). The children of vendors often came to the market after school to relieve their mothers for a few hours. Mothers proudly reported to me that "these vegetables send this one to school!" In establishing their own microenterprises, by creating a community reputation for themselves as fair traders, and by enabling their children to create a better future through education, vendors feel empowered to effect positive changes for themselves and their families.

CONCLUSION

Historically, women in Zimbabwe developed a marketing niche based upon their ability to adapt rurally generated skills to an urban environment. The labor reserve economy forced members of the household to earn supplementary sums of cash in order to ensure urban survival. Women's work ethic, however, was and remains today a constant resource in development. With little formal assistance, vendors expanded their marketing niche that today entails the purchase and resale of tons of horticultural crop commodities; and they supply more than a million urban dwellers with their fresh produce needs.

The ability of women to further develop their enterprises requires official government recognition of their integral role in the maintenance of their families, in educating the next generation, and in provisioning the urban community. Development will be highly problematic, however, if ESAP or similar policies continue to chip away at their self-reliant abilities. Instead, official policies should make several resources available to vendors: credit, training, education, appropriate facilities, and a supportive transportation system. With these inputs, vendors could access credit to implement innovative marketing strategies, be trained to become more efficient managers, purchase small shops or stalls with amenities, and be able to convey the commodities unencumbered by inflated transport costs. Official recognition would also allow women to operate their enterprises as legitimate businesses.

The critical missing element in market women's growth and development is a political environment that recognizes and emphasizes their self-reliant activities as a model for development. Their history of tenacity, blended with a work ethic that views their economic contributions as an element integral to family and community survival, should serve as a cornerstone in the creation of policies to promote growth and development.

NOTES

1. Joan May, *Zimbabwean Women in Colonial and Customary Law* (Gweru, Zimbabwe: Mambo Press, 1983); Elizabeth Schmidt, *Peasants, Traders and Wives. Shona Women in the History of Zimbabwe, 1870–1939* (Portsmouth, N.H.: Heinemann, 1992).

2. George Kay, *Rhodesia: A Human Geography* (New York: Africana, 1970).

3. Schmidt, *Peasants*.

4. M. Yudelman, *Africans on the Land* (Cambridge: Cambridge University Press, 1964).

5. Schmidt, *Peasants*; Terri Barnes and Everjoyce Win, *We Live a Better Life. An Oral History of Women in the City of Harare, 1930–1970* (Harare: Baobab Books, 1992).

6. Terri Barnes, "African Female Labour and the Urban Economy of Colonial Zimbabwe, with Special Reference to Harare, 1920–39," M.A. thesis, Department of History, University of Zimbabwe, 1987.

7. See A. K. H. Weinrich, *African Farmers in Rhodesia* (London: Oxford University Press, 1975), for some of the reasons for its abandonment in 1962.

8. Settler colonialists held very specific views about Africans in urban areas: "The native is a visitor in our white towns for the purpose of assisting the people who live in towns and that no other natives should be present in the towns unless he is of some assistance to the white people inhabiting them" (Southern Rhodesia, Legislative Assembly, *Debates* 1935: cols. 583–584).

9. Robin Palmer, "Agricultural History of Rhodesia," in *The Roots of Rural Poverty in Central and Southern Africa*, edited by Robin Palmer and Neil Parsons (London: Heinemann, 1977), pp. 221–254.

10. See Barry A. Kosmi, "Ethic and Commercial Relations in Southern Rhodesia: A Socio-Historical Study of the Asians, Hellenes and Jewish Population, 1898–1943," Ph.D. dissertation, Department of History, University of Rhodesia, 1974, for an analysis of the segregated development of this market.

11. Marshall Sahlins, *Stone Age Economics* (New York: Aldine, 1972).

12. B. Malinowski, *Argonauts of the Western Pacific* (London: Routledge, 1922).

13. At a majority of vending sites, vendors told me of the *muti* (medicine, herbs) sprinkled on a stall to lure customers or to deflect customers from neighboring stalls. The medicines used have cosmological meaning and are linked, through *nganga* (traditional healer), to the ancestors.

14. Joan May, *African Women in Urban Employment* (Gweru, Zimbabwe: Mambo Press, 1979); see Brahima D. Kaba, *Profile of Liberian Women in Marketing* (Monrovia: University of Liberia Press, 1982), for a similar analysis for Liberia.

15. Zimbabwe, Central Statistical Office, *Main Demographic Features of the Population of Zimbabwe: An Advance Report Based on a Ten Percent Sample* (Harare: Government Printer, 1985), pp. 122–130.

16. Mary Osirim, "Beyond Simply Survival: Women Microentrepreneurs in Harare and Bulawayo, Zimbabwe," in *Urban African Women*, edited by Kathleen Sheldon, forthcoming; Michael A. McPherson, *Micro and Small Scale Enterprises in Zimbabwe. Results of a Country-Wide Survey* (East Lansing: Michigan State University, Department of Economics, GEMINI Project, 1991); Katrine Saito, *The Informal Sector in Zimbabwe: The Role of*

Women, Report No. 9006-ZIM (Washington, D.C.: World Bank, 1990); Veronica Brand, *One Dollar Workplaces: A Study of Informal Sector Activities in Magaba, Harare* (Harare: University of Zimbabwe, School of Social Work, 1982); Veronica Brand, Rodreck Mupedziswa, and Perpetua Gumbo, *Women Informal Sector Workers under Structural Adjustment in Zimbabwe. A State of the Art Paper Written as Part of the Research Programme on the Political and Social Context of Structural Adjustment in Sub-Saharan Africa* (Harare: University of Zimbabwe, School of Social Work, 1992).

17. Since I did not interview husbands while conducting this research, I cannot factually report how men dispose of their incomes. According to conversations with the market women, however, all too often men waste their earnings on beer drinking and womanizing. In casual conversations with a range of individuals in Harare, I found that many men invest a portion of their earnings in enterprises that might provide the potential to increase income, such as import–export, transportation, and the like. Many also feel obligated to help siblings through school or to support them until they can be economically self-sufficient.

18. See Rae Lesser Blumberg, *Income under Female vs. Male Control: Differential Spending Patterns and the Consequences When Women Lose Control of Returns to Labor* (Washington, D.C.: World Bank, 1987 [draft]); Eleanor R. Fapohunda, "The Nonpooling Household: A Challenge to Theory," in *A Home Divided: Women and Income in the Third World*, edited by Daisy Dwyer and Judith Bruce (Stanford: Stanford University Press, 1988), pp. 143–154; Nancy Folbre, "The Black Four of Hearts: Toward a New Paradigm of Household Economics," in *A Home Divided: Women and Income in the Third World*, edited by Daisy Dwyer and Judith Bruce, pp. 248–262, for a challenge to the pooling of household resources assumptions.

19. D. H. Patel and R. J. Adams, *Chirambhuyo: A Case Study in Low Income Housing* (Gweru, Zimbabwe: Mambo Press, 1981).

20. ESAP may provide an alternative. Urban dwellers are at great food security risk since the costs of all foods have increased by more than 300 percent over the past several years because of devaluation and rising prices. In order to create a very low cost food resource, people have begun to cultivate in the undeveloped zones between high-density suburbs. During more normal economic times, this practice would be stopped and the plants pulled out of the ground by the city council. At this time, however, regulations preventing cultivation have been relaxed; G. D. Mudimu and Solomon Chigume, "Open Land Cultivation in Harare: Issues and Options," Harare, Department of Agricultural Economics and Extension, University of Zimbabwe, 1993 (draft).

21. See Jane Guyer, *"Women's Work in the Food Economy of the Cocoa Belt,"* Working Paper No. 7, Brookline, Mass., Boston University, 1978, for a discussion of how new tasks are subsumed under existing cultural activities among the Beti of Cameroon and the Yoruba in Nigeria.

22. Joan May, *Zimbabwean Women*.

23. This became such a widespread problem that new marriage laws were promulgated a few years after independence. Under the new laws, a woman can garnish a man's salary to obtain child support. This assumes that a man is employed and earning a salary that can be attached.

24. School fees were reinstated at the primary level in 1993 as a result of ESAP (Zimbabwe, *Zimbabwe. A Framework for Economic Reform [1991–1995]* [Harare: Government Printer, 1991]).

25. For a full definition of food security, see Carl K. Eicher and John M. Staatz, "Food Security Policy in Sub-Saharan Africa," an Invited Paper Prepared for the Nineteenth Conference of the International Association of Agricultural Economists, Malaga, Spain, 1985; and Katrine Saito, *The Informal Sector in Zimbabwe*.

Chapter 9

Trade, Economy, and Family in Urban Zimbabwe

Mary Johnson Osirim

Female market traders, especially in West Africa, are noted for their economic independence, their strength and ingenuity as businesswomen, and their ability to exert significant control over the process of food distribution.[1] From at least the eighteenth century, many women working in this sphere have been quite successful, particularly in terms of their major contributions to their families.[2] Their participation and achievements in this sphere are at least attributable to their significant role in agriculture on the continent.[3] In the current period, however, several structural factors have tended to limit the possibilities for women to achieve economic success, namely, continued discrimination based on their gender, including the gender-based division of labor and the economic crisis that has engulfed most of sub-Saharan Africa.

In the majority of these nations, women still face restricted opportunities in the labor market and in education because of structural inequalities and socialization based on their gender. Women are concentrated in agriculture, where they still produce about 80 percent of all crops on the continent, and informal-sector activities, where they constitute at least 39 percent of all sales workers in Nigeria.[4] Unlike men, they have fewer opportunities and receive little encouragement to obtain training in nontraditional fields, such as manufacturing and high-technology areas, in vocational schools, or through apprenticeships. Although both women and men occupy positions in trade, men generally sell manufactured goods, and women are most often involved in the less lucrative commodities of food and cloth. Thus, women are restricted not only in the niches they can fill in the broad occupational spectrum but also in what goods they can sell in the market. What women do sell often yields smaller cash payments than the trading activities of men.

The international debt crisis of the 1980s dealt an especially severe blow to sub-Saharan Africa. In the case of Zimbabwe, the decline in economic growth by 1988 led to increasing poverty and unemployment by the end of the decade.[5] Under the advice of the World Bank and the International Monetary Fund (IMF), Zimbabwe adopted a Structural Adjustment Program (SAP) in 1990 to tackle the economic problems. Such programs have frequently meant rising costs for food, the removal of government subsidies from vital social services, and the retrenchment of civil service employees. Poor women have been hardest hit by these measures since they have few employment options, are highly dependent on public transportation and subsidized health and education systems, and (as women) bear many of the responsibilities for food purchases. Women in the market experience declining sales and often increased competition from men, who often seek self-employment in the market or in small produce shops after displacement from the formal sector of the economy.

This chapter seeks to explore the realities affecting urban market women in Zimbabwe. To what extent are they limited by the economic crisis, particularly the adoption of a SAP, in their roles as microentrepreneurs? What socioeconomic factors were involved in their decisions to become market traders in the first place? What problems and successes have they experienced in their income-generating activities? What is the relationship between their status in the family or household and their roles as producers in the society? Based on extensive interviews conducted in Harare and Bulawayo, Zimbabwe, in 1991, this chapter examines these questions after a review of some earlier studies that have investigated the roles and status of market vendors in Third World societies.

WOMEN'S ROLES AND STATUS AS TRADERS

Among West African women, whose historical position in market trade is well documented, women's roles in the household and community were based on co-operation, rather than competition in the precolonial period.[6] Women (and men) occupied roles in the public and private spheres and were frequently accorded high status for their activities in the political and economic life of the community.[7] Colonialism and the emergence of capitalism altered this pattern of complementary roles to such an extent that among the Yoruba, for example, a gender-based division of labor evolved in such areas as trading. Women generally controlled items related to subsistence (e.g., food and cloth) while men dominated the trade in goods that generated capital.[8]

The origins of a gender-based division of labor in trading are not limited to African societies, nor are they linked only to the beginning of a capitalist mode of production. Turrittin acknowledges that the Bambara of Mali hold traditional beliefs about what goods are appropriate for a woman to sell: "Women deal mainly in labor-intensive locally produced raw or processed foodstuffs as well as a narrow range of craft products; men deal in items available through long-distance trade."[9] Adding to traditional beliefs concerning the gender-based division of labor among the Bambara are Muslim beliefs (adhered to mainly by those of higher status) that women should not go to the market at all, since this is a public space also occupied by men. Strict differentiation by sex of market activities has also been noted in Latin America. In rural Guatemala, Swetnam observed that women not only sell unprofitable products but are taught by their mothers to do so.[10] Women train their daughters to trade in areas they know, such as food. In addition to this mode of sex-role socialization, these women lack the resources to invest in more profitable trade in durable goods.

Despite the restrictions in market activity by gender, many women have attained success in this field. Even during colonialism, Ghanian women found market trade to be a lucrative venture. Robertson demonstrates that Ga women during the late nineteenth and early twentieth centuries achieved success by "withdrawing from other productive work and devoting themselves fully to trade."[11] One of the significant contributors to success for these women was their creation of informal organizations, such as rotating credit schemes to provide capital for their establishments.[12] According to Sanday, through the organization of trade guilds these women regulated their activities, controlled their own financial resources, and demonstrated a high degree of autonomy.[13]

Women's informal associations today are often limited in what they can achieve for market traders. While they are still important sources of financial (and emotional) support for women, they generally lack the connections to the formal sector of the political and economic institutions that can provide entrepreneurs with larger loans and access to business services for expansion.[14] Clark confirms the lack of available institutional credit for about 90 percent of the urban market women she studied in Ghana and their continued economic dependence on rotating credit schemes, known as *susu*, and on family members for the operation of their businesses. She warns, however, that in a period of adjustment smaller vendors are in an extremely precarious situation because relatives find it difficult to provide monetary gifts or loans since they are also experiencing financial strain.[15] In her study of female and male traders in Mali, Turrittin suggests that the male organization, the Association Villageoise (AV) has surpassed the women's rotating credit schemes in terms of what the female organizations have provided for their members. The AV was responsible for "building a metal-roofed warehouse plastered with concrete to store agricultural materials" and was able to secure credit with the major development bank of Mali for its members.[16]

Therefore, although market women have historically achieved economic independence through these endeavors, they do face contemporary challenges to their status attributable in part to the persistence of gender-based inequalities. Adjustment programs in many Third World nations, however, have further intensified the economic difficulties facing market traders today. In Ghana, for example, devaluation, exchange rate adjustments, and the priority given by the government to nonfood consumer items such as cocoa, have led to lower real incomes for traders since 1984. These vendors, as participants in the informal economy, are experiencing greater competition from the women and men entering this sector as a result of displacement from positions in the public and private spheres, further contributing to reduced earnings.

Although programs to mitigate the social costs of adjustment have been instituted by some Third World states, in the case of Ghana, the credit, skills, and management training provided by such programs were not extended to market traders. These women were also victimized by harassment from the military, who frequently raided the major markets in an effort to confiscate imports and certain manufactured goods that were banned.[17] Similar raids have been noted by market women in Lagos, Nigeria, once austerity measures were established in the early 1980s.[18] While the Ghanaian government applauds the improvements in market infrastructure and roads under structural adjustment, small traders have in fact become more impoverished during this period.[19]

Before the enactment of an adjustment program in Zimbabwe, women market vendors there were already encountering serious problems in operating their businesses. Economic difficulties for some traders were posed by the spoilage and waste of fresh produce resulting from the lack of refrigeration and adequate shelter from the sun, as well as the required weekly payments for stall rentals. The greatest constraint to improving the economic viability of their enterprises was posed by transportation problems in the capital. The lack of adequate buses and taxis and the distance from the major market to the wholesalers, greatly extended the workday of these vendors. These women were also exploited by price gouging from the drivers of "emergency taxis."[20]

Thus, the economic status of many African women in trade has been constrained by a myriad of structural problems besetting them during the past decade. This chapter explores the current position of urban traders in Zimbabwe and how they have tried to cope with the challenges posed by a declining economy and structural adjustment.

RESEARCH METHODS

In 1991, along with two research assistants, I conducted field work among women working as traders in Harare and Bulawayo, Zimbabwe. Interview measures were constructed consisting of four sections: (1) the personal attributes of the businesspeople—their family, educational, and occupational histories; (2) their roles and responsibilities in the family; (3) the operation of their enterprises; and (4) the role of government and nongovernment support services in their activities. In some cases, with the assistance of translators, market women were asked over 100 questions focusing on these issues. In an effort to concentrate the sample, one major market was chosen in each city: in Harare, Mbare market; and in Bulawayo, Manwele market. As part of a larger study, twenty food sellers were interviewed in these two cities.

Estimating the number of market traders in Harare and Bulawayo and their percentage of the current labor force is extremely difficult. No reliable statistics were available at the time of my research. In 1978, it was estimated that 36 percent of urban women were engaged in such forms of self-employment as handicrafts and fruit and vegetable vending.[21] The Zimbabwe labor force survey of 1986–1987 stated that over 64 percent of all informal-sector enterprises were owned by women.[22] During this period, Horn estimated that there were 3,426 vendors in the high- and low-density suburbs of Harare.[23] Given the establishment of the SAP in 1990, rising unemployment, and the mounting financial pressure on poor Zimbabwean families, my research suggests that the number of participants in urban market trade is likely to have increased.

This examination briefly explores some of the critical issues revealed by these women regarding their decisions to start their businesses, the successes and problems they have experienced, particularly under the SAP, their use of support services, and their roles and responsibilities in the family and household.

EDUCATION, MARITAL STATUS, AND ECONOMIC FACTORS IN WOMEN'S ENTREPRENEURSHIP IN ZIMBABWE

The sample of twenty traders in Zimbabwe, admittedly small, was evenly distributed over the two cities studied. Seven women in the Harare sample were Shona, the majority population of Zimbabwe, compared to four participants in Bulawayo who were Ndebele, the indigenous people of the Bulawayo region. Such a distribution is expected, given that the Shona constitute over 70 percent of the population of Zimbabwe, with the Ndebele accounting for about 16 percent.[24] Women from Malawi and Zambia were also found working in both Mbare and Manwele markets. Migrants from these nations are not uncommon, given the proximity of these nations to Zimbabwe, their shared British colonial heritage, and the fact that these three nations were linked through the Central African Federation from 1954 to 1963.

Women in the Bulawayo sample were older, with an average age of 44 years, compared to 38 for Harare. Thus, the mean age of women in the Zimbabwean sample was 41 years. The age of the respondents is an important factor to consider in assessing the educational attainment level of the sample, since older market women are likely to have had fewer opportunities to attend school. Under the Tribal Trust Land System in Zimbabwe, black women's opportunities to attend school were extremely limited.[25] To regulate the quality and mobility of labor, the British allowed black men to attain some formal education and migrate to the cities and towns to work in mines and factories, while women were restricted to agricultural work in the reserves. In some rare cases, black women could receive some formal instruction in the mission schools, which at best provided them with about four years of training in domestic skills.[26] The majority of women in this study had attained some formal education, with half of those in each city attending primary school for four years or less (see Table 9.1). Only one woman in each of

Table 9.1
Educational Attainment of Market Traders in Harare and Bulawayo

Level of Education	Number of Respondents	Percentage
No Formal Schooling	2	10%
Some Primary	10	50%
Completed Primary	3	15%
Completed Primary and Some Secondary	1	5%
Completed Secondary	1	5%
Completed A-Levels	2	10%
Completed Secondary and Teaching Certificate	1	5%
TOTAL	20	100%

the Harare and Bulawayo samples had never attended school. Three traders in Bulawayo had completed their primary studies, and one woman each in Harare and Bulawayo had received A-Level certificates.

Perhaps even more important for the fulfillment of their daily activities is the acquisition of knowledge and skills through informal educational channels. The majority of women revealed that they learned their trade from working with their mothers and other female relatives, often from an early age in the local markets. This early socialization into marketing was also observed by Swetnam in his study of traders in rural Guatemala.[27] In addition to learning "how to sell" from their female relatives, women also acquired other skills through participation in clubs and organizations, such as the Women's Embroidery Club, and government-sponsored programs. Six traders in the Harare sample and four of the Bulawayo participants had received some additional training through these programs. In most cases, women received instruction in the traditional "female" activities of cooking, sewing, and knitting. However, one woman did receive agricultural extension training from the Zimbabwean government; and two women gained skills that could directly benefit them in their marketing activities through the Zimbabwe Women's Bureau and an evening school. Training in banking, financial management, and cooperation was provided by the bureau, while another woman benefited from evening classes in accounting, math, and English at an evening school.

Although this is a very small sample, it should be noted that very few women received training from either government or nongovernment organizations (NGOs) that would directly enhance their performance as market traders. The traders interviewed were willing to participate in such programs, but for the most part they were unaware of any that existed to assist them. While there are programs in Zimbabwe to help women form cooperatives and to support those entrepreneurs establishing small independent firms, few efforts other than the provision of market stalls by the city councils have been undertaken by the state to advance the position of market vendors.[28] Training from female relatives was far more significant in this regard.

Although most vendors in these cities had some additional work experience prior to their participation in market trade, very few had attained white collar employment in the formal sector. The exception to this was one woman in Bulawayo who had earlier taught primary school. Five of these vendors had never engaged in any other income-generating activities prior to their present positions. The remainder of the sample had either been trading in other goods such as textiles or working in low-level service positions as domestics, home childcare workers, nurse's aides, or maintenance staff. Thus, the skills training and participation of these women in the labor market has been and remains along gender lines and, as discussed earlier, is further circumscribed by trade in domestic goods.[29]

Although eight of the twenty participants were married, the majority were currently unmarried single parents. The average number of children among those interviewed was five. Data on the marital status of the sample are shown in Table 9.2. The marital profiles are similar to trends observed nationally and in the region as a whole. The Southern African Development Coordination Conference has reported that 25–40 percent of all households among its member nations, including Zimbabwe, are headed by women and are disproportionately poor.[30]

Table 9.2
Marital Status of Market Traders in Harare and Bulawayo

Marital Status	Number of Respondents	Percentage
Currently Married	8	40%
Divorced	5	25%
Widowed	5	25%
Never Married	2	10%
TOTAL	20	100%

British colonial policies establishing the Tribal Trust Lands, the payment of taxes by blacks, and laws regulating the supply of African labor meant that black men had to migrate to the towns and cities in search of work when their labor was needed by whites. Although these men might have left wives and children in their respective villages, they sometimes began additional relationships with women in the urban areas, and later decided that they were uninterested in continuing their earlier marriages. Some of the market traders in this study, who had previously resided in rural areas, discovered that their husbands were involved in such relationships when they traveled to the cities in search of their spouses. Consequently, many of these women became the principal supporters of their children and engaged in urban market trade as the only available means of accomplishing this task. Others are struggling with former husbands to see children that are now being raised by their former spouses' families.

WHY MARKET TRADE?

How did these women first become involved as traders in the markets? The reason most often cited by these participants, who had been engaged in trade for an average of seven years, was to provide financial support for their families. Given the high percentage of female-headed households, there was a critical need for them to earn some cash income. The next most frequently reported response was the need to *supplement* their husbands' incomes, while others specifically mentioned that they had to provide education for their children. These market traders also explained that it was easy to enter this line of work because it required little startup capital to purchase the initial commodities. This was especially noted by those women who had learned to sew and wanted to begin seamstress shops but were prohibited from starting these enterprises because they did not have sufficient capital to purchase sewing machines and rent space.

Women in Harare who knew how to knit and crochet viewed market trade as a more profitable enterprise because the demand for knitted and crocheted goods is seasonal. Fruit and vegetable vendors were quick to point out that such trade is more lucrative because of the constant demand for food and because these goods can directly help to feed their own families: "I wanted money to put my children through school. With knitting, I only do it if someone places an order. Selling beans meets the daily needs of the local people. I will make more money doing the vegetable and bean business."[31] They also regarded market trade as more profitable than subsistence agriculture or domestic work. In the latter case for women in Zimbabwe, decent wages and stable employment seemed more difficult to come by since many whites left after independence. As one trader commented: "I prefer to spend the day here [in the market] to sitting at home. The business helps me raise my children. After my European employer left the country, it was hard to find another job as a domestic."[32] Further, market trade enabled women to more effectively fulfill their domestic responsibilities, since for example, they could care for their young children in the market:[33] "Trading was one of the easiest things you could do that you didn't need a lot of money to start off with. I could watch my child and do business. When the child gets older, I want to go back to nursing work."[34]

In addition to the lack of money to establish manufacturing or other service enterprises, these women were frequently blocked from pursuing other opportunities in the labor market. Because gender-based discrimination continues to pervade social, economic, and political institutions in Zimbabwe, women are encouraged to pursue activities related to their domestic tasks, such as cooking, sewing, and knitting, in schools and in government and privately sponsored training programs and by their relatives.

As previously discussed, British colonialism significantly restricted both the amount and type of education women could receive; and as a consequence, many older women lack sufficient formal education and skills, which severely limits the types of jobs they can obtain. Today, women still face obstacles in obtaining training for nontraditional occupations. Visits to city government training programs revealed that very few women received training in areas such as carpentry, welding, or high technical fields. Given these circumstances, women chose trading as their only viable alternative.

Because of the current problems in the national economy, these women even faced impediments when they participated in other "female" occupations. Because of unemployment, devaluation, and skyrocketing prices, poor Zimbabweans are frequently unable to purchase needed goods and services. They must seek credit from traders and other microentrepreneurs to obtain these products. One trader in Mbare market remarked that she also knitted for commercial purposes, but this proved unprofitable: "The amount of gain from knitting is very small. [Today] it is difficult to obtain money from people who have credit with you."[35]

Several women became market traders not only because they had been socialized in this trade and had fewer alternatives for income earning in the larger economy but also because they were able to continue ownership of a family member's business. Some traders had taken over the businesses of their mothers, sisters, and even a brother once they had become too sick or financially unable to manage the enterprise. Furthermore, family members had frequently encouraged these women to become traders in the first place, not just by training them in this line of work but by giving advice and showing by example that such businesses could be profitable.

In addition to their encouragement and transmission of trading skills, family members had been instrumental in providing these entrepreneurs with the startup capital for beginning their enterprises. Their parents, siblings, or husbands were responsible in whole or in part for providing the initial capital for these activities for half of the traders in Harare and for seven of the vendors in Bulawayo. In the remaining cases, women used their own savings to start their enterprises. For a few women, these savings were accumulated while working in the formal sector; but in the majority of cases, women were able to save this money from other home-based income-generating activities they had engaged in, such as sewing and knitting. Market traders in this study had not obtained any of their initial capital from

banks, government programs, or NGOs. Thus, without the financial support, training, and encouragement provided by their families, market traders in this study
are likely to have encountered greater difficulties in establishing their businesses.

Starting a business is especially problematic for many poor women today, given
the low level of government support for small businesses and microenterprises
and the increasing pressures families face for basic survival in the midst of economic crisis. The latter situation makes it even more difficult for family members
to pool their resources to enable a female relative to start an enterprise at the
same time that many male family members are unemployed or in the process of
losing their jobs under the vagaries of structural adjustment.

PROBLEMS OF MARKET TRADERS
UNDER STRUCTURAL ADJUSTMENT

Today, African market women are facing mounting difficulties in the workplace and in the household because of the economic crisis engulfing most of
Africa. In Zimbabwe, formal-sector employment growth had declined significantly by 1988, with the national unemployment rate estimated at one million
persons, or 50 percent of the potential labor force.[36] Throughout much of the
decade, the economy and the state faced many problems, including the war in
Matabeland, world recession, drought, and destabilization in the region caused
by South Africa's frequent raids on the frontline states. Zimbabwe was nevertheless able to maintain employment growth and the expansion of social services
until the end of the decade.[37] Unemployment problems in this period, compounded
by the drought that began in 1991, resulted in a decline in domestic production in
1992 of approximately 9 percent.[38]

To counter this economic decline, the government of Zimbabwe, at the urging
of the World Bank and the IMF, adopted a Structural Adjustment Program (SAP)
in 1990. Although the state claims that this program is "home grown," it includes
the same major provisions found in other adjustment programs throughout the
Third World: (1) trade liberalization, (2) reductions in government expenditures,
(3) devaluation, (4) reduced controls over foreign currency, and (5) restrictions
on trade unions.[39]

Early impact of the SAP has most adversely affected the poor.[40] The lifting of
price controls, combined with the drought, has led to food shortages, as well as
increased hunger among this group. Reductions in, and in some cases the removal of, government subsidies for education, health, and transportation have
begun to take their toll. In the short term, this situation is likely to worsen as 45 to
50 thousand workers are retrenched from formal-sector employment under the
SAP, disproportionately affecting the lowest paid, low-skilled laborers.[41]

How have market traders in the urban centers in Zimbabwe fared under these
conditions? These vendors reported many of the same problems under the SAP
that Clark's traders in Ghana previously noted.[42] Microentrepreneurs remarked
that their major problems under adjustment have been the shortage of customers,

the increased competition in the marketplace, and the rising costs of commodities and transportation. The removal of government subsidies from public transportation has resulted in increased costs to market traders, who depend on public buses to bring their goods to market. These costs, coupled with the rising prices charged by wholesalers, have made it extremely difficult for these vendors to make a profit. Their efforts to raise prices to realize even a small profit often result in declining sales. These problems were summed up by two traders in Mbare market:

The skyrocketing nature of prices have [*sic*] affected the business. Things are more expensive now. It is not only my problem but a national crisis for all the people engaged in vegetable trading.[43]

[The problems are] inflation of prices and relaxed demand. Fluctuation of wholesale supply. Price increases affect everyone.[44]

With so many traders in the markets, customers just go to the next stall and attempt to make a better deal. This increased competition is not only from market women but from men who work in such markets as Manwele selling the same goods as women. Also, as Clark has observed, increased displacement of men from formal-sector occupations under the SAP is likely to lead to increased competition not only from men in the marketplace but also from men who, because they have more capital and connections, can open produce stores.[45] While all the vendors in this sample did report that they had earned profits since they began their enterprises, the problems created by the SAP have reduced profits over the past few years.

Transportation poses even greater problems for market women in Zimbabwe today than at the time of Horn's study because under structural adjustment there are far fewer buses operating, since the government cannot afford to repair them.[46] Traders who were accustomed to waking up at 4:00 A.M. to start their business day are now frequently beginning to "line up" for buses at this time. In addition to the increased costs, these women can wait on lines for hours before obtaining transport to wholesalers and then to the market.

The location of a market and harassment by the police were also problems encountered by traders in Zimbabwe, especially in Bulawayo, that have intensified under the adjustment policies. Traders in Manwele market reported that they were experiencing declining sales in the past few years as more blacks were leaving the high-density suburbs, such as Mzilikazi (where Manwele was located), every day for employment in the central city. In downtown Bulawayo, workers could shop at large markets, in grocery stores, and in supermarkets, as well as make their purchases from street vendors at the bus depot. Although hawking their wares in the latter case is illegal, some traders reported that they and others have tried to sell goods at bus stations very early in the morning before the police arrive to fine them and confiscate their goods. This is one of the "survival strategies" market traders have used to stay in business; it involves yet greater physical sacrifices for them every day. They have to awaken even earlier to sell for a few hours at the depot in town, leave before the police come, and arrive back at their stalls in Manwele between 7:30 and 8:00 A.M. at the latest. As Horn revealed in an earlier study, police harassment of market traders is not a recent phenomenon.[47] Women who succeed in taking on this extra shift can increase their profits, but others find it an additional source of competition.

In addition to the problems cited above, many foodsellers faced daily problems of spoilage. As earlier observed by Horn, this was particularly a problem for those who sold tomatoes and some fruits.[48] Sometimes these goods would break while they were being transported; and any fresh tomatoes not sold by the end of the day would often have to be transported home or given away, since the markets did not have refrigeration. The issue of spoilage was an even greater problem for a market trader who could not afford an indoor stall or at least one protected by a roof. These women traded outdoors all day immediately adjacent to the major market with little or no protection from the elements. Traders who remained outdoors paid about Z$10 per month for the use of the space, while those indoors paid approximately Z$10 to Z$14 per month. The commodities of the former were directly subject to the environment.

Market traders at present are also encountering greater responsibilities in their families and households. Even in cases where women are married and living with their families, structural adjustment policies have meant increasing financial hardships. Although women reported that men are primarily responsible for housing, utilities, food, and educational expenses, men were more likely to be paying the full costs of housing and utilities, and they expect women to contribute to the costs of food and education. Under the current adjustment policies, it became necessary for women to increase their contributions toward providing food and education for their children, since contributions from men in these areas either remained constant or declined with the onset of the economic crisis. This occurred at the same time that government subsidies were removed in these areas.

Adjustment policies induced by the IMF and the World Bank in Africa have encouraged the export of agricultural products, often creating shortages of these commodities at home. As a result, food prices have escalated, and traders have experienced declining sales. Therefore, it is little wonder that some market traders in Bulawayo were willing to trade in different locations and take the risks that this entailed in order to contribute as much as possible to their families. These financial burdens are added to their responsibilities for housework and childcare, which remain almost exclusively the domain of women. Market traders reported that they were further plagued by increased conflict, drunkenness, and physical abuse from their husbands, who were also facing mounting pressures as a result of structural adjustment.

Are there any support services to assist women in fulfilling their productive and reproductive roles, particularly given the strains posed by the SAP? The majority of market traders believed that little if anything could be done to change their household responsibilities because these duties belonged to them as women, mothers, and wives. With respect to their tasks as entrepreneurs, over half the sample believed that neither the government, the NGOs, nor informal associations could help them in their businesses. However, the Zimbabwe government's social policies designed to improve the status of women, enacted immediately after independence, probably explain why some traders mentioned government efforts to improve their plight.

Included among these programs was the establishment of the Ministry of Cooperative and Community Development and Women's Affairs, which was charged with the responsibility of removing all forms of discrimination against women in society and supporting the creation and maintenance of women's income-generating activities. They noted that the government did provide and maintain the markets, as well as toilets and sanitation facilities in some cases. Traders mentioned that informal associations existed, such as rotating credit schemes, known as "rounds," that could, and in a few cases did, assist them by providing loans and lump-sum payments that kept their businesses afloat. None of the women in this study had ever received a business loan from a commercial bank. Thus, despite the attempts by the Zimbabwean government and the NGOs to provide support services for women in business, market traders in this study have little knowledge of what exists. Furthermore, they perhaps correctly perceived that the majority of such services were not designed for them.

SUCCESS AND ASPIRATIONS FOR THE FUTURE

As indicated earlier, although profits have declined since the establishment of the adjustment program, traders in this study had earned profits from their businesses. In addition, most respondents indicated that success was measured by their ability to support (or assist in maintaining) their families. In particular, they commented on meeting the expenses of feeding and educating their children, with the latter assuming the greatest importance for them. These women further expressed goals as businesswomen. Included among the goals in both cities was the desire to expand their current activities: "I look forward to possibly expanding this business. Then I would have to make an establishment elsewhere and have some of my kids get involved in this business. Right here in Mbare, I would like to have two stands in the market."[49] Others hoped to add products, especially handmade clothing and prepared foods, to their market activities. The vendors most often wanted to establish their own shops; and with respect to clothing manufacturing, they hoped to purchase sewing machines. As one Mbare trader remarked: "I want to diversify—[move into] knitting and sewing with modern machines. I want to establish links with influential people because of my business and establish something better than my present situation."[50]

Zimbabwean entrepreneurs correctly perceived the growth in demand for prepared meals available at low cost for urban workers. The need for such ready-to-eat foods had grown dramatically in the post-independence period with the increased migration to the cities. Several traders expressed the desire to open take-away food shops that would sell *sadza*, an indigenous cornmeal dish, especially during lunch time.[51]

The most important concern of many of the traders interviewed, however, was for their children to realize an improved quality of life:

I want my children to reach a higher stage of education and have better jobs than what I have.[52]

I don't want my children to live the life that I live. I want them to have a better life.[53]

I have no goals except taking care of my children. I look forward to their going to work. . . . I suspect that they will follow my line and end up doing what I am doing [trading]. I would prefer them going to work in the formal sector.[54]

While these traders were committed to investing in the education of their children, and thus the future development of their society, current structural barriers limited their possibilities for success in this area. The faltering economy, the adoption of the adjustment program, and a lack of attention by the state to their needs as women and as microentrepreneurs posed obstacles to the realization of these goals.

TRADE, EMPOWERMENT, AND NATIONAL DEVELOPMENT

While Zimbabwe's economic crisis has reduced the earnings and increased the costs borne by these women, market trade has empowered them and enabled them to contribute to development. Since independence in 1980, women have been able to participate more openly in the informal economy. Under colonialism, most women were relegated to the Tribal Trust Lands, where they engaged in subsistence agricultural production. In their efforts to regulate the labor supply in the cities, few women were allowed by the British authorities to trade in the urban areas.[55] Although the government continues to impose some restrictions regarding where and under what conditions microenterprises can be established, women's informal enterprises are much more clearly visible in the streets of Harare and Bulawayo today. Thus many activities, such as crocheting, food selling, and hairdressing are no longer primarily invisible, home-based activities. Increasing the visibility of these enterprises enhances the recognition of the work women do and in fact clearly demonstrates *that women are involved in income generation.*

Although the state's attempts to improve the physical conditions under which women work in the informal sector have lagged far behind what is needed, the fact that these activities are now frequently performed outdoors has led the local and federal governments to provide some facilities for vendors and other microentrepreneurs. Further, under improved economic conditions, the greater visibility of these businesses is likely to result in more customers, and consequently more income, for these women.

In fact, the empowerment of Zimbabwean women and their contributions to national development are significantly tied to income earning. Most African women believe they have important roles and responsibilities in production and reproduction and maintain that they need to work because they have children.[56] With respect to microenterprises such as market trade, women control the profits from their businesses, determine how they are to be used, and are further empowered through decision making involving the general operation of their enterprises.[57] Given African women's strong dedication to their children as a central construct of their identity, it follows that a substantial proportion of the profits from trading and other enterprises are used by women to feed, clothe, and educate their children. The majority of Zimbabwean traders in this study reported that profits were used to care for and educate their children, as well as reinvested in their businesses. In addition, these vendors do transmit their skills as traders to the next generation by taking their younger children to the market with them and having their older children assist them in obtaining and selling their produce. Through these reproductive activities, Zimbabwean traders are empowering themselves and contributing to the development of human capital.

Market traders also empower themselves through their participation in associations involving their trade, including rotating credit schemes. The "rounds" in Zimbabwe do supply women with needed cash, not only to help in the daily maintenance of their families and to buy essential commodities but also to assist them in making "lump-sum" payments for school fees. Through their organizations, market vendors can also be an important political force. As the major suppliers of foodstuffs for urban residents, they have the power to collectively halt the distribution of food in the cities in response to state actions, for example, that run counter to their interests. Market traders in several African countries have engaged in such actions through demonstrations against structural adjustment policies.[58]

Finally, as previously stated, if these traders are successful in realizing increased profits from their activities, they will further contribute to national development through the development of new service and manufacturing enterprises. These women discussed their goals to begin clothing factories, take-out restaurants, and produce shops. The establishment of these ventures would create employment opportunities, contribute to local production, and thus satisfy some of the demands of the domestic market. These actions would amplify the direct contributions of these entrepreneurs to national development.

CONCLUSION

Despite the history of economic independence exhibited by West African women traders and the dynamic roles experienced by many African market women generally, these Zimbabwean traders face several obstacles to improving their status. Among these are the persistence of a gender-based division of labor, which circumscribes women's roles both within the formal occupational sphere and within the marketplace. In addition, women's problems have been aggravated by Africa's current economic crisis.

As a result of the escalating unemployment in Zimbabwe created by the retrenchment of men from formal-sector employment and a declining economy, women have been forced to assume more financial responsibilities in the maintenance of their families. Under structural adjustment, women pay increased costs for food, transportation, education, and healthcare for themselves and their children, since the government has removed the subsidies from many vital services. As businesswomen, they are also affected by the removal of subsidies, since they are highly dependent on public transportation to bring their goods to the market. High unemployment has led many displaced men to seek opportunities in food sales, either through the establishment of produce stores or as vendors in the informal economy. Such activities have increased the competition for women in the workplace. This competition, when coupled with the rising price of commodities and efforts to pass these costs on the customers, has led to decreased sales among these traders. Thus, the state's adjustment program has contributed to the decline of women's income-earning ability and their capacity to contribute to national development.

Although generalizations are not possible from such a small sample, this exploratory study suggests that these problems still beset Zimbabwean women in the informal sector. Because of limited opportunities in the labor market, these women began their enterprises as means to assist them in supporting their families. While their families and, to a more limited extent, informal market associations have assisted them in establishing and maintaining their businesses, the stresses posed by the removal of government subsidies from many vital services, rising unemployment, and poverty will make it more difficult for such support to continue. Thus, government and NGOs must assume a more active role in providing institutional support to market women.

Women in this study have acknowledged the need for adequate market facilities such as refrigeration and shelter. This means that women sitting on the bare ground outdoors need to be provided with at least stalls in which to work. New comprehensive urban markets could not only house all of the women trading within and outside the current official markets but also provide on-site childcare facilities. Given the economic difficulties Zimbabwe is facing, such markets could be built as self-help projects, where the state provides the materials and the entrepreneurs and their families provide the labor. These women would face fewer health risks, lose fewer commodities to spoilage, and still be able to see their children in a more relaxed setting during the workday. While it might prove extremely difficult to maintain a highly subsidized public transportation system, some effort needs to be made to lower the costs of these services for market traders, who distribute essential goods and are often the poorest women in these nations. Furthermore, the government needs to end the harassment of these women by the police, especially considering the few employment options that are available to women.

In addition, both NGOs and governments need to provide market traders with training and loan programs to enable them to move into more profitable manufacturing and service activities. For such policies to succeed, traditional and contemporary barriers that restrict women's activities must be removed. Changes in socialization practices, in the home, at school, and in the workplace need to be implemented. Active media campaigns to encourage women to enter nontraditional fields should be encouraged. Also, laws that discriminate against women in the public and private spheres should be abrogated so as to enhance the status of women microentrepreneurs.

Even if such changes become institutionalized at the national level, poor women will still disproportionately bear the burdens of development as a result of the global economic system. Zimbabwe, like other sub-Saharan African nations, needs to target its programs to meet indigenous and regional needs, as opposed to the goals of the multilateral agencies and transnational capital. In this regard, rather than southern nations adopting adjustment programs to satisfy the requirements of international lenders (who are largely northerners) and supposedly to improve their economies in the long run, the focus of restructuring efforts needs to shift to the global marketplace. At this level, the Western nations and Japan should focus, at the very least, on balancing the benefits between their societies and the rest of the world. Only then can traders and others at the bottom of the social structure in African societies more fully realize an improvement in their life chances.

NOTES

1. Sée Sidney Mintz, "Men, Women and Trade," *Comparative Studies in Society and History*, Vol. 13, 1972, pp. 247–269; Peggy Sanday, "Female Status in the Public Domain," in *Women, Culture and Society*, edited by Michelle Zimbalist Rosaldo and Louise Lamphere (Stanford: Stanford University Press, 1974); Barbara Lewis, "The Limitations of Group Action among Entrepreneurs: The Market Women of Abidjan, Ivory Coast," in *Women in Africa*, edited by Nancy J. Hafkin and Edna G. Bay (Stanford: Stanford University Press, 1976); Claire Robertson, *Sharing the Same Bowl: A Socioeconomic History of Women and Class in Accra, Ghana* (Bloomington: University of Indiana Press, 1984); Gracia Clark, ed., *Traders versus the State* (Boulder, Colo.: Westview Press, 1988); Gracia Clark, "Class Alliance and Class Fractions in Ghanian Trading and State Formation," *Review of African Political Economy*, Vol. 49, 1990, pp. 73–81.

2. See Clark, "Class Alliance"; Ann Seidman and F. Anang, eds., *Twenty-First Century Africa: Towards a Vision of Self-Sustainable Development* (Trenton: Africa World Press, 1992).

3. See Ester Boserup, *Woman's Role in Economic Development* (New York: St. Martin's Press, 1970); Nancy Horn, "The Culture, Urban Context and Economics of Women's Fresh Produce Marketing in Harare, Zimbabwe," Ph.D. dissertation, Department of Anthropology, Michigan State University, Lansing, 1988.

4. The term "sales worker" in Morgan's work refers to women employed as sales clerks in shops, as well as those engaged in petty commercial activities. See *Sisterhood Is Global: The First Anthology from the International Women's Movement*, edited by Robin Morgan (Garden City, N.Y.: Doubleday, 1984); Lillian Trager, "From Yams to Beer in a Nigerian City: Expansion and Change in Informal Sector Activity," in *Markets and Marketing*, edited by Stuart Plattner (New York: University Press of America, 1985); and Seidman and Anang, *Twenty-First Century Africa*.

5. Interview with Hasan Imam, "Recent Developments in the Economy of Zimbabwe and the Role of the Informal Sector," World Bank, 1990; Interview with Katrine Saito, "The Role of Women in the Informal Sector in Zimbabwe," World Bank, 1990.

6. Simi Afonja, "Changing Modes of Production and the Sexual Division of Labor among the Yoruba," *Signs: Journal of Women in Culture and Society*, Vol. 7, No. 2, 1981, pp. 299–313.

7. Kamene Okonjo, "The Dual-Sex Political System in Operation: Igbo Women and Community Politics in the Southeastern Nigeria," in *Women in Africa*, edited by Nancy Hafkin and Edna Bay.

8. Afonja, "Changing Modes of Production."

9. Jane Turrittin, "Men, Women, and Market Trade in Mali, West Africa," *Canadian Journal of African Studies*, Vol. 22, No. 3, 1988, pp. 583–604.

10. John Swetnam, "Women and Markets: A Problem in the Assessment of Sexual Inequality," *Ethnology*, Vol. 27, No. 4, 1988, pp. 327–338.

11. Robertson, *Sharing the Same Bowl*; Turrittin, "Men, Women, and Market Trade."

12. Sanday, "Female Status in the Public Domain"; Lewis, "Limitations of Group Action"; Turrittin, "Men, Women, and Market Trade."

13. Sanday, "Female Status in the Public Domain."

14. Mary Osirim, "Gender and Entrepreneurship: Issues of Capital and Technology in Nigerian Firms," in *Privatization and Investment in Sub-Saharan Africa*, edited by Rexford A. Ahere and Bernard S. Katz (New York: Praeger, 1992).

15. Gracia Clark and Takyiwaa Manuh, "Women Traders in Ghana and the Structural Adjustment Program," in *Structural Adjustment and African Women Farmers*, edited by Christine H. Gladwin (Gainesville: University of Florida Press, 1991).

16. Turrittin, "Men, Women, and Market Trade."

17. Clark and Manuh, "Women Traders in Ghana."

18. Mary Osirim, "Is This Adjustment with a Human Face? Women, the State and Microentrepreneurship in Nigeria and Zimbabwe," paper presented for the Carter G. Woodson Institute's Lecture Series, The University of Virginia, Richmond, 1993.

19. Clark and Manuh, "Women Traders in Ghana."

20. Emergency taxis in Harare, Zimbabwe, are old, often dilapidated station wagons that provide some of the cheapest transportation in the city. Drivers typically crowd at least ten people into these vehicles and drop passengers off at requested stops along the major roads. Unlike regular taxis, they do not provide door-to-door service. For further discussion of this issue, see Horn, "The Culture, Urban Context and Economics of Women's Fresh Product Marketing in Harare, Zimbabwe."

21. Morgan, *Sisterhood*.

22. Zimbabwe Ministry of Labor, *Labor Force Survey, 1986/87* (Harare: Government Printer, 1987).

23. Horn, "Women's Fresh Product Marketing."

24. George Kurian, *Encyclopedia of the Third World* (New York: Facts on File, 1987).

25. Gay Seidman, "Women in Zimbabwe: Post-Independence Struggles," *Feminist Studies*, Vol. 10, No. 3, 1984, pp. 419–440.

26. For a comprehensive discussion of the structure and philosophy of the mission schools, see Carol Summers, "Native Policy, Education and Development: Social Ideologies and Social Control in Southern Rhodesia, 1890–1934," Ph.D. dissertation, Department of History, Johns Hopkins University, Baltimore, 1991.

27. Swetnam, "Women and Markets."

28. For example, the Ministry of Cooperative and Community Development has created several loan and training programs that could benefit women who own small microenterprises in Zimbabwe.

29. Afonja, "Changing Modes of Production"; Turrittin, "Men, Women, and Market Trade"; Swetnam, "Women and Markets."

30. Patricia Made and Myorovai Whande, "Women in Southern Africa: A Note on the Zimbabwe Success Story," *Issues: A Journal of Opinion*, Vol. 17, No. 2, 1989, pp. 26–28.

31. Interview with Maruku, a trader in Manwele market, Bulawayo, Zimbabwe, 1991.

32. Interview with Tendai, a trader in Manwele market, Bulawayo, Zimbabwe, 1991.

33. Young children were often seen accompanying their mothers in Mbare and Manwele markets, since childcare in Harare and Bulawayo costs between Z$120 and Z$200 per week. These costs were beyond the reach of the majority of traders in these cities. (At the time of this study, U.S.$1 = Z$2.30.)

34. Interview with Ncube, a trader in Manwele market, Bulawayo, Zimbabwe, 1991.

35. Interview with Wilson, a trader in Mbare market, Harare, Zimbabwe, 1991.

36. See Andrew Meldrum, "Mugabe's Maneuvers," *Africa Report*, May/June, 1989; Saito, "The Role of Women."

37. Colin Stoneman and Lionel Cliffe, *Zimbabwe: Politics, Economics and Society* (London: Pinter Publishers, 1989).

38. Roy Laishley, "Drought Dims Hope of Faster Recovery," *Africa Recovery*, Vol. 6, No. 2, 1992.

39. See the Training Aids Development Group, "Structural Adjustment: Changing the Face of Zimbabwe," *Read On*, No. 3, 1991; Jonathan Moyo, "State Policies and Social Domination in Zimbabwe," *Journal of Modern African Studies*, Vol. 30, No. 2, 1992, pp. 305–330.

40. Moyo, "State Policies and Social Domination."

41. Peter Gibbon, "The World Bank and African Poverty, 1973–91," *Journal of Modern African Studies*, Vol. 30, No. 2, 1992, pp. 193–220.

42. Clark and Manuh, "Women Traders in Ghana."

43. Interview with Chisango, a trader in Mbare market, Harare, Zimbabwe, 1991.

44. Interview with Chera, a trader in Mbare market, Harare, Zimbabwe, 1991.

45. Clark and Manuh, "Women Traders in Ghana."

46. Horn, "Women's Fresh Produce Marketing."

47. Ibid.

48. Ibid.

49. Interview with Bizure, a trader in Mbare market, Harare, Zimbabwe, 1991.

50. Interview with Chera, a trader in Mbare market, Harare, Zimbabwe, 1991.

51. Sadza is an indigenous food made from corn meal. It is usually served with a cooked green leafy vegetable and a piece of boiled meat.

52. Tendai, interview (1991).

53. Interview with Lisa, a trader in Manwele market, Bulawayo, Zimbabwe, 1991.

54. Interview with Maganasadza, a trader in Mbare market, Harare, Zimbabwe, 1991.

55. Seidman and Anang, *Twenty-First Century Africa*.

56. Afonja, "Changing Modes of Production"; Clark, *Traders versus the State*; Brooke Schoepf, "Gender Relations and Development: Political Economy and Culture," in *Twenty-First Century Africa*, edited by Ann Seidman and F. Anang.

57. Sanday, "Female Status in the Public Domain"; Afonja, "Changing Modes of Production."

58. On several occasions, market women in Ghana and Nigeria have demonstrated against the government to express their displeasure over austerity and adjustment policies. Examples of these demonstrations in the post-independence era began in the early 1960s in Ghana and have continued into the recent period in both countries, as noted in Nigeria in the early 1990s. For a further discussion of this issue in Ghana, see Clark and Manuh, "Women Traders in Ghana."

Chapter 10

The Growth and Dynamics of Women Entrepreneurs in Southern Africa

Jeanne Downing

SEARCHING FOR RELEVANCY AMONG GROWTH-ORIENTED STRATEGISTS

Africa experienced little in the way of growth during the 1980s. The near collapse of African economies was affected by events both within and outside the control of political leaders. Outside events such as the fall in commodity prices on the world market, environmental hazards, and structural adjustment policies of the World Bank and the IMF all served to depress growth.[1] Events inside Africa such as malconceived policies and corrupt leadership further eroded the economic base of many countries (Zaire, Cameroon, Côte d'Ivoire, Nigeria, Mali, Togo, Zambia,

The data upon which this chapter is based was collected by Michigan State University (MSU) under the Growth and Equity through Microenterprise Investment (GEMINI) Project. Carl Liedholm and Donald Mead at MSU developed the methodology and guided the field research, conducted by Yacob Fisseha, Michael McPherson, and others. Lisa Daniels analyzed the data generated using SPSS and worked diligently to ensure the comparability of the variables across countries. I would like to give special thanks to Steve Haggblade for his guidance and inspiration in analyzing the data. Finally, Tulin Pulley, formerly of AID's Office of Women in Development which funded this research, provided enormously helpful feedback on the multiple drafts and the final report.

and others). In light of the performance of African economies, donor strategies have sought both policy and microlevel perscriptions capable of starting an engine of recovery and growth. While macropolicies and privatization have been important foci of identified prescriptions, the informal sector has been viewed as holding potential for broad-based employment generation.

The interest of the major donors like the World Bank, the United Nations Development Program (UNDP), and the Agency for International Development (AID) in the informal sector largely relates to its potential for spurring overall economic growth. To achieve this objective, growth-oriented donors have promoted investment strategies that typically exclude women. Given the meager resources of African governments and the inability of many countries to generate growth of any kind during recent years of recession and structural adjustment, they argue, it is imperative to target available resources toward dynamic subsectors that have the greatest potential for contributing to economic growth. Invariably, subsectors within which women are concentrated do not fall into the category of "dynamic."

Women in Development (WID) researchers have argued for years that growth-oriented strategies exclude women.[2] Donors counter that this exclusion is not based on sex but on the commonly held view—one that has been bolstered by the WID literature—that women's enterprises are small, marginally profitable, and offer little potential for contributing to the macroeconomy. While the literature concomitantly points to the importance of women's meager incomes to human capital investment and family welfare, these welfare arguments fall on deaf ears of growth proponents.

This chapter argues that the characterizations of women's enterprises as small and largely lacking potential for growth are, from a policy viewpoint, dangerous. They suggest to donors and policymakers in search of cost-effective means for generating growth that women's enterprises are not worthy of attention. More important, they ignore the work that has been done in transforming women's traditional activities into dynamic ones. Women work long and hard. For this we have much evidence, and because of this WID researchers and activists have sought ways of alleviating the unpaid and poorly remunerated labor burdens of women. The challenge, particularly in Africa where growth is critically needed, is to demonstrate that the hours women work can be translated into improved opportunities with potential both to empower women and to contribute to macroeconomic growth.

The means for accomplishing this exist. Several examples stand out. Most of them are based on a subsector approach, including SEWA's work in India, CARE work in Thailand's silk subsector, the multidonor work with women in horticulture in The Gambia and, before the civil war, work by PFP/Liberia and UNIFEM in Liberia.[3] All these examples illustrate the possibility of upgrading the traditional activities in which large numbers of women are engaged into high-value product markets.

This chapter argues that in order to expand our capabilities to replicate successes, WID research needs to move beyond documentation and measurement of the constraints that women face. Understanding these constraints has been and still is critical to the WID cause, but political exigencies require that the case be made for how women can be and are relevant to growth-oriented strategies. More research is needed to document the growth patterns of female entrepreneurs, their strategies for generating income, and cases of where women have been successful in shifting out of low-growth, low-return activities into those with greater prospects. This research is needed to contribute to intervention designs that integrate women more fully into the development process. This chapter is a small step in this direction. It sets out to explore at least some of the evidence about female entrepreneurs' growth patterns.

DESCRIPTION OF THE DATA

The data used to explore female entrepreneurs' growth patterns is based on census-type surveys conducted by Michigan State University under the Growth and Equity through Microenterprise Investments and Institutions (GEMINI) project.[4] Census surveys were conducted in four countries in the Southern African region: Lesotho, Swaziland, South Africa, and Zimbabwe. The South Africa data represent a complete census of two black urban townships: Mamelodi and Kwazakhele. Nationally representative samples were selected from the other countries, and the population of enterprises was extrapolated from a geographically stratified random sample.

Evidence was gathered by means of both household surveys and street-by-street enumeration of enterprises along roads and in commercial districts, industrial districts, and traditional market areas. One exception was South Africa, where surveys were all conducted at households. Households were asked whether anyone in the compound or homestead operated an enterprise. "Enterprise" was defined as any economic activity that produces goods, half of which are marketed. The household surveys were meant to measure home-based enterprises, and the market-based surveys to ascertain market-oriented firms of 50 employees or fewer.

In South Africa, interviews with women and men were conducted separately. In the other countries, the adult present at the time of the interview was queried; however, most household interviewees were women. In South Africa, the entire population of the two townships was interviewed; nationally representative samples were interviewed in the other countries. In Lesotho, 7,292 enterprises were enumerated from canvassing 24,240 households. In Swaziland, enumerators collected data from 7,107 households or enterprises. Out of the total sample, 2,759 operating enterprises were identified. In Zimbabwe, the sample of 5,575 was obtained from visits to just under 15,000 households and enterprises.

Two instruments were used; the first was a one-page questionnaire designed to gather information from the broadest base of the population possible within the allocated time, which tended to be about six weeks. This first census-type instrument collected data on types of enterprises that were then classified according to SIC codes, employment patterns, location, sex of proprietor and employees, structure of enterprise, seasonality, and so forth. A second more in-depth questionnaire was administered to a much smaller subsample. In Lesotho, for example, this smaller sample amounted to 631 enterprises. The second instrument attempted to capture constraints, entrepreneurial characteristics, and dynamic changes. However, the short time allowed for these more in-depth interviews was still limited, and thus the findings are more indicative than conclusive.

THE SOUTHERN AFRICAN CONTEXT

Most small enterprises in Southern Africa are wedged into market niches not already usurped by large, modern South African firms. Entrepreneurs in Lesotho, Swaziland, and the black townships of South Africa are forced to seek out the few markets where they can compete or avoid competition with the low-priced, mass-produced goods of large RSA firms. Even in remote rural areas of Lesotho, for example, South African stores dominate. Basothos claim that farmers are unable to sell their locally grown vegetables because the RSA stores sell them even at the village level at much lower prices.[5]

While market economies have developed in other African countries, commerce in the black Southern African Customs Union (SACU) countries has generally been impeded, at least in part, because of domination by South Africa.[6] SACU has facilitated the penetration of South African firms into the SACU countries—Lesotho, Swaziland, and the black townships of South Africa have been more vulnerable to this penetration than Zimbabwe, which is not a SACU member. Yet Zimbabwe has its own particular history which has depressed the development of the informal sector. The system of economic controls established prior to independence gave white Zimbabwean firms monopolies and other privileges that allowed them to control markets for the most lucrative products. Many of these controls and privileges remain today in a slightly modified form. In both Zimbabwe and South Africa, laws prohibited blacks from operating businesses until relatively recently. As a result, the informal sector in these countries is underdeveloped.

The repression of the small enterprise sector throughout Southern Africa has meant that financial and other input services for small businesses and microenterprises (SMEs) are sorely lacking or underdeveloped.[7] Basotho businesspeople complain of the difficulty of obtaining bank loans; they argue that borrowing is much more difficult for Basotho than expatriates. Although small enterprise credit programs have been initiated in Lesotho and Swaziland and most recently in South Africa and Zimbabwe, significant impact has not yet been achieved. According to a World Bank survey of female microentrepreneurs in Zimbabwe, only 5 percent of sample respondents in Zimbabwe had obtained formal credit; 75 percent of female respondents received financing from personal savings or family grants.[8]

Marketing infrastructure and skills are lacking in the countries surrounding and surrounded by South Africa. In black South African townships, the manufacturing sector is relatively small. In Zimbabwe, the dominance of white Zimbabwean and European firms favored by government policies has equally affected the development of marketing and financial infrastructure and informal-sector manufacturing. One can only surmise that the market domination of RSA firms has propagated both a dependency and a barrier to the development of indigenous marketing and production systems.

The female-to-male ratio of the informal-sector labor force is relatively high in Lesotho and Swaziland because of the large number of men employed much of the year in South African mines. Although the rural areas are still dominated by women in these countries, the sex ratio in urban areas is changing as employment in South African mines drops and men return to their homelands in search of enterprise and employment opportunites. In Zimbabwe, men have been outmigrating to employment centers for decades. In the wake of these migrations, concentrations of women have been left behind in the rural areas to fend for themselves.[9] Meanwhile, divorce and abandonment rates have risen dramatically.

GEMINI data for Southern Africa reveal that 73 percent of SMEs in Lesotho are female owned. In Swaziland the share is even higher at 84 percent. In the two South African townships, the share of female entrepreneurs to male was only 62 percent; in Zimbabwe, it was 67 percent. In all countries, there is a significant number of de facto female-headed households in the rural areas, where men have outmigrated or are absent much of the year.

GENDER-DIFFERENTIATED PATTERNS
OF ENTERPRISE GROWTH

GEMINI data for Southern Africa provide two primary indicators of growth: employment growth and changes in the average number of firm employees across rural–urban strata. The latter variable, a static measure of the average size of firms, reveals changes from major city to secondary cities to smaller towns or employment centers to rural areas. It reveals changes in the size of firms with increase in size of the market center. Employment growth rates measure changes in the number of employees between a firm's startup date and the time of the interview. The resulting number is divided by the number of years in operation to yield an annual rate. The variable does not distinguish between enterprises that failed to add employees because of lack of profits or product demand and those that did not increase the number of employees but increased their output per worker and their profitability. Furthermore, it measures growth rates of enterprises that survived over the period, thereby ignoring those that did not survive.

This last characteristic is particularly problematic because of the potential for significant inaccuracies. For instance, if most enterprises in a given subsector died during the time period and those remaining grew at a healthy rate, the growth rate, calculated as described above, could be very misleading. If, for instance, men's enterprises die at a higher rate than women's and leave behind firms that grow at faster rates, the employment growth rate would bias assessments of men's enterprises as compared to women's. Unless dead enterprises are accounted for, it is difficult to draw reliable conclusions about the growth potential of an aggregation of enterprises categorized by gender or subsector.

To compensate for the exclusion of dead enterprises and shed light on death rates, the age structure of enterprises is presented in Table 10.1. If death rates are high among a category of enterprises, a very low percentage of older firms and high percentage of younger firms would be expected. The data show, however, that female-owned enterprises are virtually identical in age structure to male-owned ones, except in Zimbabwe—where the pattern deviates only somewhat.[10] Overall, the data indicate that women's enterprises are as stable and long lasting as men's enterprises. This finding is corroborated by McPherson's 1992 analysis of firm survival using the hazard modeling. In analyzing GEMINI data from Zimbabwe and Swaziland, McPherson concluded that when market-related failures are considered—as opposed to nonbusiness personal failures—women's enterprises are no more likely to fail than men's. This similarity in death rates is surprising, given the often-cited marginality of women's enterprises.

Table 10.2 presents employment growth for female- and male-owned firms in Lesotho, Swaziland, South Africa, and Zimbabwe. The data indicate that female-owned enterprises grow at rates, on the whole, substantially slower than those of male-owned firms. In the trade sector, the slower rate of growth is significant in every country for which there are data. The gap between male- and female-owned trading enterprises, however, is particularly wide in South Africa.

Table 10.1
Percentage Distributions of Enterprises by Age of Enterprise and Gender of Proprietor

Age	Lesotho F	Lesotho M	Swaziland F	Swaziland M	South Africa F	South Africa M	Zimbabwe F	Zimbabwe M
< 1 Year	12	11	25	25	21	17	6	5
1-2 Years	20	2	13	7	24	18	27	11
3-5 Years	23	36	16	22	26	26	19	17
6-8 Years	8	14	13	18	9	12	18	7
9-15 Years	22	17	15	9	11	16	19	25
> 15 Years	14	18	11	14	9	12	8	33
TOTAL	100	100	100	100	100	100	100	100
NUMBER	8145	3535	38794	6449	3239	1636	47272	35113

Table 10.2
Employment Growth Rates of Enterprises by Gender of Proprietor and Sector

Sector	Lesotho		Swaziland		South Africa		Zimbabwe	
	F	M	F	M	F	M	F	M
Manufacturing	na	na	.05	.14	.13	.28	.05	.08
Trade	na	na	.07	.11	.22	.35	.10	.15
Services	na	na	.13	.05	.27	.14	.11	.20

GEMINI data disaggregated by subsector indicate the importance of trading to women in the southern African region. In South Africa, there were more female entrepreneurs in retail trade than in any other subsector. In Lesotho, Swaziland, and Zimbabwe, the retail trade subsector ranks second in terms of absolute number of female-owned enterprises. The number of women engaged in retail trade, as compared to men in all countries, is more than twofold that of the number of men. Yet, the growth rate of male-owned enterprises exceeds that of women's retail trade enterprises in Swaziland, South Africa, and Zimbabwe. Even within the same subsector, that is retail trade, the growth rate of men's firms outstrips that of women's.

Data on "average number of employees per firm" reinforce the conclusion that women's enterprises do not grow at the same rate as men's. GEMINI data on "average number of workers" by sector and by geographic stratum, from major city to rural area show that in Swaziland, Lesotho, and (to a lesser extent) Zimbabwe, men's enterprises consistently increase as market size increases. Women's enterprises, on the other hand, remain surprisingly consistent in size regardless of location along the urban–rural continuum. Women's enterprises do not appear to respond to the larger markets of urban centers. Although they survive as long as men's do, they appear to be static in growth.

Here are some questions raised by these findings. Why are women's enterprises so consistently small sized, averaging slightly over one employee regardless of location? Are women's enterprises unable to grow despite increases in market size? Do female entrepreneurs have priorities other than growth? Are they uniformly hampered by some constraint that male entrepreneurs do not face? Can the lack of growth be explained by low demand for women's products; high concentrations of female entrepreneurs in the same business; limited access to inputs and working capital; or the constraints associated with women's combined productive and reproductive responsibilities?

GENDER-DIFFERENTIATED CONSTRAINTS TO GROWTH

GEMINI surveys explored potential constraints to growth by means of a questionnaire administered to a smaller segment of each national sample. Respondents from this smaller sample were asked about their "current problems." Table 10.3 displays the categories of problems cited and responses disaggregated by gender. Because the samples are considerably reduced, cells with only one or two cases may not be significant.

The problems most often cited by both male and female entrepreneurs were financial, market, and input-supply related. "Financial" problems were typically expressed in terms of insufficient working capital or cash flow problems. They appeared to be significant in all countries. In fact, insufficient working capital stands out as the highest priority problem for male entrepreneurs, except in Zimbabwe, where access to nonfinancial inputs is a more cited constraint. For women,

Table 10.3
Percentage Distribution of Major Problems by Gender of Proprietor

Problems	Swaziland		South Africa		Zimbabwe	
	F	M	F	M	F	M
Financial	10	62	28	24	7	16
Bad Debt	10	26	1	6	9	1
Tools/Technology	6	2	1	6	1	24
Market	43	3	29	13	23	17
Government Policy	4	1	8	15	1	1
Location or Space	3	2	5	21	5	3
Transportation	6	1	9	9	9	11
Labor	0	1	1	1	1	4
Inputs	12	0	1	3	40	20
Miscellaneous	7	3	15	3	5	4
TOTAL PERCENTAGE	100	100	100	100	100	100
NUMBER	4939	553	86	68	42400	30278

Note: Data did not include the country of Lesotho for these problems.

insufficient market demand was the outstanding problem. Inputs—that is, insufficient supplies of inputs—ranked second, except in South Africa where it was a low-priority problem for all producers. Both male and female producers in RSA have easy access to the outputs of large-scale manufacturers and farmers.

Departing from a vast body of literature indicating that gaining access to credit is far more difficult for women than for men, GEMINI data on "current problems" suggest that insufficient working capital is a more important problem for male entrepreneurs than for female. This finding, however, could be influenced by the fact that respondents were allowed to give only one answer and were forced to prioritize problems. Thus, while women may cite insufficient working capital less often than men, this does not mean they have more access to working capital. It may indicate that women's market problems are more important. Without a market, they may have little use for financing. The importance of "market"—or what was expressed by female entrepreneurs as "insufficient numbers of customers"— is curious in light of the unresponsiveness of female-owned enterprises to increases in market size. It suggests that rather than being uninterested in growth, women face obstacles. Data showing the survival rate of women's firms to be comparable to that of men's (see Table 10.1) indicate that although women may suffer more than men from insufficient demand for their products, they are able to survive as well as men. Is this because women have different survival strategies than men?

Table 10.4, revealing access to credit, indicates that relatively few small entrepreneurs, male or female, have access to formal credit. The data do not reveal consistent or significant differences between male and female entrepreneurs' access to credit. Participants from Southern Africa at the GEMINI Conference on Small Enterprise Development, February 1992, in Swaziland, argued that this "finding" did not correspond to their experience of living in Lesotho, Swaziland, South Africa, or Zimbabwe. One potential explanation for this discrepancy is the inclusion of informal credit sources in assessing access. Respondents could answer questions concerning credit access with *friends, family,* or *other*. In Lesotho, credit unions were included under the *other* category. Because credit unions rely on mobilized savings for lending funds and collateral, women—who tend to have a higher propensity to save than men—have fairly high participation levels in these quasi-formal financial institutions.[11] On the other hand, a World Bank survey in Zimbabwe reveals that 75 percent of female entrepreneurs obtained startup capital from personal savings or family grants.[12] Women entrepreneurs also receive credit from input suppliers. Research in Lesotho, for example, revealed that dressmakers establish longstanding relationships with wholesalers in Durban and Johannesburg.[13] On the basis of this relationship and trust between buyer and seller, wholesalers sold inputs to informal dressmakers on a credit basis.

GEMINI data on the percentage of respondents who had ever received training do not measure quality and obviously do not measure impact. Nevertheless, the evidence indicates that in Lesotho small female or male entrepreneurs had relatively good access to training. Relative to other countries, respondents from Lesotho also had better access to credit. Previous data, showing change in the average

Table 10.4
Percentage Distribution of Sources of Credit by Sector and Gender

Sector	Lesotho		Swaziland		South Africa		Zimbabwe	
	F	M	F	M	F	M	F	M
Manufacturing								
No credit	70	75	94	68	75	68	95	100
Friend or family	12	2	4	28	na	na	na	na
Bank	12	2	0	1	na	na	na	na
Other	6	21	2	3	na	na	na	na
TOTAL	100	100	100	100	100	100	100	100
Trade								
No credit	13	77	57	94	84	82	97	95
Friend or family	5	3	23	3	na	na	na	na
Bank	6	13	6	3	na	na	na	na
Other	76	7	14	0	na	na	na	na
TOTAL	100	100	100	100	100	100	100	100
Services								
No credit	99	67	100	97	79	86	93	99
Friend or family	0	0	0	3	na	na	na	na
Bank	1	33	0	0	na	na	na	na
Other	0	0	0	0	na	na	na	na
TOTAL	100	100	100	100	100	100	100	100
Overall								
No Credit	70	79	84	80	84	79	95	99
Friend or family	10	2	9	15	na	na	na	na
Bank	10	5	2	2	na	na	na	na
Other	10	14	5	3	na	na	na	na
TOTAL	100	100	100	100	100	100	100	100

number of employees by geographic strata, do not indicate that these inputs had any effect on growth in number of employees; nor do they show any difference from one country to the next, despite varying degrees of access to these inputs.

Data on access to credit and training overall indicate that female enterpreneurs have not translated access to credit and training into increases in firm employment to the extent that male entrepreneurs have. This could indicate that the markets to which female entrepreneurs are able to gain access, even within the same subsector, do not have sufficient growth potential to allow firm growth. This hypothesis is confirmed by data showing higher growth rates for male-owned firms in the same subsector.

The difference between women's and men's enterprises is further highlighted by data on enterprise location shown in Table 10.5. While overall small enterprises in the region are much more likely to be home based (H) than located at a traditional market (TM) or central business district (CBD), women's enterprises are more often home based than men's. A larger percentage of men's enterprises are located in the commercial business districts. Most evidence indicates that home-based enterprises have lower growth rates and profits than market-based firms.[14] Although home locations have the advantage of allowing women to combine their domestic responsibilities with their enterprise activities, they have the disadvantage of relative lack of access to customers.

Table 10.6 displays the number of female- and male-owned firms in each subsector and confirms past research attesting that women's enterprises are concentrated in a narrower range of subsectors than men's.[15] Table 10.6 shows significant crowding by female microentrepreneurs into four subsectors: food, beverage, tobacco; textiles and garments; wood-based production; and retail. Men's enterprises, on the other hand, are more evenly distributed among the same four subsectors that women dominate, as well as fabricated metal production, other manufacturing, construction, transport, and services.

A World Bank survey in Zimbabwe showed that almost two-thirds of the female entrepreneurs surveyed in Harare and one-third of those interviewed in two secondary towns were concentrated in textiles and garment making.[16] Crowding of women into a narrow band of subsectors is often used to explain the low-profit margins and depressed growth of women's enterprises compared to those of men.[17]

A more detailed disaggregation of subsector data into product markets, at the three-digit International Standard Industrial Classification (ISIC) level, is shown in Table 10.7. Each entry represents product markets in which at least 90 percent of the enterprises are female owned. GEMINI data indicate marked qualitative differences in the kinds of activities that women engage in. The data also might explain gender differences in growth patterns. Women's firms appear to be concentrated in far more traditional and less dynamic product markets than men's. Women's manufacturing activities, for example, include beer brewing, dressmaking, knitting, crotcheting, and grass and cane work. Men's manufacturing activities, on the other hand, suggest more modern product markets such as construction, welding, auto repair, radio and television repair, and brick or block making.

Evidence from a number of African countries suggests that traditional product markets face shrinking demand over time through competition with and substitution by more modern products.[18] GEMINI data on growth rates by product market support the contention that women's activities are more traditional and less dynamic than men's. The traditional nature of women's enterprises is also suggested by the different nature of their output markets. Data indicate that women's final products are sold directly to consumers more often than men's, while many of the products produced by men's firms are intermediate goods sold to as inputs to other firms.

Table 10.5
Percentage Distribution of Locations of Enterprises by Sex by Sector

Sector		Lesotho			Swaziland			South Africa			Zimbabwe		
		H	TM	CDB	H	TM	CDB	H	TM	CDB	H	TM	CDB
Manufacturing	F	88	6	2	83	6	3	88	1	3	93	2	1
	M	37	18	13	65	6	16	73	5	12	77	1	10
Wholesale	F	39	9	10	39	26	8	70	2	5	54	10	11
Retail	M	30	22	2	47	12	12	62	3	9	34	6	36
Services	F	57	32	1	93	0	4	93	–	6	91	1	7
	M	30	41	3	60	15	6	54	4	11	50	0	11

Table 10.6
Number of Enterprises by Subsector and Gender

Subsector	Lesotho		Swaziland		South Africa		Zimbabwe	
	F	M	F	M	F	M	F	M
MANUFACTURING								
Food, Beverage, Tobacco	33571	1227	3703	389	135	51	45431	15329
Textiles and Garments	12952	3513	7796	510	227	123	247319	21506
Wood-Based	3375	1096	16319	590	9	53	104948	64323
Paper, Printing, Publishing	0	4	0	12	1	0	95	128
Chemicals and Plastics	14	0	17	16	1	5	0	272
Nonmetal Mineral	271	1576	423	166	0	38	15816	15908
Fabricated Metal	8	409	12	113	4	58	13	18386
Other Manufacturing	30	759	98	420	7	144	3235	18325
SERVICES								
Construction	330	3889	9	441	0	31	2347	32147
Wholesale	326	20	0	12	9	2	79	531
Retail	18816	7913	12826	3015	2166	723	112658	61780
Restaurant and Hotel	1119	1053	68	61	363	145	2617	540
Transportation	8	467	9	152	16	122	0	1573
Services	3853	4137	493	334	204	82	7467	13539

Table 10.7
Subsectors Dominated by Women

Lesotho	Swaziland	South Africa	Zimbabwe
		Bread Making	
Beer Brewing	Beer Brewing		Beer Brewing
Dressmaking	Dressmaking	Dressmaking	Dressmaking
Knitting	Knitting	Knitting	Knitting
Other Textile Manufacturing	Other Textile Manufacturing	Other Textile Manufacturing	Other Textile Manufacturing
	Weaving		Weaving
			Crocheting
Grass Cane Work	Grass Cane Work		Grass Cane Work
	Pottery		Pottery
Vending Foods			
	Vending Drinks		
	Vending Forest Products		
	Vending Hardware		
			Vending Garments
	Retail Garments		
		Child Care	

MAJOR FINDINGS AND CONCLUSIONS

The major findings revealed by GEMINI's Southern Africa data are as follows:

1. The survival or death rate of women's enterprises is similar to that of men's. This means that women's enterprises are as long lasting as men's.
2. Employment growth rates of women's enterprises are, for the most part, significantly lower than those of men's.
3. Even within the same subsector, women's enterprises grow more slowly than men's.
4. Women's enterprises remain the same size (between one and two employees) regardless of location along the rural–urban continuum or sector. Men's enterprises, on the other hand, exhibit a fairly regular increase in the number of employees with increase in market size.

5. The most often cited problem of female entrepreneurs was inadequate market demand. For males, financial problems were more common.

6. Female entrepreneurs have not translated access to credit and training into increases in firm employment to the same extent as men.

7. A larger percentage of women's enterprises are home based. Men's enterprises are located in central business districts more often than women's.

8. Women's enterprises are concentrated into a narrow range of subsectors.

9. Women's firms appear to be concentrated in far more traditional and less dynamic product markets than men's. Furthermore, women's firms are traditional income-generating activities operating in markets that are typically shrinking rather than growing.

The GEMINI data from Southern Africa both confirm old suppositions about women's enterprises and raise new ones. The data substantiate a breadth of literature indicating that women's enterprises are smaller and less dynamic than men's. This growth differential held up when the survey was examined by sector, subsector, and product market (at the one-, two-, and three-digit ISIC levels). Subsector data, however, showed that even within the same subsector women's enterprises grew at rates that were consistently slower than men's. Data showing changes in average number of employees across different-sized markets and from urban to rural indicated not only a slower rate of growth but an apparent inelasticity to changes in market size.

Explanations for what at times appeared to be a slower growth rate and other times a lack of growth were suggested repeatedly. Women's firms suffer from insufficient market demand more than men's. This is explained by the large number of entrepreneurs producing the same products and the resultant competition and depression of profits. In addition, women's products tended to be traditional, made in and sold from the home directly to consumers. While women's firms were concentrated in a narrow range of subsectors, men's firms were distributed over a larger array of subsectors and located in commercial markets accessible to a larger number of potential buyers.

Insufficient demand for women's products probably explains why women were less able than men to translate the credit and training they were able to obtain into increases in number of employees. It may also explain the apparent inelasticity of their firms to increases in market size. As the size of markets increases from rural to urban areas, the number of firms in female-dominated subsectors may increase accordingly, thereby impeding firm growth.

Clearly these findings deepen our understanding of the growth dynamics of women's enterprises, but what do they reveal that is new? Despite the relative lack of growth of female-owned firms and what previous research indicates are meager profits, women's firms were just as long lasting as men's. GEMINI data also highlight the importance of market access to the growth and dynamics of women's enterprises. Although markets are central to economic analyses of firm growth, research on gender differences in small enterprises in economic development more often focuses on women's relative lack of access to inputs such as credit. GEMINI data underscored both the relative lack of attention paid to market demand by the WID literature, on the one hand, and its relative importance to female entrepreneurs, on the other. Another "new" finding is the apparent inelasticity of women's firms to increases in market size and access to credit and training. This "inelasticity" may indicate that female entrepreneurs have different business objectives or strategies than males.

DRAWING CONCLUSIONS BASED ON WID LITERATURE

The WID literature provides a number of explanations for the relative lack of growth of women's enterprises that complement and enrich conclusions drawn from the data. Foremost among these is women's dual domestic and productive responsibilities. Women simply lack the time to invest in the growth of their businesses. They spend as many as sixteen hours per day feeding and caring for their children, fetching firewood and water, growing and shopping for food for their families, cooking, and generating income. During peak childbearing years, the weight of domestic responsibilities can be so great as to leave little time or energy for business.

Berger, Jiggins, Otero and Downing, and Bolles all argue that the growth of women's firms is furthermore hampered by the siphoning off of profits into household consumption.[19] Women invest a significant portion of their business revenues in human capital, most important the education of their children. A woman at GEMINI's Swaziland Conference added that African women make health, education, and welfare investments that are considered the responsibility of the public sector in other countries.

Dessing, Cobbe, Tinker, and Downing suggest that women have different business objectives and strategies than men. Female entrepreneurs, they argue, tend to grow laterally, engaging in multiple income-generating activities. They do this to spread risks, even out their income stream, and manage capital needs. Tinker and Grown and Sebstad further argue that women may be more likely than men to diversify their income streams because of their greater tendency toward and need for security. This orientation is attributed to the meager resources to which they have access, women's primary responsibility for feeding and educating their children, and the threat of abandonment and divorce. These factors combine to drive women to invest profits in the security offered by kin networks and multiple risk-reducing ventures.[20]

This chapter, based upon GEMINI data from Southern Africa, argues that relative access to markets also affects the ability of women's enterprises to grow in size or profitability. Female entrepreneurs are, in essence, the last bidders for markets. They receive what is left after more powerful constituencies have claimed their market niches. The small-enterprise sector as a whole is squeezed into the market left by larger, capital-intensive firms. With the backing of government funds and policies, large firms are able to dominate the most lucrative national markets, typically in product markets that allow for economies of scale. Small producers are able to compete only where economies of scale cannot be realized by larger production units and in rural areas with markets too shallow and dispersed to interest large firms.

Within the segment of the market that small entrepreneurs are able to capture, men with their greater political and economic power are generally able to control more lucrative and less labor-intensive activities than women. Women, on the other hand, are restricted by their combined productive and reproductive responsibilities and associated labor, time, and mobility constraints. According to Saito, women in Zimbabwe are compelled to buy from distant input markets and sell in faraway output markets because of the high cost of transportation.[21]

Displacement by men further erodes women's bargaining position in the competition for markets. Displacement in Africa has been documented by many writers.[22] This evidence indicates that, where investments are made to increase the profitability and decrease the labor intensity of women's income-generating activities, these activities are more often than not taken over by men. Together with other constraints, displacement pushes female entrepreneurs into market niches that others have found the least interesting, the most labor intensive, and those with the lowest return.

Finally, structural adjustment has added to the pressure on women. As the income-generating and employment opportunities of men have been increasingly reduced as a result of structural adjustment programs and declines in commodity prices on the world market, the displacement of women from traditionally female-controlled activities has equally intensified.

NOTES

1. Riccardo Faini, Jaime de Melo, Abdelhak Senhadji, and Julie Stanton, "Growth Oriented Adjustment Programs: A Statistical Analysis," *World Development*, Vol. 19, No. 8, 1991, pp. 957–967.

2. Marguerite Berger and Mayra Buvinic, eds., *Women's Ventures: Assistance to the Informal Sector in Latin America* (Boulder, Colo.: Kumarian Press, 1989); International Center for Research on Women (ICRW), *Keeping Women Out: A Structural Analysis of Women's Employment in Developing Countries*. Prepared for the Office of Women in Development, Bureau for Program and Policy Coordination, Agency for International Development, Washington, D.C.

3. Marty Chen, "A Sectoral Approach to Promoting Women's Work: Lessons from India," *World Development*, Vol. 17, No. 7, July 1989, pp. 1007–1016.

4. The Growth and Equity through Microenterprise Investments and Institutions (GEMINI) project is funded by the U.S. Agency for International Development, Bureau for Private Enterprise, Office of Small, Micro, and Informal Enterprise.

5. William Grant et al., "Lesotho Small and Micro-enterprise Strategy—Phase II: Subsector Analysis" (Washington, D.C.: GEMINI, 1990). GEMINI subsector analyses in Lesotho showed the competition that the small entrepreneurs and microentrepreneurs face from South African firms. Interviews revealed that this competition between RSA firms also prevailed in Namibia and Swaziland.

6. The SACU member countries are Botswana, Lesotho, Namibia, South Africa, and Swaziland.

7. The repression of the informal sector in the region has accrued from legal prohibitions, in the case of Zimbabwe and South Africa, from competition with modern RSA firms, which prevails throughout the region, and from socialist policies in Zimbabwe, Zambia, and Tanzania.

8. Katrine Saito, "Women and Microenterprise Development in Zimbabwe: Constraints to Development," *Women in Development*, World Bank, Draft, 1991.

9. Ibid.

10. In Zimbabwe, there is a higher percentage of male-owned enterprises than female-owned that are more than nine years old, but a higher percentage of female-owned firms that are one to two or six to eight years old.

11. Berger and Burinic, *Women's Ventures*; Saito, "Women and Microenterprise"; Jeanne Downing, "Gender and the Growth and Dynamics of Microenterprises," GEMINI Working Paper No. 5. Prepared by the Growth and Equity through Microenterprise Investments and Institutions (GEMINI) Project for the Office of Women in Development, U.S. Agency for International Development, 1990.

12. Saito, "Women and Microenterprise."

13. Grant et al., "Lesotho."

14. W. P. Strassmann, "Home-Based Enterprises in Cities in Developing Countries," *Economic Development and Culture Change*, Vol. 36, No. 1, 1987, pp. 121–144.

15. Downing, "Gender"; Susan Watts, "Rural Women as Food Processors and Traders: Eko Making in the Ilorin Area of Nigeria," *The Journal of Developing Areas*, Vol. 19, No. 1, October 1984, pp. 71–82.

16. Saito, "Women and Microenterprise."

17. Watts, "Rural Women as Food Processors and Traders"; Downing, "Gender."

18. Yacob Fisseha, "Small Scale Enterprises in Niger: Survey Results from Dosso and Maradi Departments," a Report Prepared for USAID/Niger on a project funded by Michigan State University, East Lansing: Michigan State University, 1990; Steve Haggblade, "Proposed Subsector-Based Monitoring and Evaluation System for CARE/Thailand's Silk Promotion Efforts," GEMINI Working Paper No. 23, 1991; Strassmann, "Home-Based Enterprises."

19. Marguerite Berger, "Giving Women Credit: The Strengths and Limitations of Credit as a Tool for Alleviating Poverty," *World Development*, Vol. 17, No. 7, July 1989, pp. 1017–1032; Janice Jiggins, "Conceptual Overview: How Poor Women Earn Income in Rural Subsaharan Africa and What Prevents Them from Doing So." Background Paper prepared for the Symposium "Expanding Income Earning Opportunities for Women in Poverty: A Cross-Regional Dialogue," Sponsored by the Ford Foundation in Women's Program Forum, Nairobi, Kenya, May 1–5, 1988; Lynn A. Bolles, "Economic Crisis and Female Headed Households in Urban Jamaica," in *Women and Change in Latin America*, edited by June Nash and Helen Safa (South Hadley, Mass.: Bergin and Garvey, 1985), pp. 65–83; Maria Otero and Jeanne Downing, "Meeting Women's Financial Needs," paper presented at the Conference on Informal Finance, sponsored by Ohio State University and Science and Technology/Research and Development/AID, October 1990.

20. Louise Barrett Cobbe, "Women's Income Generation and Informal Learning in Lesotho: A Policy-Related Ethnography," Ph.D. dissertation, Florida State University, Tallahasse, Fla., 1985; Irene Tinker, "The Human Economy of Micro-Entrepreneurs," paper presented at the International Seminar on Women in Micro- and Small-Scale Enterprise Development, Ottowa, Canada, October 26, 1987; Downing, "Gender"; Caren Grown and Jennefer Sebstad, "Introduction: Toward a Wider Perspective on Women's Employment," *World Development*, Vol. 17, No. 7, July 1989, pp. 937–952.

21. Saito, "Women and Microenterprise."

22. Daisy Dwyer and Judith Bruce, *A Home Divided: Women and Income in the Third World* (Stanford: Stanford University Press); Jean Jules Botomogno et al., "Opportunities for Small-Scale Palm Oil Processing in Cameroon," prepared for the International Fund for Agricultural Development (IFAD) and the United Nations Fund for Women (UNIFEM); ICRW, *Keeping Women Out.*

Selected Bibliography

Adagala, Kavetsa, and Patricia Bifani. *Self-Employed Women in the Peri-Urban Setting: Petty Traders in Nairobi.* Nairobi: Derika Associates, 1985.

Afigbo, Adiele Eberechukwu. *The Warrant Chiefs, Indirect Rule in Southeastern Nigeria, 1891–1929.* New York: Humanities Press, 1972.

Afonja, Simi. "Changing Modes of Production and the Sexual Division of Labor among the Yoruba." *Signs: Journal of Women in Culture and Society* 7 (2) (1981): 299–313.

Afshar, Haleh. *Women, Development and Survival in the Third World.* London: Longman, 1991.

Ahere, Rexford A., and Bernard S. Katz, eds. *Privatization and Investment in Sub-Saharan Africa.* New York: Praeger, 1992.

Awe, Bolanle, ed. *Nigerian Women in Historical Perspective.* Lagos and Ibadan: Sankore and Bookcraft, 1992.

Barnes, Sandra. *Patrons and Power. Creating a Political Community in Metropolitan Lagos.* Manchester: Manchester University Press for the International African Institute, 1986.

Bazilli, Susan, ed. *Putting Women in the Agenda.* Johannesburg: Ravan Press, 1991.

Beck, Lois, and Nikki Keddie, eds. *Women in the Muslim World.* Cambridge: Cambridge University Press, 1978.

Beneria, Lourdes, ed. *Women in Development: The Sexual Division of Labor in Rural Societies.* New York: Praeger, 1972.

Berger, Marguerite. "Giving Women Credit: The Strengths and Limitations of Credit as a Tool for Alleviating Poverty." *World Development* 17 (7) (July 1989): 1017-1032.

Berger, Marguerite, and Mayra Buvinic, eds. *Women's Ventures: Assistance to the Informal Sector in Latin America.* Boulder, Colo.: Kumarian Press, 1989.

Boserup, Ester. *Woman's Role in Economic Development.* London: George Allen & Unwin, 1970.

Callaway, Barbara. *Muslim Hausa Women in Nigeria.* Syracuse: Syracuse University Press, 1987.

Callaway, Barbara. "The Role of Women in Kano City Politics." In *Hausa Women in the Twentieth Century,* edited by Catherine Coles and Beverly Mack. Madison: University of Wisconsin Press, 1991.

Campbell, Bonnie, and John Loxley, eds. *Structural Adjustment in Africa: Côte d'Ivoire, Cameroon, Ghana, Morocco, Madagascar, Tanzania, Uganda, Zimbabwe.* London: Macmillan, 1989.

Clark, Gracia. "Class Alliance and Class Fraction in Ghanian Trading and State Formation." *Review of African Political Economy* 49 (1990): 73–81.

Clark, Gracia, ed. *Traders versus the State.* Boulder, Colo.: Westview Press, 1988.

Davison, Basil. *Africa in History: Themes and Outlines.* London: Macmillan, 1968.

Davison, Jean. *Voices from Mutira: Lives of Rural Kikuyu Women.* Boulder, Colo.: Lynne Rienner Publishers, 1989.

Dorward, David. "The Impact of Colonialism on a Nigerian Hill-Farming Society: A Case Study of Innovation among the Eggon." *The International Journal of African Historical Studies* 20 (2) (1987): 201–224.

Dwyer, Daisy, and Judith Bruce, eds. *A Home Divided: Women and Income in the Third World.* Stanford: Stanford University Press, 1988.

Ekechi, Felix K. "Aspects of Palm Oil Trade at Oguta (Eastern Nigeria), 1900–1950." *African Economic History* 10 (1981): 41–58.

Ekechi, Felix K. "Colonialism and Christianity in West Africa: The Igbo Case, 1900–1915." *Journal of African History* 12 (1) (1971): 103–115.

Ekechi, Felix K. *Tradition and Transformation in Eastern Nigeria: A Sociopolitical History of Owerri and Its Hinterland, 1902–1947.* Kent, Ohio: Kent State University Press, 1989.

Elson, Diane. "How Is Structural Adjustment Affecting Women?" *Development* 1 (1989): 67–74.

"Employment, Incomes, Basic Needs and Structural Adjustment Policy in Uganda, 1980–87." In *The IMF, the World Bank and the African Debt,* vol. 2. Edited by Bade Onimode. London: Zed Books, 1989.

Engels, Frederick, ed. *The Origin of the Family, Private Property and the State.* New York: International, 1972.

Faini, Riccardo, Jaime de Melo, Abdelhak Senhadji, and Julie Stanton. "Growth Oriented Adjustment Programs: A Statistical Analysis." *World Development* 19 (8) (1991): 957–967.

Falola, Toyin. *The Political Economy of a Pre-colonial African State, Ibadan, ca. 1830–1893.* Ile-Ife: University of Ife Press, 1984.

Falola, Toyin. "Salt is Gold: The Management of Salt Scarcity in Nigeria during World War II." *Canadian Journal of African Studies* 26 (3) (1992): 412–436.

Fapohunda, Eleanor R. "The Nonpooling Household: A Challenge to Theory." In *A Home Divided: Women and Income in the Third World,* edited by Daisy Dwyer and Judith Bruce. Stanford: Stanford University Press, 1988.

Gladwin, Christine H., ed. *Structural Adjustment and African Women Farmers.* Gainesville: University of Florida Press, 1991.

Gough, Kathleen. "The Origin of the Family." *Journal of Marriage and the Family* 33 (4) (November 1971): 760–770.

Gray, Richard, and David Birmingham, eds. *Pre-Colonial African Trade: Essays on Trade in Central and Eastern Africa before 1900.* New York: Oxford University Press, 1970.

Green, Reginald. "The Broken Pot: The Social Fabric, Economic Disaster and Adjustment in Africa." In *The IMF, the World Bank and the African Debt,* edited by Bade Onimode. London: Zed Books, 1989.

Hafkin, Nancy, and Edna Bay, eds. *Women in Africa: Studies in Social and Economic Change*. Stanford: Stanford University Press, 1976.

Hansen, Holger Bernt, and Michael Twaddle, eds. *Changing Uganda*. London: James Currey, 1991.

Hansen, Karen Tranberg. "The Black Market and Women Traders in Lusaka, Zambia." In *Women and the State in Africa*, edited by Jane Parpart and Kathleen Staudt. Boulder, Colo.: Lynne Rienner, 1989.

Hay, Margaret Jean. "Queens, Prostitutes, and Peasants: Historical Perspectives on African Women, 1971–1986." *Canadian Journal of African Studies* 22 (3) (1988): 431–447.

Hay, Margaret Jean, and Sharon Stichter, eds. *African Women South of the Sahara*. London: Longman, 1984.

Henn, Jeanne K. "Women in the Rural Economy: Past, Present, and Future." In *African Women South of the Sahara*, edited by Margaret Jean Hay and Sharon Stichter. London: Longman, 1984.

Hill, Polly. *Population, Prosperity and Poverty: Rural Kano 1900 and 1970*. Cambridge: Cambridge University Press, 1977.

Hill, Polly. *Rural Hausa*. Cambridge: Cambridge University Press, 1972.

House-Midamba, Bessie. *Class Development and Gender Inequality in Kenya, 1963–1990*. Lewiston, N.Y.: Edwin Mellen Press, 1990.

House-Midamba, Bessie. "The United Nations Decade: Political Empowerment or Increased Marginalization for Kenyan Women?" *Africa Today* 37 (1) (March 1990): 37–48.

Jamal, Vali. "The Agrarian Context of the Uganda Crisis." In *Changing Uganda*, edited by Holger Bernt Hansen and Michael Twaddle. London: James Currey, 1991.

Jamal, Vali. "Coping under Crisis in Uganda." *International Labour Review* 127 (6) (1988): 679–701.

Johnson, Cheryl P. "Grassroots Organizing Women in Anti-colonial Activity in Southwestern Nigeria." *African Studies Review* 25 (2/3) (June/September 1982): 137–157.

Johnson, Marion. "The Slaves of Salaga." *Journal of African History* 27 (2) (1986): 341–362.

Kea, Ray A. *Settlements, Trade and Politics in the Seventeenth-Century Gold Coast*. Baltimore: Johns Hopkins University Press, 1982.

Kenyatta, Jomo. *Facing Mount Kenya: The Tribal Life of the Gikuyu*. New York: Vintage Books, 1965.

Kiteme, Kamuti. "The Socioeconomic Impact of the African Market Women Trade in Rural Kenya." *Journal of Black Studies* 23 (1) (September 1992): 135–151.

Kongstad, Per, and Mette Monsted. *Family Labour and Trade in Western Kenya*. Uppsala: Scandinavian Institute for African Studies, 1980.

Lewis, Barbara. "The Limitations of Group Action among Entrepreneurs: The Market Women of Abidjan, Ivory Coast." In *Women in Africa: Studies in Social and Economic Change*, edited by Nancy Hafkin and Edna Bay. Stanford: Stanford University Press, 1976.

Longhurst, Richard. "Resource Allocation and the Sexual Division of Labor: A Case Study of a Moslem Hausa Village in Northern Nigeria." In *Women and Development: The Sexual Division of Labor in Rural Societies*, edited by Lourdes Beneria. New York: Praeger, 1972.

Lovejoy, Paul E. "Concubinage and the Status of Women Slaves in Early Colonial Northern Nigeria." *Journal of African History* 29 (2) (1988): 245–266.

Loxley, John. "The IMF, the World Bank and Reconstruction in Uganda." In *Structural Adjustment in Africa: Côte d'Ivoire, Cameroon, Ghana, Morocco, Madagascar, Tanzania, Uganda, Zimbabwe*, edited by Bonnie Campbell and John Loxley. London: Macmillan, 1989.

Macharia, Kinuthia. "Slum Clearance and the Informal Economy in Nairobi." *Journal of Modern African Studies* 30 (2) (June 1992): 221–236.

Mamdani, Mahmood. *Imperialism and Fascism in Uganda*. Trenton: Africa World Press, 1984.

Martin, Susan. "Gender and Innovation: Farming, Cooking and Palm Processing in Ngwa Region, South-Eastern Nigeria, 1900–1930." *Journal of African History* 25 (4) (1984): 411–427.

Martin, Susan. *Palm Oil and Protest, An Economic History of the Ngwa Region, South-Eastern Nigeria, 1800–1980*. Cambridge: Cambridge University Press, 1988.

May, Joan. *Zimbabwean Women in Colonial and Customary Law*. Gweru, Zimbabwe: Mambo Press, 1983.

Mba, Nina Emma. *Nigerian Women Mobilized: Women's Political Activity in Southern Nigeria, 1900–1965*. Berkeley: Institute of International Studies, University of California, 1982.

Moore, Henrietta L. *Feminism and Anthropology*. Minneapolis: University of Minnesota Press, 1988.

Morgan, Robin, ed. *Sisterhood Is Global: The First Anthology from the International Women's Movement*. Garden City, N.Y.: Doubleday, 1984.

Mullings, Leith. "Women and Economic Change." In *Women in Africa: Studies in Social and Economic Changes*, edited by Nancy J. Hafkin and Edna G. Bay. Stanford: Stanford University Press, 1976.

Muriuki, Godfrey. *The History of the Kikuyu 1500–1900*. Nairobi: Oxford University Press, 1974.

Nash, June, and Helen Safa, eds. *Women and Change in Latin America*. South Hadley, Mass.: Bergin and Garvey, 1985.

Nelson, Nici. "Female-Centered Families: Changing Patterns of Marriage and Family among the Buzaa Brewers of Mathare Valley." *African Urban Studies* 3 (Winter 1978–79): 85–103.

Nelson, Nici. "How Women and Men Get By: The Sexual Division of Labour in the Informal Sector of a Nairobi Squatter Settlement." In *Casual Work and Poverty in Third World Cities*, edited by Ray Bromley and Chris Gerry. New York: John Wiley & Sons, 1979.

Nzomo, Maria. "The Gender Dimension of Democratization in Kenya: Some International Linkages." *Alternatives* 18 (1) (Winter 1993): 61–73.

Nzomo, Maria. "The Impact on the Women's Decade on Politics, Programs and Empowerment of Women in Kenya." *Issue: A Journal of Opinion* 17 (2) (Summer 1989): 9–17.

Obbo, Christine. *African Women: Their Struggle for Economic Indepedence*. London: Zed Press, 1980.

Onimode, Bade, ed. *The IMF, the World Bank and the African Debt*, vol. 2. London: Zed Books, 1989.

Oppong, Christine, ed. *Female and Male in West Africa*. London: George Allen & Unwin, 1983.

Oppong, Christine, ed. *Sex Roles, Population and Development in West Africa*. London: J. Currey, 1987.

Osirim, Mary. "Gender and Entrepreneurship: Issues of Capital and Technology in Nigerian Firms." In *Privatization and Investment in Sub-Saharan Africa*, edited by Rexford A. Ahere and Bernard S. Katz. New York: Praeger, 1992.

Oyugi, Walter O., Atieno Adhiambo, Michael Chege, and Afrifa K. Gitonga, eds. *Democratic Theory and Practice in Africa*. Portsmouth, N.H.: Heinemann, 1988.

Parpart, Jane L., ed. *Women and Development in Africa*. Halifax, N.S.: Dalhousie University Press, 1989.

Parpart, Jane, and Kathleen Staudt, eds. *Women and the State in Africa*. Boulder, Colo.: Lynne Rienner, 1989.

Plattner, Stuart, ed. *Markets and Marketing*. New York: University Press of America, 1985.

Robertson, Claire. *Sharing the Same Bowl: A Socioeconomic History of Women and Class in Accra, Ghana*. Bloomington: Indiana University Press, 1984.

Robertson, Claire. "Traders and Urban Struggles: The Creation of a Militant Female Underclass in Nairobi, 1960 to 1990." *Journal of Women's History* 4 (3) (Winter 1993): 9–42.

Rosaldo, Michelee Zimbalist, and Louise Lamphere, eds. *Women, Culture and Society*. Stanford: Stanford University Press, 1974.

Schlegel, Alice, ed. *Sexual Stratification*. New York: Columbia University Press, 1977.

Schmidt, Elizabeth. *Peasants, Traders and Wives. Shona Women in the History of Zimbabwe, 1870–1939*. Portsmouth, N.H.: Heinemann, 1992.

Simms, Ruth. "The African Woman as Entrepreneur: Problems and Perspectives on Their Roles." In *The Black Woman Cross-Culturally*, edited by Filomina Chioma Steady. Rochester, Vt.: Schenkman Books, Inc., 1985.

Stamp, Patricia. *Technology, Gender, and Power in Africa*. Ottawa: International Development Center, 1989.

Staudt, Kathleen. "Women Farmers in Africa: Research and Institutional Action, 1972–1987." *Canadian Journal of African Studies* 22 (3) (1988): 567–582.

Strobel, Margaret. "African Women." *Signs: Journal of Women in Culture and Society* 8 (1) (1982): 109–131.

Sudarkasa, Niara. "The Status of Women in Indigeneous African Societies." *Feminist Studies* 12 (1) (Spring 1986): 91–103.

Sudarkasa, Niara. *Where Women Work: A Study of Yoruba Women in the Marketplace and in the Home*. Ann Arbor: University of Michigan Press, 1973.

Swetnam, John. "Women and Markets: A Problem in the Assessment of Sexual Inequality." *Ethnology* 27 (4) (October 1988): 327–338.

Tinker, Irene, ed. *Persistent Inequalities: Women and World Development*. New York: Oxford University Press, 1990.

Turrittin, Jane. "Men, Women, and Market Trade in Mali, West Africa." *Canadian Journal of African Studies* 22 (3) (1988): 583–604.

Utas, Bo, ed. *Women in Islamic Societies: Social Attitudes and Historical Perspectives*. Copenhagen: Scandinavian Institute of Asian Studies, 1983.

Vansina, Jan. "Lessons of Forty Years of African History." *International Journal of African Historical Studies* (IJHAS) 25 (2) (1992): 391–398.

Vansina, Jan. "Trade and Markets among the Kuba." In *Markets in Africa*, edited by Paul Bohannan and George Dalton. Evanston, Ill.: Northwestern University Press, 1962.

VerEecke, Catherine. "From Pasture to Purdah: The Transformation of Women's Roles and Identity among the Adamawa Fulbe." *Ethnology* 28 (1988): 53–73.

Wipper, Audrey. "Reflections on the Past Sixteen Years, 1972–1988, and Future Challenges." *Canadian Journal of African Studies* 22 (3) (1988): 409–421.

Wipper, Audrey. "Women's Voluntary Associations." In *African Women South of the Sahara*, edited by Margaret Jean Hay and Sharon Stichter. London: Longman, 1984.

Index

About the Editors and Contributors

JEANNE DOWNING, Ph.D., is Program Development Director for Africa at the Appropriate Technology International, Washington, D.C. She is a former assistant professor of Geography and Regional Planning at Western Washington University, and specializes in gender studies. Her publications include *Women in Rural–Urban Exchange: Implications for Research and Intervention Identification*, with Jennifer Santer (Worcester, 1988); "Gender and the Growth and Dynamics of Microenterprises," in *Small Enterprise Development* (1991); and "Women in Small and Microenterprises in the Eastern Caribbean" (Washington, D.C.: The Futures Group, 1990).

FELIX K. EKECHI, Ph.D., is Professor of History, and Coordinator, African Studies Program, at Kent State University. He is the author of several books and articles, including *Missionary Enterprise and Rivalry in Igboland* (London, 1972); *Tradition and Transformation in Eastern Nigeria* (Kent, 1989); and "The Cassava Palaver: The Gender Problem in African Economic Development," *Proceedings* of the 12th Annual Third World Conference, vol. 1, 1986.

TOYIN FALOLA, Ph.D., is Professor of History at the University of Texas at Austin, and Coeditor, *African Economic History*. His numerous publications include *The Political Economy of a Precolonial African State: Ibadan, 1830–1900* (Ile-Ife, 1984); *Religion and Society in Nigeria* (Ibadan, 1991); and "The Place of Women in the Yoruba Pre-Colonial Domestic Economy," Ife University, *Seminar Proceedings* (1978).

NANCY E. HORN, Ph.D., is Associate Professor of Anthropology, and Coordinator of the Women's Resource and Research Center at Washington State University.

Her publications include *Women in Agriculture in Botswana* (Michigan State, 1985); *Cultivating Customers: Market Women in Harare, Zimbabwe* (forthcoming); and "The Informal Fruit and Vegetable Market in Greater Harare: A Working Paper" (1986).

BESSIE HOUSE-MIDAMBA, Ph.D., is Assistant Professor of Political Science at Kent State University. Her publications include *Class Development and Gender Inequality in Kenya, 1963–1990* (Lewiston, 1990); "The United Nations Decade: Political Empowerment or Increased Marginalization for Kenyan Women?" *Africa Today* (1990); and "The Legal Basis of Gender Inequality in Kenya," *Journal of the African Society of International and Comparative Law* (1993).

NAKANYIKE B. MUSISI, Ph.D., is Assistant Professor of History and Women's Studies at the University of Toronto, Canada. Her research focuses on Baganda Women of Uganda: "The Transformation of Baganda Women from the Earliest Times to the Demise of the Kingdom 1967," Ph.D. dissertation, University of Toronto (1991).

ONIAWU W. OGBOMO, Ph.D., is a Postdoctoral Fellow at the Frederick Douglass Institute of African and African-American Studies, University of Rochester. His recently completed dissertation at the University of Toronto (1993) entitled, "Men and Women: Gender Relations and the History of Owan Communities, Nigeria c. 1320–1900," is being prepared for publication.

MARY JOHNSON OSIRIM, Ph.D., is a Lecturer in Sociology at Bryn Mawr College and the author of *Resource Guide to the Study of Third World Women/ Women of Color*, with Mili Cisneros (Bryn Mawr College, 1987); "Gender Entrepreneurship and Privatization: Issues of Capital and Technology in Nigerian Small Firms," *Private Investment* (1989); and "Characteristics of Entrepreneurship in Nigerian Industries That Started Small: Some Preliminary Findings from the Lagos Case," *Perspectives in International Development* (1986).

CLAIRE ROBERTSON, Ph.D., is Associate Professor of History and Women's Studies at the Ohio State University. Her publications include, *Sharing the Same Bowl: A Socioeconomic History of Women and Class in Accra, Ghana* (Bloomington, 1984); *Women and Slavery in Africa*, with Martin Klein (Madison, 1984); and "Developing Economic Awareness: Changing Perspectives in Studies of African Women, 1976–1985," *Feminist Studies* (1987).

CATHERINE VEREECKE, Ph.D., is Assistant Director of the Center for African Studies at the University of Florida, and former Assistant Professor of Anthropology at Ohio State University. Her publications include "From Pasture to Purdah: The Transformation of Women's Roles among the Adamawa Fulbe," *Ethnology* (1987); "Cultural Construction of Women's Economic Marginality: The Fulbe of Northeastern Nigeria," *Michigan State University Papers on Women* (1989).

ISBN 0-313-29214-0

9 780313 292149

90000>